C000001554

LIFE IN THE WEST.

LIFE IN THE WEST:

BACK-WOOD LEAVES AND PRAIRIE FLOWERS

𝕽𝔬𝔲𝔤𝔥 𝕾𝔨𝔢𝔱𝔠𝔥𝔢𝔰 𝔬𝔫 𝔱𝔥𝔢 𝕭𝔬𝔯𝔡𝔢𝔯𝔰

OF THE

PICTURESQUE, THE SUBLIME, AND RIDICULOUS.

EXTRACTS FROM THE NOTE BOOK

pseud — OF

MORLEIGH‸ IN SEARCH OF AN ESTATE.

" The ancient proverb 's come to pass :
The priest, as he performs the mass,
Forgets that ever clerk he was,—
He knoweth not his estate."—OLD BALLAD.

" Gratum opus agricolis."—VIRGIL.

" And when pleasure begins to grow dull in the east,
We may order our wings, and fly off to the west."—T. MOORE.

" And deem the woods will be our home at last."—BYRON.

LONDON:

SAUNDERS AND OTLEY, CONDUIT STREET.

1842.

TO

THE OUTWARD BOUND,

THIS WORK

IS RESPECTFULLY INSCRIBED

BY

THE AUTHOR.

PREFACE.

I CONSIDER a Preface to be a work of supererogation, and never read one with common patience in my life. Nevertheless, I think it right to inform the reader, that three of the following papers have already met the public eye, in the pages of a leading London periodical.

THE AUTHOR.

DIRECTIONS TO THE BINDER.

———

ERRATA.

4, *for* " genus" *read* " genius."

15, *for* " cook" *read* " cock."

45, *for* " monstrous" *read* " monotonous."

149, *for* " marquetiere" *read* " marqueterie."

152, *for* " crawling" *read* " crowding."

173, *for* " schute" *read* " chute."

179, *for* " cadenas" *read* " cadences."

261, *for* " pottawattomers" *read* " pottawattomies."

295, *for* " death's door" *read* " Death's Door."

350, *for* " provider" *read* " providor."

CONTENTS.

CHAPTER I.

CHAPTER II.

CHAPTER III.

CHAPTER IV.

CHAPTER V.

CHAPTER VI.

CHAPTER VII.

CHAPTER VIII.

CHAPTER IX.

CHAPTER X.

CHAPTER XVI.

CHAPTER XVII.

CHAPTER XVIII.

LIFE IN THE WEST,

ETC.

CHAPTER I.

Embarkation — British Queen — Passengers — Foreign habits—
Sympathizer and Sufferer—Quaker and West Indian—The boon
companions—Tea—Ship books—Scot's advice.

Off Portsmouth, March 12, 1841.

MY DEAR ———,

Here I am at last, safe and sound on the
promenade deck of the longest steamer in the world—
The British Queen. Forward they are getting up the
anchor with a dolorous song—the steam is up already
—the dwarfish crank and comfortless little steamer,
in which we sought refuge at Southampton from the
harpies hovering about the pier, frets and vapours
alongside, impatient to be off; aft and amidships a
general shaking of hands, earnest conversations,
brief snatches of sentiment, abruptly broken off by
the shrill tinkling of a bell. " Passengers for Southampton all aboard," is the cry. " Stand by the hand-
ropes there."—" Ay, ay, sir"—" Take care of the
lady's muff'"—" Ay, ay, sir"—" My bonnet! oh, my
bonnet!"—" Be steady, my dear,"—" Crush'd out of
shape"—" Put your foot down here, ma'am." " Ay
de mi," murmurs a Spanish youth, looking over the

3   B

side—" Todos las damas"—" all the ladies are going away"—" Gott befohlen"—" Gehabt euch wohl"—" Bon viaggio, piensa de me me cara"—" Adieu, adieu, ma chere"—" Vaya con Dios"—" Take care of yourself, old boy"—" Write soon"—" You have an onion in your handkerchief"—" Send me up a bottle for my tears, *luv*"—" Ah, you're a sad fellow !"—" Put your letter in a bottle, do"—" I'll send it by the first sucking whale we meet." Thus, amidst a Babel of strange tongues and sounds we separate the homeward and the outward bound, waving hats, caps, and hand-kerchiefs, as we glide over the Solent sea. I thank my stars I have a berth, a state room, all to myself—an unexpected piece of good fortune—a luxury, which can only be appreciated by those who have been doomed to share that cage-full of lockers and baggage, pomp-ously called a state room, with a strange invalid, or a stout gentleman of very irregular habits. Buttoned up to the eyes in my old pea-jacket, in the armour of resignation I post myself near the chimney, and eye askant the rest of my fellow passengers. They have finally fixed upon and settled down bag and baggage in their berths, and now come tumbling up the hatchways to look at the Needles and Hulse Castle. Sixty passengers, male and female, strut about the decks in their fancy costume; here we have a group of officers bound for Canada; one sports a long white nightcap, long bodied drab jacket, and ferocious mustachios; another shews his shapes in tight tartans; a third envelopes his head and shoul-ders in a brown Bernoose, his nether man being en-cased in long Indian leggins and moccassons—there goes a Greek cap and long tassel to feed the fishes; but we have still a high Turkish cap amongst us, three Welsh wigs, one quaker broadbrim, and a variety of sow-westers. Yon tall Frenchman in the sweeping white Bernoose would insinuate that he has been fighting with the Arabs, while the band of Germans on the paddle-box exhibit their bizarre chacos and gnarled pipes to the evening sun, as they "roar a catch" from Robert le Diable. "It is a party of pleasure," cries a Baltimore lawyer, with a face like an overgrown capsicum, naval cap and button, worn knowingly over his worst eye. "A party of pleasure," echoes a bench of ladies in black, most mysteriously veiled. The Captain makes his best bow to his passengers, flatters himself we shall have a most delightful passage, and one of the steward's men, bleating forth Rory O'More on a Kent bugle, calls us *possè comitatus* down to dinner.

There is a general rush for seats—the Captain's table is soon beset by French, Germans, Italians, and Americans, while the rest are fain to set themselves down at the mate's table, at which all the odd fellows and disjointed members of society cut their mutton. The French and Germans know how to enjoy themselves—the champagne begins to circulate, and men who were total strangers to each other half-an-hour ago, push the bottle back and forwards, laugh, jest, jeer, and quaff together like sworn brothers. "Je suis Francois moi," is deemed a sufficient introduction among the French; but "Je suis Parisien," pronounced with a sonorous voice, the right hand laid upon the embroidered vest with *empressement*, penetrates the heart of every Frenchman, and illuminates his face with the sunshine of gladness. Not so the English; it is not enough to hear that your neighbour is a cockney, and that this indeed is his first voyage—the very first—that you, born within the sweet sound of the Bow bells yourself, should take such a sudden interest in your compatriot as to ask him to drink wine, and enter into familiar conversation with him. Stand off and steer clear is our motto, *entre nous*; though among foreigners we relinquish our conventional ice, and while we barely exchange monosyllables with friends, lovers, and countrymen, launch forth into the wild extravaganzas of our neighbours. But from the sublime to the ridiculous. Soup, fish, flesh, and fowl, and the long bill of fare, having flown through the salon and disappeared in a tremendous clatter of plates, knives, and forks, the foreigners swallow a chasse café, and rush on deck to smoke, leaving the natives to sip their wine, and munch their nuts and almonds in sober sadness.

" It is our duty to finish it," said a very stout gentleman near me to his son, as he pushed a decanter of port to that meagre youth, who, by his Frenchified airs and impatience, seemed bent upon following the smokers *la haut.* " Broke a tooth, sir ?" inquired a florid-faced, bald-pated, black-whiskered genus with a sanguine eye, which he bent commiseratingly upon a hungry-looking pilgarlic in a buffalo-skin coat, who, with as many grimaces as a poisoned baboon, relieved his jaws of fragments of nut-shells, &c., and declared he was subject to shooting pains from his gums to the back of his head, and so forth. " I'm not surprised to hear it, sir," replied the sanguine inquirer, who, for brevity, I may call the sympathizer; " when men will sport with their teeth, break nuts and stones;" and the twain draw nearer and enter into a learned disquisition on teeth, to which myself and others, seeking information and amusement, attend. " You have suffered a deal with your teeth, sir," said the sympathizer, as he listened to the sufferer's tale of woe. " Now let me look into your mouth," continued he, and as the sufferer complied, the sympathizer assisted him to keep his mouth open, holding his black moustache firmly with one hand, while with the other he introduced a crooked steel instrument with a white handle into the other's mouth, and invited us to observe the decayed and neglected state of the gentleman's masticators—an unpleasing sight. " But it is not too late—it is not too late," said he, cheerily, probing the poor devil's stumps; " all this damaged row may be filled and put into good working order—fact, gentlemen—without heat or pressure. Ha, what have we here? a sheep's trotter or the tip of a cow's horn!" The sufferer imperfectly signifies the new discovery in his mouth is merely a false tooth, put in by a first-rate hand in America. " I beg your pardon," cried the sympathizer, tapping the false tooth merrily—" I thought it must be a fragment of a horse's hoof"—and the sufferer, having been tickled and probed about the mouth much longer than he liked, was suddenly seized with dire qualms and misgivings in another direction, broke loose without apology, and bolted into his berth. Further down the table sit three canny Scots sipping whisky-toddy, while a tall West Indian youth, with fine black eyes, and dressed à la Byron, seems listening most deferentially to a thick-set, hale, severe looking Quaker, the formal cut of his brown coat and drab waistcoat, his austere brow chiselled by thought, the strict schooling and rigid control of the muscles of his face, round and rubicund, formed by nature for mirth and good fellowship, shews the unrelenting stuff of the inner man, and the victory achieved over the outer man. Now with quaint and studied action he draws from the depth of his capacious pocket a book, from which he straightway reads a passage, then plunges his hands below the table, and produces sundry clumsy black looking rings, which at first I thought were a variety of hall-door knockers, carried off as the trophies of a midnight lark in the great metropolis; but that a quaker could be guilty of such a backsliding affair seemed impossible, and I was induced to draw closer to that society, and inspect some ponderous fetters which this upright quaker assured me had been forwarded from the Havannah to Birmingham, with an order for several tons' weight of fetters of the same make for the legs and arms of slaves; but, to the credit of the Birmingham manufacturers be it spoken, they have rejected the order, said the quaker, who I soon discovered to be the philanthropist S⸺e, a most zealous and uncompromising abolitionist.

At the foot of one of the tables our attention is engaged by a very noisy group of boon companions, not inappropriately named by a young Virginian, Bacchus, Silenus, and Jonathan Wild. Bacchus, a sad old winebibber, with a heavy yet Listonian countenance, a greasy suit of black, barely embracing his bloated tun-shaped figure; he called himself the great reporter, special reporter to the Times. Silenus, an ever-green old roysterer, quite out of his element when out of liquor; he vociferously applauded everything the great reporter said and did, and in an unguarded hour revealed certain portions of his history to his boon companion, who lost no time in publishing that this merry Silenus was a renegado baker from

Marylebone. Jonathan Wild, a tall, very lank, hair-brained fellow, full of pranks, mischief, and diablerie, was the happy link between Bacchus and Silenus ; he sat between the pair, in his white mackintosh and sow-wester, with his son, a very fine two-year old, on his knee, and a glass of champagne in his hand. And thus this happy trio hob, nob, sing, swear, and blaspheme together, till the steward and expert waiters roll in the tea-cups and force the trio to retire from the table.

"Tea, sir ? Black or green, sir ?" Neither, good barber, or *barbare*, as the Frenchmen call that excellent black waiter. Oh my prophetic soul ! what heavings, what dire commotions, will follow the guzzling of hot tea which I see before me, as, seated on the lofty divan near the stern windows, I look through the odd volumes, the scraps, and backs of books, miscalled the library ; truly the ship's books have been very badly kept ; here I find dozens of a neatly bound thin octavo, kicking about in every direction ; a nice book truly, " Swaim's Panacea," an interesting and disgusting history of all the miraculous cures performed by Swaim's panacea; and fronting the title page we have a full-length portrait of a lady, or skeleton in a ball-dress, grinning horribly. If this lady is cured, thought I, it would be very advisable for her to stay at home. Faugh! the very portrait has made me ill. I threw the book aside with scorn, little thinking that in a few day's hence, when the book mysteriously disappeared, I should earnestly seek for a copy, and devour the contents with as much gusto as a starving sailor would munch an old shoe.

Following the advice and example of a friendly Scot, I had just swallowed a rummer of whisky-toddy, and notwithstanding his assurance that it was the verra best thing in the warld, when the "*first blush*" of sea quakishness was over, I felt dire misgivings as I looked at the lamps swinging to and fro, and the waiters' heads bobbing up and down in the saloon.   Stretched at full length upon a sofa, unwilling, and indeed unable, to move, I listened "to the tale of love" which a buffalo man—-I mean, a gentleman in a buffalo robe coat—bleated unto a grey mackintosh, who, in turn, an amorous descant sung, until the bonne fortunes of the happy pair was lost or silenced by the loud and obstreperous laughter of a knot of merry wags seated at a table close to my sofa.   "Your health, sir—Sir, your health," echoed round the table. "Thank you, gentlemen," said a grave-looking man, bowing stiffly, and coolly replenishing his glass from a jug of mulled port which stood before him; he had been relating some rigmarole story about the purchase of a Yorkshire estate, odds and ends of which had entered my ear together with the bellowings of the buffalo-man, the advice of the Scot, and the general buz of the saloon.   "Five hundred acres in the vale of York."   "Put a wee drop mair whisky in it, mon." "She winked divinely at me in church." "I resolved to visit it privately." "She dropped her handkerchief, I picked it up." "Be a stirring the spoon and putting in a wee drap mair." "Taken in a man trap." This last sentence, pronounced by the grave gentleman, had "set the table in a roar;" he had been relating his personal adventures in search of an estate, and being recruited with a generous glass, at the urgent entreaty of his boon companions began to read aloud from the blotted pages of his note book.

CHAPTER II.

Adventures of a gentleman in search of an estate—Galway coach-
man—Reverend passenger—His opinions, zeal, and wisdom—
Athlone inn—The barber and the squire—Visit to Killmoran
—A mob—Awkward predicament.

" It was not my intention to remain in Dublin a day
longer than was absolutely necessary. I proceeded
to business at once, read all the advertisements of
lands for sale in the newspapers, filled my notebook
with the addresses of lawyers and solicitors, and the
very unpronounceable names of sundry eligible pro-
perties. Cornelius P. Meehan, Esq., was the first
solicitor I visited in Dublin. I found that gentleman
in his office, surrounded with parchment and little
japanned boxes, " chock-full of business," as he said
himself. I inquired about the Killmoran property.

" Here is a sheet of particulars," said Cornelius,
(commonly called Corney.) " May I ask who is your
man of business in this city ?" continued he.

I replied I had not employed a man of business,
nor did I intend till I had found something likely to
suit me.

" I merely asked that question," said Corney, " as
a matter of course. I don't want to force my services
upon any man. Now, just look here, sir," continued

B 3

he, unrolling a map, not the cleanest in the world ; "there, I unfold before you Killmoran, three thousand acres, be the same more or less. Look to the right, and you will see the bright green fields and arable land, two hundred and seventy-five acres, three roods, and nine perches, more or less ; this swipe of blue is the bottom, and under my forefinger, and round, halfway round the table, that vast brown tract is bog—every bit improvable bog ! There, sir," continued Corney, drawing himself up, " there is a field, a surface for a young man of spirit to embark his capital upon. People talk of going to America, and spending their lives in pulling up roots of trees as firmly imbedded in the soil as the molares in my jaw; when here, sir, at home, in our own native isle— I say native, though I presume you are not a native ; but no matter, you soon will be when you purchase Killmoran, and become wedded to the soil."

My objections to this property, and they were not a few, were met and combated by the potent Cornelius. I doubted the practicability of reclaiming the bog.

" Go to Chatmoss," said Corney ; " look at that."

" But the railroad runs through it," said I.

" Wont we have railroads through our own bogs ?" said he.

" Perhaps not," said I.

" Be easy on that score," said Corney ; " wont we have the great Atlantic, and all its branches, passing within ten miles of Killmoran ? I saw the line myself hanging up in the company's office, and, with our family interest, we might have a branch from the main trunk to Killmoran."

" But I mean to reside," said I ; " where is the

dwelling-house? the land is in the hands of tenants already."

" Tenants at will, every mother's son of them," said Corney; " you can turn them out, or leave that to me. I'll eject them forthwith; though if you like to give them plots in the bog, they'll burrow like rabbits, and be thankful to get leave; but as to the dwelling,—let me see, there is one thumping big farm-house, with a complete lawn in front of it; you could fit it up for a shooting-cabin, make quite a romantic spot in a short time, till you thought of bringing your wife; but I see by your face you are not married yet; all in good time, though. And now, what can be cheaper? We only ask twenty-one years' purchase of the present rental, three hundred and fifty pounds a-year, seven thousand three hundred and fifty pounds. Now, sir, supposing I take upon me to say that I'll throw off the odd money, and leave it the bare seven thousand," said Cornelius, with an alluring smile.

" I am not prepared to conclude the bargain immediately," said I; " I should like to see Killmoran first."

" O, as you please, sir," said he, very coolly, " it may slip through your fingers; meantime, however, don't mind what those tenants say about high rents; make no promises, judge for yourself."

" I mean to do so," said I, putting on my hat; and wishing Cornelius P. Meehan a good afternoon, sauntered towards mine inn.

Having secured the box-seat on the Galway coach, I set out in quest of this land of promise; but the strong southwester took away much of the pleasure I hoped to enjoy, as far as seeing the country went.

Our road ran close to the Phœnix Park for a mile or two; on our left ran the Liffey—an insignificant stream; beyond it lay the wide expanse, a richly wooded, thickly inhabited, beautiful country, backed by the picturesque Dublin and blue Wicklow mountains.

"Look at the biggest milestone in the kingdom," said the coachman, as we passed the Wellington testimonial.

I believe it was George IV. called it an overgrown milestone, which, indeed, it strongly resembles; there is an unfinished baldness about the whole concern, but *tout les gouts sont respectables.* The coachman was an original in his way, a very Falstaff in his person, and one of the most loquacious whips I had ever shared a box-seat with in my life: he kept up a running conversation with the outside passengers, wayfaring men, labourers in the fields, pretty girls, when they shewed their faces at the doors and windows of the houses and cabins we passed; in short, every one knew him, and returned his greeting joyfully. He addressed his horses by name; and one team in particular were his favourites: he vowed there were not their equals in the united kingdoms, nor this side Christendom.

"Now, sir," said he, "look at that off leader; he's a cross-made, coarse garron, I own, to look at, but, by my song, the work is in him yet. Whewgh, cheer up, Daniel, my jewel! I call him Daniel, sir, after our own great patriarch; he's a real liberator, able to pull all the rest after him. The cantering hack alongside of him I call the Spatterer; when the roads are heavy she fairly blinds me. This off wheeler I call Stanley. I like to have something shew the off-side, and this steady grey horse I call the Peeler. I like to have a stanch tug under my hand, though he's always trying to catch the leader by the tail. Whew! clear the road, Daniel!— keep to it, Spatterer!—no capers, Stanley; keep in a good honest trot, or maybe I wont be coming over your ears with the heavy end of the lash. You see, sir, before I got Stanley, they had him leader in the mail; they didn't know what he was up to till one night, as he was going down the hill at Lucan, having nothing better to do, he began to cut capers, and then fairly bolted, upset the mail, and the passengers were all, more or less, incovenienced, dirtied, and unseated; true for you, parson, one gentleman got his nose broke upon that occasion."

This last reply was made by the jolly coachman to a thin lath of a clerical prig, with a face like a hatchet, and a nose like a lobster's claw; he had taken his seat right behind the coachman, and made more rout at being disappointed in not getting an inside seat than forty old women. The coachman took him very quietly, told him he was better outside than inside upon a fine airy morning like this; assured him, with a vast deal of vehemence, that we were all pro-testants, sound protestants, outside, but he could not answer for the inside at all, at all. This jest seemed to be relished by the passengers on the back seats, though I afterwards heard they were Romans, as the catholics were called in Ireland.

We passed the Duke of Leinster's park and the bleak-looking town called Maynooth. The famous old castle rises, in a ruinous mass, out of a brewery-yard, and behind it stands the college, a plain-looking building, without the slightest attempt at architectural ornament or classical design.

" Since the time of Cardinal Wolsey to the present day, more than beer has been brewing under the walls of that ancient fortalice," said the parson, as we whirled out of the town.

En route we passed two canals, and, according to the coachman, they were not happy speculations.

" But, for all that, the fly-boats have taken, and will take, the best part of your passengers from you," said the parson; " I intend to patronise the boats myself, in future," said he.

This provoked the coachman's ire; he said, " There was a mighty great difference between travelling like a gentleman on top of a sporting coach, and sneaking up a bit of a ditch, like an old woman fishing for pinkeens."

But the parson declared the boat was preferable; " in it a man might stretch his legs, read his newspaper, write his letters, without being hampered with great coats and nasty old women inside a coach; or exposed, as he was at present, to the cold wind and ribaldry of an ignorant fellow outside a coach."

There was no replying to this; but when the parson got down he remembered the coachman, and handed him half-a-crown, demanding the change immediately, one shilling and sixpence. The coachman quietly put the money in his pocket, exclaiming, " Long life to your reverence."

" Give me my change!" vociferated the parson.

" Protestants for ever!" shouted the coachman, handling the ribbons.

" Come, none of your nonsense, sir," cried the angry parson; " hand me down my change."

" I'll remember your reverence when you're returning to Dublin," cried the coachman; and, exclaiming "Protestants for ever!" we drove off, leaving the enraged parson, bag in hand, by the road side.

"Now, he'll think more about that paltry one-and-sixpence," said the coachman, "than if he lost a year's tithe. I have whipped him up and down for the last twelve years, inside and outside, and I never get more than a hog at a time from him. He has a snug living down here, but it wont satisfy him, he wants to be a bishop; cook him up with a mitre and crook, like the swinging sign of St. Patrick. Indeed, to be sure, he has great interest, they say, at the castle always, no matter who reigns there. All the fat is in the fire, unless the parson, with the long nose, takes his share of the cookery. He's called, on the road, the castle hack; and a good one he is, too, for many a good pannier of game he carries up to the castle folks; I often wonder where he finds so much wild-fowl, but they say he keeps a score of pot-wollopers beating over other men's grounds for game, and bagging every feather in the country; to be sure it must cost him a sight of money, but it's a good speculation, for all the time, I hear, he's feathering his nest."

"He don't belong to any particular party?" said I.

"No, by my song," said the coachman, with a laugh; "he would persuade a saint he was always on the right side of the question, as long as he was in the same boat with the governor. If you heard him, as I have, taking up the cudgels for the new man in office, whoever he happened to be, you'd say not a wink was on him. It's a good while ago since I heard him defending that little governor some fellow threw a bottle at in the theatre; he was all in all with him. They say that governor got the living for him; but when he

went out, and another man came in, the parson was
quite as useful to him. I have heard him say, ' We
have now a man of sterling worth and wealth at the
head of affairs.'   But the sterling man went out, and
made room for another,—then sure enough I thought it
was all over with my parson.   I whipped him up to
Dublin, and not a word had he to throw to a dog, for
the new lieutenant was as different from the old as
day and night; but three days after I took him up in
Parliament Street as usual, so full of good news that
he could not keep it to himself.

"' We have at last a gallant, generous, and enterprising spirit at the helm,' said he, to a bothered Connaught man, who sat beside him, who mistook what
he said, and told him he never carried the like about
him; but, as the morning was cold, he'd join him in
a naggin of spirits at the next public-house.

" But I took him up rightly; ' Your reverence,'
says I, ' I don't think this man is as true blue as the
last.'

"' He's a stanch supporter of the church, though a
man of the people,' was his reply; then he whispers
in my ear, ' Did you ever dream of driving a bishop's
coach—you dog, you?'

" Well, sir, the man of spirit was obliged to walk
off, and then some of the old hands came back again.
How the parson had the face to face them I don't
know, but when I whipped him down again, he talked
of having been to the castle to congratulate his old
friends upon their speedy return; but when their
backs were turned, and a new man cocked his bonnet
at us, we had the parson singing like a blackbird from
Dublin to Kilcock, and from that to the Bridge and
down to his glebe.   ' We are all right now; we have

a man with a mind, and a heart, and a soul at the head of affairs; we must prosper.' But a Roscommon grazier took him up mighty sharp upon that.

" ' Why,' says Michael Balff, ' this great man of yours must be no great shakes, after all; for I never heard of anything that had neither a mind, nor a heart, nor a soul, barring a wheelbarrow with a screeching gudgeon.' But when that governor shewed us the back seams of his stockings, and was fairly gone, the parson was just as proud of his successor, for he now says, ' This is the man we were looking for—a great genius, a man of wit, a man of the people, a supporter of church and state, a philosopher, a field-officer, and'—(calling to a man on the back seat)—Jerry Mac Manus, what's this Lanty Doolan, the great schoolmaster in your town, calls himself?" " A lithe-rary character," was the reply. " That's it," continued the coachman; " so I suppose the litherary character has promised him a bishopric at last; but I'm afeard he wont make me his coachman, because I took the eighteen-pence from him; and the divil a pin I care, for I would rather die in harness, driving gentlemen on my own big coach, than be dog to any big man's coach, in the castle or out of it."

We now approached the ancient town of Athlone. I had been led to expect something very superior to any of the towns we had already passed, from the coachman's brilliant description of his native city; indeed, he waxed poetical as we approached it, bursting out into quotations from a poem, he called the " Battle of Aughrim, or Siege of Athlone." According to him, Athlone was lost through the obsti-nacy of the Irish general, St. Ruth, who refused to advance his army from Aughrim to assist the besieged, when an officer from the besieged, on his bare knees, entreated St. Ruth to send immediate aid to the besieged.

"St. Ruth answers—'Tell them St. Ruth is here, and that will do.'

"But the messenger answers—'Your aid will serve much better than your name.'

"'Bear back my answer, friend, from whence you came,' replies St. Ruth.

"And now, sir, I lave it to you, wasn't that a pretty answer to send into a starving and unfortunate garrison?"

"Not very satisfactory," said I, "at all events."

"You may well say that," continued the coachman; "but when the town was lost, and taken by the English, General Sarsfield gave it to St. Ruth in prime style; he burst out into tears of anger, and exclaimed—

> 'O heavens! Athlone is lost, that lovely seat,
> The pride of empire, and the throne of state.'

"I am sorry I can't finish it for your honour, for here we are at the turnpike of the town;" and we rattled into a beggarly account of thatched cabins, half-thatched and slated houses, thrusting their gable ends, fronts, and rears upon the road, leaving barely room for our coach to pass between the bay windows, barbers' poles, swinging signs, that adorn for ever the main street of that "pride of empire and throne of state," the antique borough of Athlone. Nevertheless, here I resolved to halt for the night, and being set down at the door of what he called the only decent house in the town, I remembered him, and followed a waiter into the hotel.

"This way, sir," said the waiter; "up stairs, if you

please—all the parlours are full of gentlemen refreshing themselves, as it is market-day; but we will be empty enough before night."

The waiter threw open a bed-room door, and was told to bring up materials for four jovial farmers sitting round a table.

"Come this way," said he, hurrying to another door, which he opened with the same success, and at another received a torrent of abuse from some ladies who were thus unceremoniously intruded upon. Another room was found occupied by the fashionable hairdresser of the town, who had caught a young squire from the country, and had enveloped the sufferer in a large patch-work quilt, pinned firmly round his neck, as he sat staring at the singular twists of his countenance in the wavy looking-glass.

"Step through this room," said the waiter, "into the closet, until the gentleman gets his hair cut, and then, sir, you'll have the whole room to yourself."

I apologized, and begged of the gentlemen not to hurry themselves.

"Very polite man, that," said the barber to his patient, as I shut myself into the closet, and, throwing open the window-sashes, looked down upon the crowded street.

The market was over, yet the people lingered about the public-house's corner and gateways, drinking, laughing, and shouting; while ever and anon rose high in air the dolorous scream of pigs homeward-bound on cars, or urged through the crowd with blows and imprecations by their indignant masters; while the bellowing of kine, bleating of sheep and goats, songs of ballad-singers, and the loud and long blessing of the beggars, made the welkin ring. My

attention was soon turned to my next door neighbours, the hairdresser and squire, adding their quota
to the general uproar; indeed I might as well have
been in the same room with them, as the slender par-
tition between us, wood and canvas, and a door unconscious of a lock, did not at all prevent me from
being almost one of the party. I had observed, *en
passant*, that the hairdresser was an original in his
way—an idle, slouching, yet consequential personage,
with a physiognomy that at once reminded me of old
Liston's tragi-comical expression. The squire was
all impatience to be off, but the hairdresser was in no
hurry to let him slip so easily. He had thrown open
one of the windows, and frequently made his appearance, leaning very leisurely upon the window sill,
speaking to his friends below, and nodding familiarly
to the crowd, till the squire's rage rose; then would
the hairdresser return, and endeavour to mollify the
hasty squire.

" Come out of the window, and cut my hair," roared
the squire; " I'll never be home in time for dinner."

But the barber still continued at the window.
" Handsome day this, Corplar Dempsey—very."

" I'll tell you what it is—by the virtue of my oath,
I'll throw you down upon the heads of the people
you're talking to, instead of minding your business!"
cried the squire.

" Arrah—don't make a Judy of yourself, Master
Thom. There, sit quiet, and I'll finish you out of a
face. Don't speak of throwing me upon the head of
that orderly man, Corplar Dempsey; if he was
killed, the people would say it was a barbarous action.
Don't slap my head again, I say, in that impertinent
manner."

" Stop, rascal !—you have given me a clip on the ear ; and do you mean to cut all the hair off the back of my head ?"

" 'To be sure I do—better to be out of the world than out of the fashion, as Corplar Dempsey says."

" But I wont have my hair cut like a corporal."

" Not you, indeed ; you must have it cut like Ensign Fubb's in rear, and curled up in front, like Blucher's in my front window. Now, stop a bit till I regale my nose, as Major O'Flannagan says when I'm shaving him. Do you snuff, Master Thom ?"

" Confound your snuff—you have let some of it fall into my eye."

" Bear it, child, bear it ! as my grandmother, rest her soul, used to say when I burnt my fingers. Now I'll just look out of the window, and take the liberty of blowing my nose. There goes three officers of the *deepot*. Ah, the nice fellows ! gaping like three turkeys after one another, with three chins in the air, because they can't link, on account of the pigs and the people. There stands my old friend, Sir John B., commander of the forces ; shall I salute him ?—No. And why ? —because he's not on duty, and it would be irregular in me to notice him. Drest his wig this morning— gave me four shillings for the same. Now he's talking to Sir James, the rich subaltern lately joined us. Sir John and Sir James—how fashionably they laugh ! —the two sirs throwing back their heads, and knocking their heels together. Easy to see they are nobility. If that musical ballad-singer would be quiet, and that farmer's wife just hold her pig's mouth, I might hear what they are saying."

Again did the squire protest he would throw the

lazy barber out of the window, and again did the barber persuade him to sit quiet.

"Now stop! Ah, Master Thom, you're a wag. I'll put your hair in irons. I'll not singe as much as a cat's hair. There's a curl—keep that for Sunday, and it will be the making of you. Now for another!"

"You are burning my hair; I smell it."

"It's rashers you smell, child. I suppose the leedies are taking a whet in the next room."

"There, I knew it—you have burnt my hair—stop!"

"Change that tune, as your uncle Anthony said to the fiddler."

"Mind your business, and never mind my uncle."

"Well, but you're growing mighty cantankerous, Master Thom, though I never cut your hair but it reminds one of your uncle's bay wig. He was a quare man—so fond of music that he maintained a blind fiddler, whose occupation was to sit scraping his fiddle from morning till night outside the squire's door. Every morning while the squire was dressing himself, there sat Teddy, rasping away on the stairs; but one morning while the squire was shaving himself, he fell to humouring the jig, keeping time with the razor upon one cheek, and then upon the other, then upon his chin, and the faster old Teddy rasped the faster the squire rasped, till Teddy, thinking he was playing for dancers, cried out as usual, giving a stamp with his feet upon the stairs, 'Right and left, set partners—whew, my jewel!' With that the squire whips the razor from his right cheek to his left, and back again, for-getting that his nose stood, like a fool, in the middle; but, by my sawkins, he was long sorry, for he had whipped a good inch off the end of it, but he had too great a spirit to give in: so, ' Change that tune,' says he to blind Teddy, and went on shaving his throat to the Kinnegad Slashers."

" I don't believe one word of it."

" Now, Master Thom, if any one else told you, you would believe it. But sit quiet for one minute, and I'll make you look like a lion. I say it, though I lost the best place ever I had by telling my master he looked like a lion. That was when I lived with the Roman Count O'Gauley, long before you were born. I was his wallet—though now they have Frenchified it into valet, but wallet it ought to be, because what has a single man's servant to do but take care of his portmantle, as they call the wallet, but in my time I had to carry the count's wallet upon my shoulder after him. Wherever he went he rode on horseback, for he said it was the only way a knight should adventure himself from one country-seat to another; and certainly it was the cheapest way in the world, for the count adventured himself into many a snug dinner-party, and then I adventured myself with his wallet into the kitchen, and the old horse adventured himself upon the lawn at the first hay-stack he met, and so we got on in the country. But when we went to Dublin, times were altered, for we paid for everything at the Brazen Head, except the count's dinners, and he dined out every day; but I had a hard life of it, for the count became as cross and bitter as soot. He had the terriblest tongue I ever heard, and no wonder; for when he was by himself he whetted it upon French, and hardened it upon German, and case-hardened it in good old Irish, till he got the sting of all the languages upon the tip of his tongue. But

before he was dressed in the morning he was quiet
enough rolled up in his big banyan with a fur collar;
but the moment he was dressed—ou wow! nothing
was too good for him then—he became as proud and
fine as Brin Borohme; in short, there was no speaking to him, so I took to humouring him, like a cross
child.   I compared him to Nelson's pillar one day,
and he put his hand in his pocket and gave me a ten-
penny bit.   I took the hint, and every evening before
he went out I compared him to something grand and
handsome, till at last the old wasp began to think it
was part of my duty.   Well, I wore out all the church
steeples upon him, to the round church that has
never a steeple at all; and then, being hard run, I
told him not one of the seven champions of Christendom could hold a candle to him, but not a rap he
gave me for that, nor yet for the nine worthies.   He
boasted he was a better man of business than any
merchant in Dublin, born with a pen behind his ear,
because he forced the landlady to take some dittos out
of his bill.   He was very proud that evening, and no
wonder.

"'Count,' says I; 'you beat the measurer,' and
till now I thought he was the completest man of business in Dublin.'

"'Who's he?' said the count, looking very mis-
trustfully at me.

"'He stands, sir,' says I, 'behind the counter in a
grand shop in Dame Street, and indeed it would do
your honour good to stop at the glass door, and look
in at him transacting business—he'll take the yard so,'
says I, taking up the count's cane, 'and he'll welt out
a piece of dimity along the counter, till it looks like
a running stream, reflecting all the roots, and posies,

and branches upon its banks ; and I defy any man to say how many yards he has measured when he stops, tears off the selvidge with a screech, rolls it up in paper, twists the ends, jingles the change, bobs his head at his customer, with "anything else to-day, ma'am ?" and all this, while a cat would be licking her ear.'

" ' Soo,' says the count, as if he smelt something unpleasant. ' He's some low shopkeeperish rascal—a cheat, I'll warrant, " a thing of shreds and patches." '

" ' May be he is,' says I, and the next day I stood outside his shop door, I watched the measurer closely. There he was, as brisk as a bee, throwing out mull muslin, like sleet, to an easy country gentlewoman ; then he flops down a roll of bombazine upon the counter, and handles his yard.'

" ' Now,' says I, ' I'll watch you, my man ;' and away we pegged together—he measuring, and I counting out loud, for the bare life. ' One, two, three, four, ten,' says I.

" ' Twenty-five,' says he.

" ' Ten—it's only ten,' says I, bawling at him.

" ' Oh, measure that again,' says the lady, ' I beg !'

" ' Of course,' says he, ' anything to please, ma'am ;' and, in a pop, he came over the counter, and made at me with the yard. ' Go along out of that, you black-guard,' said he, ' blocking up my door with your bandy legs and ugly face ;' and he hits me upon the shins with the yard till I roared out " murder !"

" ' O, you rascal,' says I. ' Till now I thought you were a complete man of business ; but I agree with master—you're a vile shopkeeperish rascal—a cheat, I'll warrant, " a thing of shreds and patches." '

" ' I despise the pair of you,' says he,

C

" ' The Count O'Gawley shall hear of your disre-
spectful conduct,' says I.

" ' I'll charge you on the watch,' says he.

" ' Wait,' says I; ' you'll sup sorrow for this,' and
away I ran to the count. ' Count,' says I, ' for the
honour of your family, take your sword, and skewer
that rascally measurer behind his counter.'

" ' Why should I draw my sword upon the plebeian?'
said he, mighty sharp.

" ' Because,' says I, ' he spoke lightly of you, and
snapped his fingers in derision at you.'

" ' And how dare you introduce my name into your
low runcounter, your plebeian brawls,' says the count,
in a rage; and with that he hits me a spiteful rap
across the knees with his cane—it went to my very
heart.

" ' Count,' says I, ' that's the sorest touch of all—
you beat the measurer.'

" But that's true. I must tell you how we parted.
The count was going to the Castle ball one night, and
I had been working like a slave for five or six hours
before he was dressed to his satisfaction, for we had
got a long swinging looking-glass in the room, and
the count would stand squaring before it for half an
hour at a time to see if his clothes fitted him to his
liking. But at last, I got him altogether; and indeed he was a picture to look at, from his shoe-
buckles to his knee-buckles, his thin laths of legs in
pink silk stockings, with yellow docks, his flowered
silk waistcoat, the flaps drawn down convenient to his
knees, then his mulberry and tan silk embroidered
coat, between the long tails of which his slender court
sword stuck out for half a mile behind; but his head
beat all the rest. I had his hair frizzled out, and at

the same time, swept back from his face, and confined in a noble club at the back of his neck, then the three round patches upon his face to mark the beauty spots. He thought he had a sweet expression in his face; but any one with half an eye would think he had steeped his face in lemon-juice every morning, and dried it again in a north-east wind; but when he was putting his cocked hat under his arm, I stepped back and addressed him. ' Count,' says I, ' you look like a lion.' He liked that.

" ' Yes,' says he, squinting sideways in the looking-glass, ' there is something royal in my bearing; but, apropos,' says he, very briskly, ' where did you see a lion, my good fellow?'

" ' I saw one,' says I, ' with the showmen in Sackville Street.'

" ' In Sackville Street?' says the count.

" ' Yes, indeed,' says I, ' and by the same token, he danced upon the tight rope when the band played Tatter Jack Welsh.'

" ' Why, that was an ape,' says the count, growing as black as my hat.

" ' I ask your honour's pardon,' says I. ' I heard one of the showmen say it was one of the lions of the European world.'

" ' It was an—ape, an ape!' cried the count, grasping his cane, and cutting capers with fair spite.

" ' Well, it was an ape,' says I, ' and barring your honour, I never saw a more outlandish and fine-dressed gentleman.' With that the count became wild with anger.

" ' To my face to compare me to a rascally monkey —your benefactor!—an ape, an ape!'

" I threw myself upon my knees, but the count

c 2

made a blow at me, then up with the cane for another welt, and he smashed the big looking-glass behind him, and I dived under the bed.

"' Come out—come out !' says he.

"' Spare my life,' says I.

"' Varlet,' says he, 'you presume upon my leniency too far. I have the temper of an angel to bear with you.'

"' A saint—an apostle,' says I, from under the bed.

"' After all I did for you !' says the count.

"' True for you, count,' says I, beginning to sob. ' Barm of my existence—true for you, count."

"' Pest to society.'

"' True to you, count.'

"' Sink of iniquity,' says he; ' but I wont ruffle myself—I wont derange my dress.'

"' Don't, count,' says I, ' remember your ruffles— don't derange yourself.'

"' I perceive you're more knave than fool,' says the count, mad that he couldn't strike me without getting covered with feathers.

"' Anything your honour likes, for peace' sake,' says I.

"' Then you confess you're a rogue,' says he, drawing his sword, and striking an old boot from one end of the room to the other. ' You have robbed me, confess the fact and die,' says he.

"' The chairman wont wait any longer,' says the chambermaid, outside the door; and the count went off, leering back at me like an old terrier pulled away from a badger.

"' Is he gone ?' says I to the chambermaid, tumbling out from under the bed.

" He is,' says she ; ' they have carried him round he corner.'

" And indeed I didn't come to myself for an hour after, till the landlady sent me a good glass of spirits to revive me, and then I took my bundle under my arm and quitted the count's service, and before he came back to the Brazen Head, I was at home in my own hotel—a house I recommend you to stop at when you go to Dublin, Master Thom, the Wig, in Stoney-batter."

While the barber ran on thus, the squire frequently lost all patience with him, and at last started up, tearing off the quilt, and putting aside the barber, prepared to depart.

" One moment more," cried the barber; " sit down till I put a drop of oil on your hair."

" You have no oil," replied the squire.

" Plenty," replied the barber.

" Then where is it?" cried the squire.

" Oh, here it is! I have it now; how cunningly Mike had it hid on the top of the press! You perceive, I always leave a depôt with the waiter."

" That's not oil," said the squire, as the barber began shaking a large bottle.

" It's the royal vegetable curling fluid; there, now your head is well soaked with it; depend upon it, your curls wont go out till Sunday."

" Confound your fluid, you have burned my head," cried the squire; " what have you poured on my hair, you rascal?"

" Well, there's no harm done," said the barber; " it tastes like bitters."

" Bitters, you rascal!—how dare you pour bitters on my head?"

" It's not bitters, Master Thom; but I'll ask the waiter—it smells like black bottle."

A sudden brawl and outcry in the street saved the barber from the honest indignation of the squire.

" It's a row—it's a row," cried he, stretching out of window, " they are at it in Doolan's, fairly murdering one another; there go three Connaught men looking for stones; how they fly out of the house as thick as bees; success to you, Pethereen Casey, you're a proper behaved man at the end of a two-handled wattle—flail' them right and left—there will be wigs on the green; I can't stand it, I must be off, whoo."

And the barber rushed out of the room, followed by the squire, who had been scrubbing at his head with a towel; but the row drove his own grievance out of his head, and catching up his hat and whip, he made his exit also.

At last, bless my stars, I have got safe out of the borough of Athlone, though, at starting upon my hack jaunting car, I despaired of getting across that national grievance, the bridge, with whole bones; indeed the outside car, commonly called bone-setter, because of the roughness of its motion, seems to court destruction on every side, presenting the legs of its occupants to each approaching car, cart, carriage, caravan, and projection likely to fasten upon, and rend off our lower extremities; but he that crossed the bridge of Athlone—

" Where two wheelbarrows tremble ere they pass,"

upon an outside bone-setter, will not forget that bridge of both sighs and groans. The most expeditious way of crossing the bridge is practised by the young townsmen, who mount boldly and step fearlessly from Leinster to Connaught, and back again upon the heads, shoulders, and horns of countrymen, cows, sheep, swine, donkeys, corn-sacks, barrels, and baskets, wedged in dense mass between the parapets, struggling forward with might and main, or pausing in wrath, while the light-heeled and familiar towns-men trip over them at pleasure. We progressed some eight miles into Connaught, gradually leaving green fields, plantation, and civilization behind us; we entered a waste of bog and swamp, enlivened with solitary potatoe patches, and cabins rivalling wigwams.

" Is it to Killmoran your honour's going ?" said the Whip, pulling up his brown hack:

" Yes," said I.

" Because," said he, " it's over forninst you now; there ought to be a booreen (lane) somewhere here-abouts, but maybe they have broke down the bridge."

" Where is Killmoran ?" said I.

" Don't you perceive it just before you ?" said the Whip—" that little hill in the bottom, about a quarter of a mile across the bog ?"

My first impulse was to return at once; but having come so far, I resolved to see it out—leaving the jarvey to follow as best he might, upon the booreen. I leaped a wide dike or trench by the road side, and the next second found myself knee-deep, firmly planted in the peat or bog, from which I extricated my legs, minus one boot, and experienced consider-able disagreements in recovering said boot from the tenacious bog. Having regained my equilibrium, I adventured across the morass, hopping from one tuft of heath to another, eschewing the black and decep-tive bog: the surface, forsooth, upon which a young man ought to embark his capital, according to Cor-nelius Meehan. I was soon hailed by a noisy pack of cur dogs; they scampered to meet me from the doors of smoky low-thatched wigwams, built upon the rising ground or island in the bog; I kept them at bay with my walking-stick, and presently a wild-looking woman appeared at the door of one of the cabins; she screamed in Irish at a man who was digging in his potatoe patch, and pointed significantly at me; the man threw down his spade, and ran off into the bog as fast as his long legs could carry him. I now beheld a swarm of half-clad children emerging from every cabin; presently men and women gathered in knots, speaking with considerable vehemence in their native tongue, and gesticulating as wildly as a lazzarone in a storm. I observed, moreover, that they receded as I advanced, and, ignorant of the cause, I halted as soon as I had gained *terra firma*, accosted an old woman who shewed her smoke-dried visage at the door of the nearest cabin, and inquired if this was not the townland of Killmoran.

The beldame answered with a sneer, " And well you know it is."

I drew the rent-roll and sheet of particulars from my pocket to refresh my memory.

" My good people," said I—for the tenants, men, women, and children, had advanced to support the old woman—" my good people, can ye inform me where is Phil Connor, and please to point out his house and holding. I"—An angry laugh and a shout of derision cut short my inquiries.

" My good people," said I, " I am surprised. Cornelius Meehan, Esq., informed me that—(cries of Go back again to sweet Corney!) " After coming so far," said I, " to see the place——"

" Well, sure you're paid for it?" said a brawny, red-headed labourer.

" Paid for what?" said I, with unfeigned surprise.

" You know for what, and so do I," he replied—
" to sarve us to be sure."*

" I mean to serve you all as far as lies in my power," said I, with a glow of philanthropic zeal, which was speedily checked and extinguished, when I observed the aforesaid men, women, and children, picking up handfuls of mire, clods, peat, and stone ; then came the courteous invitation, " Make yourself scarce, and we'll give you a fair start across the bog."

Prudence is said to be the better part of valour—

> " He that fights and runs away,
> May live——"

The " may live" of that dry distich stuck in my throat. If I had found it a difficult task to walk across that quaking bog in sober sadness, how much more difficult and impracticable to run for my life, pursued by a blood-thirsty crowd of regular bog-trotters and cur dogs!   I loathed the thought.

" My good people," said I, " you think I am an enemy ; if I was, would I trust myself alone amongst you ?   I don't understand Irish, but if you can read English, take this paper, and satisfy yourselves as to my intentions."

" Well, there's some sense in that," said the red-haired swain, but his movement in my favour was quickly overruled by his wife.

" Don't touch his paper !" she screamed.

Matters now looked as bad as ever ; I threw a furtive glance on the bog to see if my retreat was still open, when a tall sickly-looking countryman, wrapped up in his big coat, entered the crowd.

" What's the matter ?" said he.

* Give notice to quit.

" Matter enough," cried a dozen of voices ; " here's a Peeler in disguise, looking for Phil Connor."

" No, he's a rebellion officer," said another ; " didn't you hear him say he wanted to sarve us a minute ago ?"

" Shew me the paper," said the tall farmer.

I handed him the rent-roll and sheet of particulars ; he glanced over it, and then took off his hat.

" I ask your honour's pardon," said he ; " but we never see a man in this part with a paper in his hands, but we sup sorrow long enough after it."

He now explained to the people that I was a real gentleman, come down to buy Killmoran out-and-out entirely. On hearing this, matters cleared up immediately ; the woman who had been loudest in her abuse slank away, hanging down her head, and declaring she had ruined her man entirely. I followed her, and insisted upon her recalling her man from his hiding-place in the bog ; and finding that I treated them and their demonstrations as a capital joke, confidence was restored, and I had many humble petitions for pardon, and pressing invitations to enter their cabins and take an air of the fire. I now requested the tall farmer, whose name was Jem Dillon, to walk over the lands with me, and point out how the marshes, the uplands, and arable lands were divided and subdivided into small holdings and enclosures. On crossing every ditch and dry stone wall, Dillon gave me a history of the nature of the holding, and the reason of the division of acres, roods, and perches, " The soil is worn out and exhausted ; it wants rest," said Dillon, " but we have no time to give it rest ; if it wasn't for the bog stuff, warmed with a trifle of manuring gravel, we couldn't raise oats enough to feed a goose, upon the whole of Killmoran." I now looked upon the bottoms and vast extent of bog.

"It's a grand place for snipe-shooting and duck-shooting, in winter," said Dillon.

"But it might be drained and improved," said I.

"Ay, if there was fall enough for the water," said Dillon; "but it would take a power of money to open a canal through that bog all the way down to the river; and, after all, may be it would be·of no service to the bottoms here; they would be good for nothing if they were dry in summer, and the grazing cattle is all we depend on for the rent."

"Why don't you plant a few trees," said I, looking round in vain for a sheltering bush.

"Much encouragement we have to plant trees," said Dillon; "threatened with ejectments every day, why should we improve the appearance of the land, to have the rent raised higher and higher every day?"

"But if you had a lease, I suppose you would improve the place?" said I.

"Lease, indeed!" said Dillon—"lease!—how are you? When I had a lease, I didn't keep it."

"Why not keep it?" said I.

"Because I was a fool," said he, shattering his stick upon a fragment of rock that lay before us; "but it's useless to talk about it now."

I begged to know how he lost his lease, and he replied, with a little hesitation—

"I wouldn't like to say anything that might prevent your honour from having any dealings with the man that wants to sell this place, for it's myself would be proud to see our landlord walking simply through his tenants, like yourself; but there's no hiding it—our landlord is no gentleman; a few years

ago there was a great election in this county, and a
contest; you heard talk of it, of course. Well, sir,
before the election, down came the landlord himself,
and it was the first and last time that ever he darkened
my door. "Phil Dillon," said he, "you must register your vote."

"And welcome, sir," says I; "who'll get it before
my landlord?" Well, sir, I agreed to meet him next
day, at the Court-house, and so did M'Dermot and
Phil Connor, for we were the only men that had
leases on the lands: we went into the Court-house,
and there we sat cheek-by-jowl with the barrister and
the magistrates upon the bench; and when the master
saw us, he tapped an attorney on the head, and sent
him over to where we were sitting, near the dock.
'Hand over your leases,' said the attorney; and, like
three big fools, as we were, we handed them to him;
we waited long enough to be called on to register, but
not a word did we hear about it; and that evening we
just had time to say a word to the landlord as he was
stepping into the mail; we asked him to return our
leases.

"'Dillon,' says he, 'there's an informality and ille-
gality about those instruments, that must be looked
into and rectified.' You see, though he set up for a
gentleman, he wasn't above taking a drop too much;
and seeing there was no help for it, and that he didn't
know what he was talking about instruments and balderdash, we helped him into the coach—and that was
the last sight I got of him; for after that he went off
to France, and left everything in the hands of Corney
Meehan; and the next rent day we asked Corney to
return our leases, and the kennat up and tells us, our
leases weren't worth a rush; then says I, 'Jerry Mal-

lowney's life is not worth a rush;' 'nor Judy Mac-
Quades,' says my brother; 'nor my own,' says Phil
Connor; and we rehearsed the lives in our leases."

" ' Well, be quiet,' says Corney, in a soothing voice,
' and I'll do my endeavour to get your leases back
again, if they are not lost;' so we paid the rent, and
the next rent day it was the same story, and then we
went to father O'Brien, and told him our story.

" ' Why did not you come to me at first?' says he,
very sharp; 'no, you promised, you volunteered, to
vote against your country and conscience; so go be
hanged, and I hope you'll never get what you're looking for, and you'll be examples in the country.'

" ' The last attempt we made was to hire an attorney: we clubbed better than ten pounds, and went
to consult a very good head-piece in the town,
Attorney Skrewle. He asked us if our leases were
registered in Dublin; and when we said not, he began
to whistle; so he put the money in his pocket—' And
I'll not lose sight of you, my good fellows,' said he, as
he banged the door in our faces; and from that to
this, everything has been going to the bad in Killmoran; we have no heart to make up even a gap in a
stone wall; when we were served with ejectments we
sub-letted and divided our farms as you see, because
the agents find it harder to turn out whole villages
than they did formerly with the sodgers at their
backs."

We now entered Phil Dillon's bawn—a large farm-
house, in the last stage of dilapidation—a large dunghill before the door, and a pool of stagnant water.

" Why don't you remove that abomination, and let
off the stagnant water?" said I—" it's enough to breed
fever and pestilence in your family."

" You know little about farming in these parts,"
said Dillon, " or you would not say that, sir."

I had seen quite enough of this wretched place ;
and having taken an air of the fire, and hot potatoes
with my friendly guide, I wished him a better landlord,
and resumed my seat upon the car, which the jarvey
had had the prudence to keep upon the main road
till I returned, not liking, as he said, to hazard passing up through the boreen, which was the father of
all the bad old boreens in the country ; and thus
ended my first hunt after an Irish estate."

CHAPTER III.

Whist parties—Smokers—Italian Counts and stokers—Mexicans—
Virginian—Cockney—German professor — Here-we-go—Quaker's mishap.

THE French, Germans, and Italians, soon make up
whist parties, the shattered chessmen are ranged in
battle array by others, and the tables re-echo with the
racket of backgammon ; meantime, the motion of the
engines is barely perceptible, the lamps swing lightly,
and our royal vessel walks down the star-lit channel
like a phantom-ship.

Supper, sir. Cold beef, broiled bones, a night-cap,
and then turn in at half-past ten, amidst the perfume
of extinguished lamps and candles. Breakfast at
half-past eight; sea not quite so smooth; wind a-beam;
the passengers say they have got their sea legs on, and
keep marching up and down the decks as if for a
wager, the majority puffing cigars. I can smoke a
cigarrito or meerschaum against any don or Dutchman
ashore, but deliver me from the vapid odour of half-
smoked cigars at sea—bilge water and burnt cabbage
are preferable to it.

The great business of the day seems to be eating
and drinking, and the quick succession of meals—

breakfast, luncheon, dinner, tea, and supper—keep
the salon in a perpetual clatter; a constant jingling
of plates, glasses, knives, forks, and spoons; waiters
rushing to and fro, and frequently meeting full tilt
with a crash in the midst of their zeal to serve the
voracious passengers. Visit the engine-room with
two Italian counts, who are filled with amazement at
the grand scale of the machinery, and the light and
ornamental frame that supports it: the stokers are
more to be pitied than galley slaves, in my humble
opinion—exposed to intense heat; in case of accident
they are sure to suffer. As we looked down upon
these men, covered with sweat and coal-dust, one of
the Italians observed that the meanest of his countrymen
would not endure such severe work for any money—
same time dropped some silver into the cap of one of
the stokers, a buonamano; the engines are said to be
not sufficiently powerful for the vessel, and the next
trip they are to be taken out and replaced with eight
hundred instead of four hundred horse power.

The berth next to mine is occupied by a young
Spaniard or Mexican, who, with his uncle and aunt
and a splendid little fellow, followed about the deck
by a swarthy Muchacha, in the costume of the Asturias,
are quite a society in themselves. With this youth I
speedily scraped an acquaintance, on purpose to convince him of the folly of throwing away his valuable
time playing that devil's bellows or bagpipes, a French
accordion; and sooner than endure the whinings,
howlings, and gruntings of that instrument, undertake
to teach him English through the medium of an old
Spanish and French vocabulary. The young Italian
count assists me in this pious attempt to beguile the
Mexican from his melting mood: we have succeeded,

and now the happy pair are inseparable, and, neither of them understanding French enough to hold conversation, they follow each other about apropos to nothing, bleating " Mexicanito, Italianito—Mexicanito, Italianito."

" I say it is impossible to know the English," said a heavy Virginian gentleman, looking sternly round him, after dinner; "I have been four months in England with my son—we went to England to see the old country, and become acquainted there; but, I solemnly declare, we left it without making a single friend or common bowing acquaintance."

" Indeed! how very odd," replied a hungry-looking cockney, who had lent his ear to the Virginian's complaints.

" I do not think I am at all singular, sir," said the Virginian, haughtily. "I had a letter of introduction to a banker; well, sir, he never took any notice of me. I might have been introduced at court by our minister, but I declined the honour. ' No,' said I, ' I am determined to make my own way.' We lodged at the London Coffee-house, then moved to the West End—to the Hummums."

" I hope, sir, you don't mean to say the Hummums is in the West End," said the cockney.

" It is in Westminster, is it not?" said the Virginian. " We dined in the same room with country gentlemen and citizens, and never received the least notice, or were treated with the least attention."

" Probably they thought you were English yourself, sir," said the cockney, with a leer.

" No, sir, I made it a rule to converse with my son about our native land, and the people of the house knew all about us; and when we went down to

Cheltenham we were quite isolated in the crowd, and further than ever from the bosom of private society."

Here a shrewd-looking Scot begged to remark, that without proper letters of introduction from friends to friends, it was impossible for a stranger to get into private society anywhere ; for his own part, he had been like a fish out of water long enough, in New York, Boston, Philadelphia, and other cities of the union ; and though, as mercantile traveller to a first-rate house, he had plenty of business to transact, never ate or drank save at his own expense and at a public table, yet in America.

" But you never visited Virginia, the old dominion," said the Virginian.

The Scot replied in the negative, but a severe-looking German, who had hitherto held his peace, said he had travelled through Virginia, and had paid his way everywhere he went in hard dollars ; he had been to the red, white, green, and blue sulphur springs, and believed the Virginians spent more money there than the English did at Cheltenham, or the Germans at Baden Baden or Weis Baden.

" There is a wide difference between the northern and the southern states," said the Virginian, somewhat perplexed. " In the north they believe every man to be a swindler till they find he is a gentleman ; in the south they believe every man to be a gentleman till they find out he is a swindler."

There was a laugh raised at the conclusion of this table-talk, which provoked the German ; shutting up a book, with great emphasis he begged the Virginian to repeat his words, as he did not clearly understand him. The Virginian good-humouredly complied, whereupon the German said the word "swindler" did not apply to him; he was well-known in both worlds, as an author and professor of ————, and, rising from the table, this learned mufti withdrew in high dudgeon.

This morning the sea is reported to be getting up, before breakfast the weather is pronounced dirty, and the wind, which for the last three days has been most favourable, now chops round right in our teeth. The captain, mates, and the rest of the men-of-war's men, look out for squalls, and return short and gruff answers to the querulous bleatings of the passengers, who are fain to satisfy their curiosity with the card suspended over the mate's cabin door, from which the latitude, longitude, and the number of miles our good ship has steamed, is soon ascertained. First day we steamed 156 miles; second, 210; third, 220; fourth, 170; fifth, only 40 miles; sixth, the *card* is blown overboard, and observations are out of the question. The creaking, straining, and groaning noises in the saloon, and the crashing of plates and glasses in the steward's department, do not at all enliven the long faces reflected in the mirrors on every side; even our trumpeter seems to be out of sorts and out of tune, jumbling "Jim Crow" and "Auld lang syne" together. The dinner was ushered in with a variety of capsizes, soup spilled, legs of mutton and rounds of beef broke loose, sucking pigs attempting to escape from table to table, from chair to sofa. The German professor, who, since his set-to with the Virginian, spent more time at his toilet, and looked as starched and stiff in his white cravat and black silk waistcoat as a lobster on his first appearance, looked unut-

terable things when half a calf's head sought refuge
in his bosom, helping his waistcoat and frill to
more sauce and brains than the learned mufti bargained for.

" Why will you persist in setting pigs before me ?"
thundered the sanguine sympathizer, as the waiter requested a slice of the roaster, which the sympathizer
resolved to get rid of by putting whole on the plate ;
the result of that plenteous helping was the upsetting
of three decanters, as the pig flew over my head
and fell between two delicate ladies at the opposite
side. · The stiff and uncompromising conduct of the
unbending quaker, in the midst of all this growing
riot, was admirable.   He would not bend his back, I
verily believe, to evade the blow of a falling mast,
much less flinch or swerve aside from a flying cauli-
flower, or wavelet of soup——the consequence was, that
his brown coat and drab continuations began to exhibit
marks and tokens of the culinary wars, which he bore
as meekly as a martyr.   Once or twice, however, I
caught him crouching in wild alarm and bodily fear.
The first time it was at dinner, when his chair broke
loose, and carried the quaker twice backwards and
forwards from one side of the saloon to the other, the
third time it was secured by two waiters, and bound
by the leg to a table, and our friend continued his
dinner, more frightened than hurt.   The next time I
saw him surprised into exclamations on deck, when
the vessel rolled from side to side like a beer barrel,
and every one on deck was forced to lay hold on ropes,
stanchions, or bulwarks, and not a few threw themselves down on their hands and knees; but the unbending abolitionist was forced to run ; and away he
went, full tilt, against the bulwark, and would have

toppled right into the yawning abyss had not an old sailor caught him by his broad skirts ; after that escape our friend confined himself to the saloon. " Here we go, and here we go !" those monstrous words are " ever ringing in my ear ;" the burden of the song of " Here we go"—the name by which we recognise a keen card player and nail-nibbling cockney, who, from the moment the gale began, swings from side to side with the rolling and pitching of the vessel, sometimes catching hold of the next person to him, no matter who, exclaiming — " Here we go !" and invariably dragging him on, full gallop, from bulkhead to bulwark, post to pillar—even a pair of broken skins and a black eye did not steady him ; but once he had a narrow escape, even at the card table, which even the raging of the tempest could not clear, till the bench or sofa on which Here-we-go and three others were seated broke loose, with a tremendous lurch, and away they went—Here-we-go singing out, as he dragged the card-cloth, counters, money, and tricks, along with him—the partners rushed to relieve their friends in need, and met the anxious bench returning full surge with its cargo and passengers : down they went, sofa, chairs, and the card table, gamesters, cards, counters, and cash, and, like a living billow, dashed backwards and forwards upon the smooth oilcloth, till half the waiters and several passengers picked them asunder. Poor Here-we-go was a severe sufferer in that rolling match—next day he was stiff as a crutch, and covered with sticking plaster.

In the midst of all this turmoil I find the old set, the knot of odd fellows rallying round that inveterate land-louper, the gentleman in search of an estate— their mirth is less boisterous than it was a few evenings ago, they hold their glasses with both hands, and lean upon their elbows with looks of intense anxiety ; they seem to tread the green fields and wild hills with the gentleman in search of an estate, as he reads in his hum-drum way and sotto voce tone another adventure.

CHAPTER IV.

Adventures of a gentleman in search of an estate—Tipperary property—Absentee tenant—White-boys—Attack on the house—
Fly-boat—Passengers—Rough diamond.

" THE next estate I visited was situated in the wilds of
the far-famed county Tipperary. I had been invited
to look at it by its absentee landlord, who was anxious
to dispose of it for the ostensible purpose of concen-
trating his possessions in another part of the kingdom,
where, he said, " the bulk of his property lay. You
will find Altadugh a most desirable thing, in the midst
of the fine sporting county, Tipperary."

" Where the ' finest peasantry' knock down landlords, parsons, and agents, *en passant*," I observed.

" O, my good sir, that's all *passé*—threadbare subject—old song—newspaper malevolence," retorted the
absentee, very briskly ; " outrages, accidents, and
offences occur everywhere, at home and abroad ; then,
sir, look at the size of Tipperary, and its contiguity to
Cork and Limerick !"

In short, the absentee said so much in favour of the
county he wished to cut for ever, that my curiosity
was excited, and, even without the faint prospect of
finding a home in the wilds, I resolved to visit Tipperary.

I had slept at the small town of ————, about ten
miles from Altadugh; started after breakfast, and
arrived in good time to reconnoitre the premises.   I
liked the appearance of Altadugh " passing well;" at
first sight, the place seemed much larger than it really
was; clumps of trees and plantations springing up
round the verdant lawn and rising ground upon which
the house stood, an old-fashioned, high-gabled, long-
roofed building, enlivened with a singular variety of
narrow windows; a grotesque and massive Gothic
door-case seemed out of keeping in this modern struc-
ture, for doubtless it had been taken from some venerable walls, where it had defied the tooth of time, till
the hammer of the builder of Altadugh House, heedless of the " fitness of things," battered it into its present situation, and doomed its key-stone to bear a
noble pair of stag's or elk's horns, instead of the banners, shields, and spolia of its former lords, who may
have been the redoubtable knights of the Red Branch.
A neat garden and flower-knot, enclosed by a beech
and thorn hedge, might be too near the house to please
every one; but there was an air of quietness and still
life about the place that pleased me much.   A large
Newfoundland dog basked on the broad flags before
the hall door, and a peacock displayed his noble fan
to the sun.   The grating wheels of my car soon roused
the former; he lifted up his nose from his fore-paws,
and, without deigning to stand up, challenged the in-
truders upon the premises; but his loud bark was soon
changed to a doleful whine, when a shrill workman's
bell began to toll, the peacock to squall, and labourers
from the farm and yard at the back of the house ran
home to their dinners.   Then came Mr. Truemore, a
hale, good-natured-looking gentleman, turned fifty,

dressed in shooting-jacket and cords. He had been stewarding his men. When he understood the object of my visit, he politely volunteered to shew me the lands and boundaries himself. " I hold but a small part of the land in my own hands," said he, as we entered a large tillage-field.

" I thought," said I, " you rented the whole of it."

" And so I do," replied Truemore; " but latterly I have sublet the greater part of it. There," said he, pointing to a cluster of cabins, " are some of my tenants' houses."

" And how do they pay their rents?" said I.

" Punctually in labour," said he; " they perform all my farm-work, and the produce pays Mr. ——'s rents, and sometimes not even that."

" You think the rent too high, I suppose?" said I.

" Certainly," he replied; " much too high now-a-days; but the lease was taken out by my father during the war, when land and the produce were enormously high. After the war, prices came down at once; we felt a sad change; we were tied up and bound by our lease to pay a heavy rent. My father was a man of education and a gentleman; we had to keep up appearances and live like gentlemen, keep servants and horses, and pay for everything; but we had to sell our produce in the same market as our neighbours, who were all small farmers, and could afford to undersell us, because they lived like labourers, and refusing to pay their high rents, got abatements from their landlords, while our rents were raised to the last farthing. During my father's life, we expended a great deal of money on this place; we planted those trees, and built extensive offices, enclosed yards, and built sundry small additions to the dwelling-house;

D

but since our lease has expired, and the landlord refuses to renew it, or grant us a new one, even upon the same hard terms, I have sublet part of the land; in fact, I never would have done so, had I the smallest chance of having a lease; but, as tenant at will, I am at the mercy of my landlord, and have lost all thoughts of improving, or even keeping up my former improvements. I do acknowledge I am attached to this place; here I have spent the happiest days of my life. I cannot purchase the property, but I have made tempting offers to my landlord for a new lease; I have offered him a considerable fine (premium) and rents in advance, all to no purpose; we differ in politics, and that is the secret."

Having walked over the lands, and approved of Mr. Truemore's system of farming, and the explanations he entered into thereon, we returned to the dwelling-house. Truemore introduced me to his daughters; the eldest, a beautiful girl, not more than nineteen, reclined upon a sofa, and apologized for not rising. Poor girl! she was in the last stage of consumption; the hectic rose upon her cheek, and the brilliancy of those dark, blue eyes, shaded with the longest eye-lashes I ever saw, long alabaster fingers, and pallid brow, all bore the stamp of that insidious and ruthless destroyer of the "fairest flowers."

"Come, Helen," said Truemore, in a cheerful voice, "you look better to-day, love; Dr. Dowall says you ought to keep up your spirits: now the winter's over, and spring come again, you must get out in the air, and a little change of scene will be of service." (Here the youngest girl, a light, aërial creature, left the room.) "Jane is the housekeeper," said Truemore; "and here comes my brother," continued he, pointing to a tall, carelessly-dressed man, who lounged past the drawing-room windows, and entered the room. He neither spoke nor seemed to observe any one. " Jack!" said Truemore, with a loud voice, " why, Jack, don't you see Mr. Morleigh, come all the way from London to see us ?"

Jack, who had seated himself, looked earnestly at me, and repeated slowly, " Mister Mor-leigh, come all—the way from Lon-don—Lon-don ?"

He paused, then passed his hand over his brow, and repeated the same words twice over again. There was an anxious and eager expression about his hazel eyes for a second; he became silent, and looked at me with a vacant stare.

" Poor fellow !" said Truemore, " he has been in London too, but that was before his head was injured; indeed we all wondered how he survived."

" An accident, I suppose," said I to Truemore, who glanced at his daughter, and changed the subject; he spoke of stock, the prices of farm-produce, farming, and politics, then apologized for leaving me, while he went to give some directions to his out-door labourers; and the moment he left the room, John took his place close by the sofa, took his niece's hand, and looked at me with a sorrowful countenance.

" My father cannot bear to speak of his misfortunes before me now," said Helen, addressing herself to me, " and my poor uncle cannot speak for himself. O, sir, if you had known him a few years ago, full of life and hope, you would feel the sad change as much as we do, I'm sure. Some years since, my uncle went to London to speak to our landlord about renewing the lease of this place; he received much attention from him, and indeed the landlord seemed to take an interest

D 2

in poor John; he was amused by his anecdotes, and called him his original tenant. We certainly thought he would have succeeded about the lease. When John came back he kept us alive, telling us all about London; but after all we could get no satisfactory reply from the landlord, and John took a farm about five miles from this. He lived with us as usual, and rode to his farm every day; but one day he was way-laid by some villains; they fired at him, wounded him in the arm, and then beat him on the head; his skull was fractured; they left him for dead, but he recovered, after a long illness, and has ever since been just as you see him."

"And were the miscreants punished?" said I.

"Never," replied Helen; "though several people were working in the fields near the spot, and heard the shots, and must have seen the assassins, they never interfered. We offered a reward, but it was useless, no one would come forward; though the people loudly condemned the act, still the assassins escaped."

I was greatly shocked at this sad tale, and while I was expressing my indignation Mr. Truemore returned, and a servant announced luncheon. We adjourned to the parlour, leaving the poor invalids by themselves.

"You must not think of leaving us to-day," said Truemore; "you have not seen enough of the property yet. You may count on a well-aired bed."

I said I was anxious to return to Dublin in vain. Truemore pointed to the clouds on the Keeper Mountain and the dismal brow of the Devil's Bit; and as the rain began to fall, and Truemore vowed no man with a roof over his head should venture out, I agreed to become his guest, and remain at Altadugh till next morning.

I spent the afternoon as agreeably as circumstances would permit, but a shade of melancholy stole over everything; the forced gaiety of my host, the faint smiles of Helen, and even the Irish melodies Jane played on the instrument were melancholy.

" I dare say you will recognise some old friends in this bookcase," said my host; " though we live in an out-of-the-way place, we have some resources; and here," said he, opening a small cabinet, " if you are fond of antiquarian researches, you will soon discover the value of these time-worn bits of metal; this trayful of old coins was dug up from the top of the round hill you admired so much. I assure you it was no easy matter to prevail upon the workmen to dig the holes in which I planted the trees; and till I set them the example, and promised to bear all *the harm* and anger of the *good people* myself, they would not disturb the soil. The coins bear the rude stamp and superscription of your Saxon kings, Edwy and Athelstan. My poor brother, who read a great deal, and indeed, collected the greater part of those antiquities, said the coins were concealed there by the Danes, after having plundered the English coast. I am sure these thin pieces of silver were not worth fighting for. I found this bronze cup with two handles about three feet under the coins. Doctor Dowal, who is a great antiquarian in his way, says it is a Druidical censer, and attempts to prove that it belonged to the priests of the Sun, from the little hill named Belbeg; Bel being the Irish for sun, and Beg little. Some miles from this, we find the hill of Belmore, or the Great Sun Hill; we have often meditated an expedition to that hill, to seek for antiquities by moon or torch light. The farmer on whose land it is situated

would as soon see his house levelled to the ground as
see a single sod of that green mould disturbed, because his old grandmother told him she heard a
strange man tell a queer story about a simple colleen,
or girl, who *was called* for breaking a branch from a
white thorn tree on the hill side, and soon after disappeared for ever."

" How *called ?*" said L.

" Oh, *called* by the *fairies*, of course !" said Helen ;
" but Jane can sing you a song about it, if she likes."

Jane did not require much pressing.   She sat down
once more at the piano, and played a wild and melancholy Irish air I had never heard before, and sang a
few verses of the ballad.

> " She lay by the side of the mountain-stream,
>   Like a fair wild flowret strown ;
> Her mind was astray in a fairy dream
>   And she lived in the mountains alone.
>
> " She had followed her love from her own dear land,
>   Where our villagers never had been ;
> But the false one had gone with his martial band,
>   Far, far from his own Eveleen.
>
> " She sat beneath the shade of the hawthorn tree,
>   That grew on the hill fort green,
> And she heard a voice singing, ' Come follow me,—
>   Follow me, Eveleen—Eveleen !'
>
> " She followed, she followed, the villagers say,
>   And never, never came back again ;
> We anxiously sought her for many a day,
>   And we called her, but called her in vain.
>
> " They say that she lives with the good people still,
>   And oft 'neath the hawthorn green
> The young maidens hear her wild song in the hill,
>   And sigh for the lost Eveleen."

When her " wood-notes wild" died away, I would have cried " encore !" As it was, I was not sparing in my plaudits ; while Jane, blushing at my bravas, merely said she had not done justice to the words; they had been composed and set to music by—— ; and here my inquiries made the poor girl blush, and her sister smile, seeing that she had a reason for concealing the author's name. We turned once more to the cabinet. My host shewed me a coin his brother had found near a round tower. He said it was Phœnician or Egyptian, from certain hieroglyphics on it. I had seen some Egyptian coins in the museum of the Vatican, and gratified my host not a little by confirming his opinion as far as the faint resemblance those grotesque characters bore to others I had seen in the Eternal City. We glanced over a variety of spear and arrow heads found at sundry times in divers parts of the country, by John. One old weapon arrested my attention ; my host informed me it was a middoge, or an ancient dagger worn by the Irish kings. " That hoop in your hand was found in a small lake by a boy who was looking for wild ducks' nests," said my host; " doubtless it was one of the collars worn by the Saxons and Danes. I am sorry it is not the collar of gold Moore sings about."

" But you have a link of that celebrated chain, papa," said Helen.

" True, my love, and here it is. Mr. Morleigh. look at this link of gold, and fancy what a pretty fortune a chain of such links, full a cloth yard long, would be for a country maiden. That link weighs four ounces, but the man who found the whole chain brought me this link, only to ascertain if it were gold. I bought it from him by weight. He went to Dublin, and sold the rest to a goldsmith, returned to the country, took a large farm, stocked it, and from being a very poor labourer became a wealthy farmer; but a cloud, they say, hangs over the money-finder, and what comes easily goes easily. We are still superstitious in this country. The chain-finder became an unhappy man—lost his stock, his farm, and has frequently solicited a day's work as a common labourer. He has since pointed out the place where he found the chain to the country people; and for once their love of money has triumphed over their superstitious fears. Parties of treasure-seekers have frequently burrowed and dug 'deeper and deeper still' into the Doon more, or great cave, with little success, I suspect; at least, I have never heard any favourable reports, and the people are seldom silent when they are successful; indeed, if a man labouring in a field turned up a stray halfpenny, a report would soon get wind that he had made his fortune, and might never handle a spade again. Indeed, I once heard a poor man taken to task very sharply by the land agent for not delivering up a mass of virgin silver he was said to have discovered while making a ditch; however, the matter was dropped when it was found to be a lump of lead which had escaped from a tinker's budget, or forge, which had been at full work on the premises a few years before. Since I am speaking about forges, I once—but I am wearying you Mr. Morleigh."

I protested not, and my host continued.

" I once met a country fellow sauntering towards a blacksmith's forge to get a handle or hasp for his cowhouse door, fashioned out of a twisted bar of dingy-coloured brass he had found in a bog.

" ' I found it,' said he, ' a year ago, and pitched it under the dresser along with some sticks and rubbish, and this being an idle day with me, I thought I'd slip up to the forge, and hear the news, and get the handle made. I would rather have iron to be sure, but the times are bad—I'm not able to buy the length of my hand of ribbon-iron.'

" I now took the bar in my hand," said my host, " and was convinced it was heavier than brass.

" ' Barney,' said I, ' this wont do for a handle for your cowhouse door.'

" ' I thought as much myself,' said he.

" But if you really want a handle for it, I have an old one at home, and I'll give it to you for this, and welcome."

" You were always a good warrant to help a man in distress,"²said he.

" And now, Mr. Morleigh, Jane must finish the story; you must excuse me; I see the rain continues, and I must send the workmen home."

Jane resumed the story. " My father soon discovered the value of the bar—it was pure gold; he brought it to Dublin, and sold it for thirty guineas—no great sum, but quite sufficient to make the finder happy, for Barney had aspired to the hand of a rich farmer's daughter; her father would not consent to the match—he objected to Barney merely on the score of his poverty; but the thirty guineas which my father handed to the rejected suitor acted like a charm. The farmer was no longer inexorable; in short, they were married, and live very happily not far from this. My father thinks it was fortunate he met Barney before he entered the forge, from which it might never have been restored to Barney, or even served to fasten his cowhouse-door."

And thus the afternoon was spent, agreeably enough, though at first it wore a heavy aspect without and within doors. We sat down to a plain but well-dressed dinner. I say *we*, because I felt as one of the family, already quite at home. Uncle John sat at the foot, and carved away at a leg of mutton with judicial gravity; he retired with the girls shortly after the dessert. My host touched his head significantly.

" He cannot bear wine now," said he ; " time was, when he could take his two bottles, and sing his song, with the merriest and the best of us."

We now drew our chairs to the fire, placed a table between us, filled our glasses, and set the wind, rain, care, and sorrow, at defiance.

" Blow winds and crack your cheeks," said my host, as the windows rattled and the storm howled round the old house.

I like a good turf fire—I prefer it to coal; nevertheless, turf and fuel, generally speaking, were scarce in that part of the country. My host informed me that some of his tenants suffered much during the winter, when they had not laid in a sufficient stock of hand-turf during the summer. He explained the difference between hand-turf and cut-turf—the former being by far the most troublesome and expensive, made up like bricks in deep marshy bogs ; while the latter is cut with a slane, or sharp-edged spade, frequently used in the rebellions as a most formidable weapon.

" You saw the pike, in the next room ?" said my host.

" It is certainly a dangerous weapon," said I ; " but I hope the pike is only preserved as an object of curiosity in this country now."

My host assured me such was the case :   " The

pike," he said, " was found to be a most inconvenient weapon; even during the rebellion, the pikes encumbered the rebels more than anything else. No;" said he, " the gun, pistol, and blunderbuss are the weapons most eagerly sought after by the evil-minded now-a-days."

I was naturally anxious to learn something genuine about the present state of the country; but my host evaded my queries, and attempted to turn the conversation. Baffled in my endeavours for the present, I glanced at the past, and found my host was much more willing to " look back through the vista of time," at some startling scenes which had flashed before his eyes in Tipperary.

" You have already heard the particulars of my brother's misfortunes from Helen," said he. " Shortly after that vile attempt to assassinate as honest and true-hearted a man as breathes the breath of life, this country was very much disturbed; large bodies of armed men traversed the country, day and night, searching for arms, breaking into gentlemen's houses, with various success. Hitherto I had escaped—my house had been respected; I had not meddled with politics, or taken new farms; in short, I had given those agrarian legislators no fair pretext for attacking me. Nevertheless, I deemed it necessary to be prepared for the worst, and declared my intention to keep my fire-arms, perhaps a little too openly. Every night we barricaded the house, and prepared for a regular siege; and it is to this night-watching, and the perpetual state of alarm and anxiety in which we lived, I attributed the low, nervous fever which attacked my poor wife at this period. She had a strong presentiment that she would not be long with us; and her tenderness for her children and love for me increased daily. We endeavoured to raise her spirits in vain; her thoughts were all serious. The physicians declared that a change of scene and sea air might restore her; but I urged her to follow their advice in vain.

" ' Here we have loved, and here we have passed the happiest hours of our lives,' she would say, pointing to our little lawn and garden; ' it is a sweet spot, and here let us part in peace.' I could not reason with her when she spoke in this way—my heart was always too full. The disease soon made fearful ravages; she became too weak to leave her room, and at last could not bear me from her sight. She always said I should be attacked as my poor brother was—but I weary you, sir," said my host, pausing.

I begged him to continue, and declared I was much interested, and filled my glass, while my host resumed in a firmer tone.

" One beautiful cloudless day," said he, " the birds sang in the trees and the labourers sang in the fields, and everything looked bright and happy; even my poor wife, who had not slept for several nights, smiled as she sank into a sweet sleep. I left my daughter beside her, told my brother to remain in the house, while I ran into the fields to look after my labourers. I felt rejoiced in heart; the physicians had given me some hopes; they said, if she could sleep, she might recover. I crossed a tillage-field in which several workmen were digging: they inquired after the mistress's health in their usual warm-hearted way, hoping she would soon be able to walk out with me. I stayed with them a short time, giving directions to my old westard. While we were talking together, the dismal howl of a dog was heard, and the sharp report of a gun-shot echoed through the plantation; while my favourite spaniel ran up to me, bleeding to death from a wound in the side. My anger kindled, and I exclaimed to the workmen: 'Boys, come on! let us secure those poachers, who, not satisfied with shooting my game, kill my dog also.' Not a labourer stirred; but my steward, being a privileged person, threw his arms round my waist, and endeavoured to restrain me from entering the plantation. A horrid idea flashed upon my brain, as I tore away from the old man, and rushed towards the dwelling-house. 'I may be in time to secure the door,' I exclaimed, over and over again, as I rushed madly through the fields. But there—ay, even in the broad daylight, before my own door, stood several armed men; they presented their guns at my head—what cared I for their weapons? —they bid me keep back. 'We don't want your blood,' said the miscreants, 'we could have had that long ago; we want your arms.' I grappled with the speaker, and received a stunning blow on the back of my head. I was overpowered and placed on my knees opposite my own door; the house was filled with armed men, ransacking every hole and corner for arms and ammunition.

"My fire-arms were easily found, and I rejoiced to see the gang quitting the house, in obedience to the command of their captain. In this wretch, I soon recognised the son of a drunken farmer, who had held forcible possession of his land for several years, without paying either rent, tithes, or taxes; drunkenness and night-walking had given his countenance a cadaverous hue, while his bad gray eye burned with all the evil passions and imaginary wrongs of his race. I knew I had nothing to expect from him—I felt that my doom was sealed, even when he addressed me in a vulgar and familiar tone. 'We have got all your tools now,' said he, 'and this brass blunderbuss I'll carry myself; but the little pistols you bought in Dublin, I want them—hand them here.' I protested I had them not. 'Search him,' was the reply—and my pockets were searched in vain. In my pocket-book they found my half-year's rent in notes and gold, and as they forced it into my pocket again, I conjured them to keep it. 'Take all—take my property,' I exclaimed, almost frantic, 'but let me go to my wife —let me see her once more.' 'Ho, ho—ho, ho!' exclaimed the captain, 'the pistols are in his wife's room—I'll soon ask her where they are,' said he. 'Honour, captain!' said a tall dark-haired man, who was called the lieutenant, 'honour, captain,—don't disturb the dying woman.' 'D——n to your b——y soul,' cried the captain, striking his lieutenant upon the face with the butt of the blunderbuss, as he rushed into the house, while the lieutenant wiped his bleeding visage with his coat-sleeve. 'Ha, ha!—take that Shan Ruan,' exclaimed several of the gang; 'none of your Munster tricks up here, gossoon!'

"Hitherto those ruffians had respected my wife's apartment, and hearing the noise below, my daughters had locked the door and sat trembling around their poor mother. My brother had also kept his post; he remained in her room also; but when the last of the gang had retreated from the house, a maid-servant announced the glad tidings, and my daughter unlocked the door just as the savage captain rushed up the stairs, and the next moment leaped into my wife's chamber. My wife sat up in her bed, and the miscreant rudely demanded where the pistols were concealed. ' But I'll soon find them,' said he ; throwing up the window-sash, and hallooing to the gang below, he desired them to shoot the prisoner, while he counted three, if he did not name the exact spot where the pistols were concealed ; and pronounced in a loud voice, ' One, two'—then leaning upon his elbows, he looked down upon me with a fiendish grin, while the sharp clicking of the gun-locks round me told me my fate hung on a hair.

" At that breathless moment, while the eyes of the gang were raised to the window at which their captain stood, a loud explosion and a shriek broke from the house, the captain's arms dropped, the blunderbuss escaped from his hands, his chin touched his breast for a second, he sprang forward with a wild yell, and fell from the window upon the hall-door steps, a mutilated corpse. The gang rushed to raise their captain, while in the confusion I escaped into the house, and entered my wife's room ; it was filled with smoke. John was kneeling in the middle of the floor, laughing, as an idiot may laugh ; he held a pair of pistols which he had just discharged, extended towards the window. I turned to the bed, but it was all over ; her spirit had departed—she was at rest."

My host paused ; he turned his face to the wall : I had no consolation to offer. I withdrew from the parlour, inwardly regretting that I had recalled such heart-rending recollections.

I made up my mind that night before I slept—and certainly I did not fall asleep as soon as I wished, after hearing such a tale of woe—I leisurely made up my mind to have nothing to say to Altadugh. " It would be a good investment, to be sure," reasoned prudence ;

"but I wish to reside—and as to turning out the tenant, no man, save a Russian despot, would even dream of such a thing; but there are such men in the British empire, cold, calculating fellows—the place will be bought by one of them—the man turned out. What then? I was not afraid of the Rockites—nay, had I been here when the miscreants had attacked the house, ye gods, how I would have fought!" Three several taps at the window cut short this tirade, and my heart became as weak as water. *Dieu merci!* it's only a shower of hail, I soliloquized. "Yes it is in my power to keep this amiable family at home—I purchase the land, marry the daughter, and—alas, poor dear Helen! your eyes are too bright for this wicked world. No! she's the bride of heaven." Next morning, in spite of my host's kind and pressing entreaties that I would pass another day with him, I took leave of my hospitable friends. My host walked with me to his lawn gate.

"If you like this place," said the poor fellow, "don't let me stand in your way. I am ready to turn out, and give you possession whenever you wish to reside here; but whether you become a purchaser or not, whenever you come to this part of the country, make my house your home."

I grasped his hand, sprang upon my outside jaunting car, and now left Altadugh far behind me.

Returning to the metropolis, I performed some thirty miles of the journey in the canal or fly-boat: the grand cabin, which, by the way, reminded me of an omnibus, with a plank running through the middle by way of a table, was filled with respectably-dressed people. However, they closed up with a little more good-nature than the occupants of an omnibus—

Bank side Temple Bar—but before I could take my place, I was addressed by one of the passengers.

" Be steady, sir ; look at the brass pendulum—the regulator, sir ; don't you perceive it inclines to this side already ; you can't sit on this side, sir ; but the ladies opposite will accommodate you, otherwise our lives will be jeopardized."

" Oh, sit at this side, sir—sit here, sir !" squalled the said ladies ; and I got seated at last.

" You don't understand the fly-boat, sir," said the last speaker, addressing me again ; " but before you get through the next double lock, you'll be wide awake, as I am, to the danger of——

" Oh, is there any danger ?" said a bilious little woman at my side.

" Why, for my own part, I never like to alarm people—I hate that ; but, when accidents will happen in the best regulated families, why not in this very irregular ?"

" Oh, queen of heaven ! we're upside down !" exclaimed a very fat woman, as the boat jarred suddenly against the towing-path, and glanced under a bridge.

" Be calm, be resigned, Mrs. Doolan ; keep your eyes upon me, and when you see me bolt through this window, it will be time enough for you to follow my example."

" But you're such a brave man, Mr. Malone—I declare I feel as weak as water."

" Try a drop of the native, Mrs. Doolan ; I see you have a bottle in your lap."

" Ah, fie for shame, Mr. Malone !—it's only a sup of bitters I carry for my daughter, poor thing !"

" Well, Mrs. Doolan, you must take a glass of stout with me." Thus saying, Mr. Malone rang the bell, got a bottle of Guinness and two tumblers.　His good example was followed by the rest of the passengers; and some excellent bread and cheese was laid on the board.　Mr. Malone seemed to be the master-spirit of the passengers: he was one of those reckless rough diamonds, from which the sensitive recoil—a nice man for a small party, some six feet three in his shoes, big boned, and clumsily built.　His countenance was not the most prepossessing in the world, though adorned with a rich profusion of carbuncles, abrupt-nosed, wide-mouthed, beetle-browed, long-visaged, sandy-haired.　He thought he was a perfect Adonis; in a white hat with crape, and a full suit of black; so, at the ripe age of fifty-four, he gave himself the airs of twenty-four.　Emboldened with the double X he had swallowed, he made every one in the boat—his own precious self always excepted—uncomfortable, pulled a crumpled newspaper from his pocket; and, to the great annoyance of a very quiet old clergyman and romantic young lady, who had books, the fellow began to read aloud, *pro bono publico*, as he said, the prices current of the *Dublin Market* note—Alum, Alders, Antimony, Butters, Corks, Carlows, per Cool, Bacon, Bees-wax, Hides, Leather, calf, sole ditto, kips; Lead, white, black, pig; Liquorice, Lemon-juice, Lard, bladdered, bleached; Raisins, muscatel, sun, in casks; Skins, goats, sheep, kids." Goss— Here the clergyman laid down his book, and calmly entreated Mr. Malone to read to himself.

"Why should I?" was the polite reply—" why should I be so selfish as to monopolize all the news to myself?"

"Excuse me, sir," replied the other—" I, for one— and I think I may answer for this young lady,—we are very little interested in the news you have just been reading; it may be news to you, but defend me from such news!"

"Upon my word, I'll venture to say, that the ladies and gentlemen would rather listen to my price-current than to your dry sermon, parson; but since you request it, I'll put up my paper. Now, then, are you satisfied? I make it a rule never to make any man uncomfortable. I was just getting into the births, deaths, and marriages; but no matter."

Mr. Malone now favoured us with an account of his visit to his landlord, who had just returned from the Continent, where he had resided for many years, married a woman old enough to be his mother, and that ceremony being performed, returned to his country castle in Ireland, where Mr. Malone found him doing the great man.

"His lordship," said Mr. Malone, "is a slight, fair-haired young man, something like you, sir," turning to a gentleman, who blushed to the ears with pleasure, and said—

"Like me, sir? How curious!"

"Yes, sir, like you, and not two removes from a fool,—the greatest ass in existence. But her ladyship, she's a duke's daughter, they say; yes, positively, she is the very picture of that lady near the door."

"O, indeed, sir, you flatter me!" said the lady.

"Yes, madam, her ladyship is a stout, red-faced punchy old woman."

The poor lady did not look so flattered.

Hitherto I had escaped from the lash of this Goliath, but now it was my turn to enter the lists with him. He heard me speaking about land to one of my neighbours, an intelligent Scot, who had a large farm on the banks of the canal, and clasping his hands together, and leaning forward upon his elbows on the board, Mr. Malone looked up and down the cabin, smirking and winking, as he inquired, " Why we got on so slowly with the survey."

I could not pretend to answer that question, especially as I did not understand what survey the gentleman meant.

" General survey, of course," was his reply.

" I was not connected with——"

" Poh! tell me you're not a land-surveyor?"

" No, sir, I am not."

" Humph!" grunted Mr. Malone, looking very serious and austere. " In my younger days—and I'm not very old—it was the custom for every man to say what he was, like a man; no dandy clerks passed themselves off as officers upon the natives. I didn't say you were a clerk nor an officer, sir; but I premise——"

" Neither," said I, hastily.

" Humph! Bagsmen formerly, in the good old times, absolutely carried a bag; yes, a bag of patterns and samples, Mrs. Doolan; tea and sugar, Mrs. Hopkins; shewed their wares, and asked orders on all occasions, Miss Prike; now, hoity toity! the bagsman is a traveller, if you please—carries a book. I'll trouble you for your book of patterns, sir."

" Sir," said I, " I have no book of patterns."

" Humph! call it a book of prints; your book of prints, sir," persevered Mr. Malone.

" I have no book of prints, sir."

" Humph! in the tea line, I suppose. I dare say you could give us a hint about bohea. Now, here sit three ladies, I know, going to lay in stock—good opportunity for you—shew your samples—open your case—do a little business—I'll help you. What say you, Mrs. Quade, shall we look at this gentleman's samples?"

Mrs. Quade replied, with a toss of her head, " Indeed, she preferred piercing a chest at Kinahan's."

" But consider this young man, and his most respectable house—his hyson, and fine black and green, his flowery pekoe, and——"

" I beg your pardon, sir," said I, not relishing the jest at all ; " I am not a mercantile traveller."

" Humph ! I remember the time, and it's not very long ago—it was a troublesome time, sir—last rebellion, sir—when, as officer of the Merchant Yeomanry Cavalry, it was my duty to arrest every suspicious character ; and though I have retired from business, bought a farm, and the corps is broken up, yet I feel an inclination to resume my authority whenever I smell the air of my native city. Yes, sir, I once arrested a very suspicious character in a canal-boat."

" Oh, for love of the Vargin, don't proceed to extremities," squalled the nervous Mrs. Doolan.

" Mrs. Doolan, be calm—keep your eye upon me ; if you see me produce—(putting his hand into his waistcoat)—a warrant——"

" I'll faint, I'll faint, Mr. Malone ; you're not in earnest, but you look so savage."

" You grow complimentary, Mrs. Doolan—savage ! I flatter myself no lamb could be more peaceably inclined, nor look more sweetly."

" Then you do flatter yourself, Mr. Malone ; you ought to be ashamed of yourself, so you ought—frightening the life out of a weak, nervous woman like myself."

"How nervous you are, Mrs. Doolan!" retorted Mr. Malone, drawing a short pipe from his pocket; "'conscience makes cowards of us all.'"

"Speak for yourself, Mr. Malone."

"A little for myself, and twice as much for you, Mrs. Doolan."

"For me, sir! I scorn your base insinuation."

"Ay, now you're behind your own counter, ma'am."

"What do you know about my counter? I defy you; it never was cut up by the Lord Mayor, like your own."

"You're mistaken, Mrs. Doolan—you're thinking of your father's counter and short measure."

"No, sir, I'm thinking of your sandy sugar and light weights."

"A penny for your thoughts, then, though it's more than they are worth, ma'am," continued Malone; "no, ma'am, I'm aboveboard in all my dealings; fair play was always my motto—live and let live. Come, shake hands, Mrs. Doolan. I have a very great regard for your husband—decent man. I recollect the time when no loyal man in Dublin would wear a stocking to his foot unless he bought it at Doolan's. Fact, sir, that man might have commanded thousands before he took the benefit of the act."

Peace having been declared between these neighbourly folks, Mr. Malone, impatient at being cooped up so long, lamented the folly of the company, who had given up the old leg-of-mutton boats for those fly-away cockle-shells.

" In the old leg-of-mutton boats you progressed steadily, sir," said he; "if you felt inclined to walk, you could stretch yourself along the towing-path, for a mile or two, without any inconvenience; you might sit on deck and enjoy the prospects; you might write your letters, eat your leg-of-mutton dinner, make your tumbler of whiskey punch, in peace and quietness; but now a hasty bottle of ale, and, mayhap, a scrumption of bread and cheese, is all you have to comfort you; and, positively, I would as soon sit in the pipe of a bellows—such a draught of air, since they have got the fashion of taking the doors off the hinges, by way of giving more room to the passengers; and, observe, sir, we have the full benefit of a stream of flies from the stagnant pools, and dust kicked up by the horses from the towing-path; but this is more of your reforming plans—everything must be done in a hurry now-a-days. ' Marry in haste, and repent at leisure,'—good proverb that, Miss Pryke, (Miss P. was an old maid)—but I never talk politics before the ladies."

I was not sorry to hear the bell proclaiming our arrival in the good city of Dublin, nodded at my familiar Goliath and his friends, and once more returned to the comforts of Gresham's Hotel."

CHAPTER V.

THE storm still rages with unmitigated fury; every
sail has been blown out of the bolt ropes. The
sailors, engineers, and stokers look wild, weather-
worn, and exhausted. The captain looking anxious
and care-worn, the mates dejected; the promenade-
deck deserted, and frequently washed with seas;
forward, the sailors complain that their berths are
frequently inundated. It is an awful—a sublime sight,
to look from aft the binnacle, as the vessel rolls on her
side till her spars and the tall chimney almost touch
the water, and the paddle-box is plunged into the
waves, with a report like the roaring of cannon; then
slowly regaining her equilibrium, our royal vessel
mounts a broad billow, till the streaming figure-head
of our sweet sovereign turns to heaven; then
plunging down, as if to port for ever into the " hell
of waters" beneath our trembling feet. Our situation
grows critical—every hour we lose some floats from off
our paddle-wheels. Indeed, the starboard wheel is
already stripped of her floats, and the iron-rings and

bare arms of the wheel whirl round perfectly useless. By an unpardonable oversight, we have not a single spare float on board, even if the sea was smooth enough to permit us to rig up the wheel again. This is a sad affair; and now the floats on the starboard side begin to drop off, and we lose steerage way. This fearful intelligence has divers effects on the passengers: some maintain a good countenance, others sink at once into the deepest despondency; the women are too ill to move, and the men crawl about the saloon, whispering their fears. Bacchus, Silenus, and Jonathan Wild, and another of that precious clique, still cling together, drinking, singing, and uttering the most awful oaths and blasphemies. The hapless wife of that mad reveller Jonathan Wild, sits near him, holding an infant in her arms; the poor heart-broken young woman begs her husband to return from the table, to give her the boy he holds on his knee, and down whose infant throat he forces wine or brandy every time he fills his own glass. He answers his wife with an oath, consigns her to perdition, snatches the infant from her bosom, tells her to get to her berth, and be d—d, amidst the cheers of his boon companions. She listens to all his abuse, but will not leave her children. He threatens to strike her, and his companions restrain him; at length the rage of the rest of the passengers breaks forth, and the unnatural father throws his children to his wife, and returns with his boon companions to his old haunt, the bar, a dismal hole in the hold, under the saloon, from which Bacchus, Silenus, and Jonathan Wild are dragged almost nightly, by the waiter, in a state of beastly intoxication.

E

On Sunday the storm still continued to rage. Some spoke of prayer, and a Bible was opened, but no man could read aloud. The captain held a brief conference with us—stated the quantity of coal, the crippled state of the wheels, the damaged state of the sails; he asked us if we did not think it advisable to run for the Azores, and try to reach Fayal. Several of the passengers said it was the only chance we had, but a gentleman from the Far West declared it would be madness to run before the wind through such a sea, with such an unmanageable vessel. "We talk of running to the Azores," said he, pointing to the wall of waters on either side—"why, gentlemen," said he, "we are actually in the trough of the sea, at the mercy of the waves!" His words made a deep impression on all. This day we lost steerage-way for five hours at a spell. "A sail—a sail!" was the cry towards sunset. We ran on deck, and descried the dim outline of a ship to leeward. "Perhaps it is the President," said one. "The President is twice as large," said another; and in the twinkling of an eye a broad billow hid her from our sight.

Monday morning dawns auspiciously—there is a lull in the storm, a breathing pause; the engines are stopped, and all hands set to work, rigging up the paddle-wheels; one-third of the floats still sticking on the larboard wheel, are transferred to the starboard, and with some loose planks made fast, *malgré* the rolling and pitching of the vessel. Providentially, before the storm came on with fresh vigour, the last bolt was screwed home, and I never joined more heartily in a wild cheer than the moment the words "go a-head" set our gallant vessel in motion. And we did go a-head, in the very teeth of the gale, and considered the danger over, though our paddle-wheels were still in a crippled state.

What a strange compound of vanity and selfishness we poor, tempest-tossed mortals are made of; by the starting of a plank, or the failing of a rivet, we may be plunged beneath the boiling waves, and sleep, cheek by jowl, stoker by captain, first-class passenger with greasy butcher, for ever. Notwithstanding all these sad reflections, there is a great deal of grumbling and ill feeling stirred up among us, when the third-class passengers, who mess with the first and second classes, are forced to evacuate their berths forward by leakage, and share the cabins and state-rooms of the happy dogs who have hitherto enjoyed single blessedness. I escape from the honour of being saddled with a damp passenger through a nail-hole, a small leakage rendering the upper berth untenable. But loud words pass between a greasy Israelite and a fastidious West Indian, while old Here-we-go is at loggerheads with a bear-headed blue-nose—certes the blue-nose took up his quarters chez Here-we-go rather unceremoniously, and threw his saddle-bags into that gentleman's berth without leave or licence. Here-we-go jumped up in a rage, threw the saddle-bags down the hatchway, shook his fist in the blue-nose's face, ran down to the saloon, laid the whole case before the captain, snapped his fingers, spoke of law and logic. The captain, distracted enough already, answered testily; Here-we-go retorted uncourteously; and it is " a very pretty quarrel as it stands."

As the storm abates the cold increases, and we are getting into higher latitudes. Having all our Northing to do yet, the want of stoves in the saloon is keenly felt, and we have only to stamp about the decks, blowing our fingers to keep up the natural heat. It is to the absence of stoves that I attribute the pugnacious spirit which seems to gain ground amongst us with frightful rapidity. The blue-nose (who, by the way, for a reserved tee-totaller of Scottish extraction, seems to blunder into scrapes faster than any man on board)—this gentleman did dare to twit the sanguine sympathizer upon his antipathy to pork, and to the carving sucking pig; but the sympathizer took him in hand *sur le champ;* an angry altercation ensued—the words Jew, quack, Scot, renegade, were bandied backwards and forwards, till the sympathizer, turning up his coat cuffs, offered to crack the blue-nose's neck for the good of society. This generous offer the blue-nose declined, and shrunk back from the tug of war with a very bad grace. This day, after dinner, coffee is refused by the steward. The French and Germans raise a great clamour, much jabbering and bombast, till the steward, a foppish prig, makes his appearance, and studiously arranging his ambrosial curls, tells the French they cannot have any more coffee after dinner. Had a bomb-shell fallen on the table before them, it could not have created a greater outcry. They sprung up, and rushed on deck with a whirlwind of *sacres! quel horreur! betise! sottise! c'est epouvantable! detestable! incroyable! sacre! sacre!* Thus the French, having ramped about, and expended their violence upon the winds, calmly listen to the captain, who says that the steward is in fault, and they shall have coffee as usual in future. *Bravo! bravissimo! c'est tres bien! c'est bien! bon! bon! bon! vive la café! vive le capitain!* A violin scraper makes his appearance, our trumpeter joins him, and in five minutes French, Germans, and

Italians go capering and capricoling about the slippery decks, to ,ʾ,trauss's bal Raccatin galop, mingled with O'Keefe's hornpipe. *Vive la bagatelle!*

Crossing the Banks, the cold still increasing, water frozen in our water-bottles, the ship's bows and fore-castle a mass of glittering ice, several sailors ailing, one frost-bitten in the fingers; we are bound for Halifax now. The Baltimore lawyer and others are seen whisking about the state rooms and saloon, with sheets of writing-paper in their hands, and pens behind their ears, or mysteriously conferring together in little knots; the result of their lucubrations and consulta-tions is soon made manifest, and the passengers being mustered in the saloon, the Baltimorean takes leave to read an address from the passengers on board the British Queen to the captain, congratulating him, &c.; upon which another seedy individual—whose face we have not seen since the storm began, and now glides about the deck, recording the doings of the young Italian count, with whom he seems anxious to scrape a close acquaintance—" Monsieur le Count is skipping about! Monsieur le Count, he is dancing like our-selves! Monsieur le Count is quite a sailor!" all this marvellous intelligence is bleated about by this bleak-looking individual—who now thrusts himself forward, and reads a proposal that a subscription be forthwith entered into—a purse raised—a few pounds subscribed by the passengers—to purchase a small testimonial, a piece of plate, for the captain. This proposal, ema-nating from such a source, is not as heartily responded to as that of the Baltimore lawyer; however, the paper was laid on the table with a solicitation for signatures. The wording of the address is the next knotty point, the quaker objecting to flattery *in toto*, others thinking the address too long, others thinking it premature; and in the midst of the debate, Mr. Jonathan Wild rises with his child in his arms, and reads a letter which he has penned, to the company, the proprietors of the British Queen. He began by stating a number of grievances; that he had paid upwards of one hundred pounds for his state room, and should have been treated with more respect; that he had been insulted by the captain, who threatened to put him in irons if he did not behave himself; appeals to the passengers if his conduct has not been that of a gentleman, requests their signatures to his letter, and sets his child on the table while he hands the letter to one of the passengers. The Baltimore lawyer desires Jonathan Wild to take his child out of the light, and a very edifying, though not very elegant, conversation ensues; the lawyer calling Jonathan Wild a disgrace to humanity and his nation, and a pest to society, while the other is not slow to return the compliment, old slave driving bachelor; mean, fawning lickshoe, shy, sly, slippery, canting hypocrite, being the chosen words and epithets lavished upon the lawyer. Meantime a French New Yorker, with a face like a hungry catamount, springs upon Jonathan; the child is snatched up from the table, and is saved from being crushed between the grappling foes. The Frenchman's assault is uncalled for, and Jonathan, if he is to be kicked, must not be kicked by a Frenchman. His unfortunate wife makes her *entrée* with the screaming infant, and her words and sobs fall like oil upon the angry waves. Jonathan is advised to retire, but he refuses; the captain is sent for, and he says that if the rest of the passengers desire it, Jonathan Wild shall be put in irons. Most votes carry; the French are anxious for the example to be made, but the lately abused Baltimore lawyer, to his credit be it spoken, enlists the Americans on his side, and Jonathan is saved from the clutch of the quartermaster, and permitted to return to his cabin. Meantime our steward has been fighting behind the scenes, and received a tremendous black eye from an exasperated waiter, who is sent forward in irons.

The French and Germans have got up a separate address to the captain, lauding his conduct and courage to the skies, but condemning the conduct of the steward, who has treated them with great impertinence. This letter is handed round after dinner for signature, and disappears very mysteriously at that end of the table where the ancient people are seated. The French are furious, and this will grow a brawl anon. Several English and Americans now make common cause with the French, and the letter is angrily demanded, and it is traced to the aforesaid quarter. The steward has been seen drinking with Bacchus, Silenus, Jonathan Wild, the sanguine sympathizer, and his clique of ancient people, and being on our legs, a spirited and plucky little German roundly charges the sympathizer, in his tiger-skin waistcoat, with having made away with the letter. That great philanthropist answers in brief and most unparliamentary language; he tucks up his coat cuffs, doubles his fists, and strikes out at the little German, who takes up an imposing position also; but Jonathan Wild throws himself between the pugilists; flinging his sow-wester at one and his mackintosh at the other, he offers to fight them both; while another German and the steward are at loggerheads to leeward, shaking their fists in each other's faces, and threatening to wring each other's noses off. In the midst of this *party of pleasure* a gun is fired, and a cry of land acts like a charm on the belligerents. We rush and scramble up the hatchways, and look upon the bleak and frosty shores of Maine at a distance—a cheerless sight, said to be the contested land about which so much has been said and sung. " We'll not quarrel with you about it, gentlemen," said an American, as he looked at the desolate coast, from which a piercing blast hissed over the freezing water. We want a pilot, and espying a small coaster, send a boat after her, but strange to say, the fellow sheers off with all sail, and we haul up our boat again, the poor fellows quite stiff with cold, and the quartermaster, who sat in the stern sheets, frost-bitten. A pilot at last—go-a-head! All right; we have him on board, and crowd round the tall blue-nose as eagerly as if he was a South Sea islander.

"A captain bold at Halifax,"— Halifax, immortalized in the world of song by the misfortunes of Baily—" unfortunate Miss Baily." Where did she live—shew me her house. Stop her—ease her—stop her—let go—a crash drove Miss Baily out of my head. We are along-side of Cunard's wharf, scrambling over the Queen's side, and dropping into the arms of the mob of Hali-faxonians, waiting to receive us with broad stares. Away we go, racing up-hill, to the Freemasons' Hall, led on by a gallant bewhiskered dragoon, attired in a bernoose, fur boots, red sash, a red skull-cap adorning his bald pate, bestriding a cart-horse, tugging at full speed, and a reeling load of Germans and French-men waving their caps and handkerchiefs, while the mob bring up the rear, shouting like so many devils let loose. " Verily, Freemasons' Hall hath not received such a singular visitation for some time, I calculate," said a Yankee, as we took that hotel by storm, and frightened the black waiters into a state of lamentable stupidity.

Happy is the man who can get a bed in the Freemasons' Hall; first come first served. We early birds may go to roost, while the late arrivals are doomed to gallop all over Halifax in quest of bed, and, finally, several return, much against their will, to sleep on board the British Queen. Here, for the first time, I taste that truly American beverage, egg-nog, a goodly jug of which is prepared by a jovial Virginian, who frequently directs our attention to the number of niggers in Halifax; he declares they are runaway slaves, every one of them. Certainly they are the ugliest race of men I have ever seen—all lips and eyes. Visit the House of Assembly, Governor's house, barracks; &c., the town seems to be little better than an unsightly jumble of grog-shops. House rent is said to be very high, the country round about barren and cheerless. I was not sorry to hear that our royal vessel was ready for sea again, the smiths and carpenters having worked all night at the wheels, and the best part of the inhabitants of the town and country poured through the hatches and gangways, till, their curiosity at length satisfied, we hoist our blue peter, and get up the steam, amidst the farewell cheers of the good people of Halifax; but even here, and at such a critical moment, our worthy captain is doomed to be disappointed. He stood triumphantly on the starboard paddle-box of his royal mistress, and doffed his bonnet to the assembled multitude; the crew cheered, the passengers cheered, the red-hot poker was sent forward, the gun fired,—" stop, stop—ease her. Stop her; and we make an inglorious pause, and stop short in confusion, in the midst of all the

E 3

cheers. A few fathoms from the wharfs, a long cable has been entwined and entangled round one of the paddle-wheels; axes are procured, and the tedious process of cutting up a hawser gone through; this is pleasant—off—off; fairly started now, at all events. "Don't whistle till you're out of the wood," says the Iowa man. I hate croakers. We have two pilots on board, our own old fellow and the long blue-nose. Sitting down to tea at dusk, we are all thrown on our beam-ends with a sudden jerk, followed by a rumbling noise, and a trembling, quaking motion under our feet. Hello! what's the matter? A general rush on deck, when, running aft, we gratify and satisfy ourselves with looking back at a black-headed rock, against the base of which our ship's bottom or side has been scraped; meantime the blue-nosed pilot has made his escape, and gone ashore. In the general confusion, fortunately for himself, he has saved his bacon before it was generally known that through his close shaving and obstinacy we should have run right on the rock, had not our own wary old pilot seen it. Some proposed that we should return to Halifax and report his conduct; others proposed that we should pursue the renegade ashore, and reward him with a good rope's-ending: and, talking of reward, a subscription is entered into forthwith for our own old pilot, who saw the rock, and sung out to the men at the wheel, to which, as an amendment, some propose to reward the men at the wheel; others, to hang a medal round the neck of the royal figure-head, and thus reward the Queen, because she obeyed the helm so promptly. Only one man speaks in the renegade pilot's behalf; he says the pilot wanted to go ashore—his supper was waiting for him—he wished to save us the trouble of lowering a boat—he only wanted to run the bowsprit of our royal vessel right up to his own door, so that he might, without loss of time, step into his wife's bed-room window.

This being the last night we are doomed to spend on board the British Queen, a tone of joyous hilarity expands among us; mirth, smiles, and laughter, in lieu of frowns, and fear, and rage. It is a most delectable change, and I find the grave gentleman has resumed his seat at the little table, where, amidst the congratulation of the knot of odd fellows who have set themselves round him, and inspired with a goodly rummer of bishop, he favours us with his last " moving tale."

CHAPTER VI.

Adventures of a Gentleman in search of an estate—Dennis M'Gwiggan and his valet—A mountain farm—The gold mine—My whip —The seekers—Botanists versus Geologists—Race to Dublin.

" To be sold by private contract, part of the lands of Ballycragmorris, containing sixteen hundred and ten acres, two roods, and nineteen perches, more or less, delightfully situated in the romantic, picturesque, peaceable, and sporting county Wicklow," &c.

"This reads pretty well," said I, throwing down the ' Mail ;' " it is, moreover, slily hinted that the lands will be sold considerably under their real value ; and though I perfectly agree with Sir Hudibras, that

> ' Th' intrinsic value of a thing,
> Is just so much as it will bring,'

I may stumble upon a prize, a real good bargain, such as civilized wiseacres made with the natives in the good old times." And having finished my breakfast, fortified with tongue, chicken, and an extra cup of *café noir en avant*, I shouldered my umbrella, because, even in the month of June, " the weather is not the most secure" in the sister island, and marched with hasty strides to the house of Dennis M'Gwiggan, solicitor, and found that gentleman in green slippers and pie-balled dressing-gown, shaving himself at his black bureau.

" Sit down, sir," said he, when I entered his office ; " sit down, sir. Your case must be desperate, since you drop in so early ; but *nil desperandum,*" sputtered this limb of the law, as he plunged his face into a large basin of water, and then, turning round, like Niobe, all in tears, sought for a towel to hide his blushes ; the towel, to use a legal term, *non est inventus,* and Mr. M'Gwiggan rang the bell furiously, till the meagre youth who had ushered me into the office made his appearance. Here a most refreshing dialogue passed between master and man, the latter declaring he had left the towel upon certain deeds and papers, and the former vowing vengeance upon his negligent and deceitful servant, ending by assuring him—" By the virtue of my oath, and as sure as my name is Dennis M'Gwiggan, I'll warm the wax in your ear, if you don't get me something to wipe my face while I say Jack Robinson."

" Take my praskeen, take my praskeen, till I run up to the mistress for a towel," cried the youth, hastily divesting himself of an apron, once white, which he threw towards his indignant master, and escaped from the office, round which the attorney moused for the lost towel, tossing deeds, papers, and parchments to and fro, and ever and anon directing some of his rambling conversation to me.

" Sit still, sir—don't let me disturb you—that boy will be hung. I'll attend to your case immediately. Nothing's too hot or too heavy for him. I'll give him a mark of my affection one of those days, the scurvy hound ! You want to have a writ marked, or a letter——"

Here I thought it high time to declare the object of my visit as briefly as possible. Never was Dennis M'Gwiggan more confounded. He blushed to the ears as he grasped the rejected apron, scrubbed his round potato face withal, twisted an orange and green silk shawl round his short bull-neck, buttoned his pie-balled dressing-gown, ejaculated " Ballycragmorris !" and without further delay caught up the newspaper, and read the advertisement in a loud and sonorous voice, though I begged to assure him I had already read the advertisement, and wished to hear the particulars.

" Sixteen hundred and ten acres, two roods, and nineteen perches, be the same more or less," said he.

" English or Irish measure ?" said I.

" Plantation, plantation, sir !" quoth he.

" Is the property open ?"

" It lies in a ring fence," replied the solicitor.

" I mean, is it entailed ? In short, has the advertiser a right to sell it ?"

" Right, sir !" said Dennis, with a stare ; " have I a right to sell this house ?"

I supposed that was best known to himself.

" Well, sir, I have a right to sell my own property."

I was happy to hear it, and hoped the advertiser enjoyed the same privilege ; I was induced to make the observation from the well-known fact, that it was easier to advertise a property for sale than shew good title to a purchaser. I spoke from experience, having gone through many fatiguing preliminaries, and all but purchased an estate, a chancery suit, and the onus of providing for nine younger children, and a widow into the bargain.

"Make yourself easy on that score," said Dennis, "for the widow and children are already provided for in this case, and my client is free as air to do what he likes with Ballycragmorris. The title is most unexceptionable. I have the skins under my thumb. The land is part of the confiscated property of the O'Toole. In fact, Ballycragmorris was the favoured retreat, the fastness, the stronghold, of that arch rebel——"

"Here's the towel, sir," said the trembling lad, peeping into the room.

"D—n your towel!" thundered Dennis, indignant at this futile interruption to his peroration. "D—n your impudence!" exclaimed the man of law, hurling a bundle of deeds at the head of the intruder, who scamped off like a rabbit, while Dennis resumed. "Where was I?" said he; "O'Toole—the O'Toole, as I said before. D—n that boy—he provokes me. Indeed, I must apologize to you, sir, a stranger, though I flatter myself we will be better acquainted when you purchase Ballycragmorris. Here is the map. You perceive the great military road runs through the heart of the property; and then, it is all in hand. That mark, like a brick, is the shooting lodge —capital shooting on the hills, you know."

"But the arable land," said I; "please to inform me how many acres of arable land. I cannot discern any marks or tokens of enclosure on the face of the map."

"This is an old map," said Dennis. "I admit the property is not very highly cultivated; if it was, we would ask a larger price for it. Twenty years' purchase is no great price for one of the best mountain grazing farms in Wicklow, and besides, *entre nous,*" said Dennis, mysteriously lowering his voice, "the property must be sold, and whoever gets it will get a precious bargain."

"I doubt it much, for mountain farms in this weeping climate are very unproductive, I understand."

"And what signifies a mere farm, the dirty acres, the crops and superficies of the richest lands in Meath or Kildare, when compared with the high bold headlands of Ballycragmorris," said Dennis, with a smile. "In fact, sir, it is impossible to say what this property may be worth in the hands of an active and enterprising capitalist. No, sir," continued he, "I will no longer keep you upon the thorns of suspense. Know, then, young man, that you are upon the eve of buying what my client (God pity him!) is compelled by the tide of misfortune to sell—a mine of gold," said Dennis, sinking his voice into a deep whisper, and thumping his fist upon the desk before him.

"Indeed!" said I, not expecting to hear such a valuable communication.

"You may well cry indeed!" said Dennis. "Bless your stars, my good sir, you are on the high road to Fortune's lap. Once in possession of Ballycragmorris, you'll sink a shaft in the hill-side, and reap a golden harvest. O, if I had the money, the gold mine should not go a begging," said Dennis, who then informed me, that the country people had found bits of gold in the gravel and sand washed from the hill-side by a torrent; and further, that several miners had declared that from the aspect of the country a second Potosi might lie beneath a very unpromising exterior.

Look before you leap being my new maxim, I declined making a written agreement or verbal promise with the sapient M‘Gwiggan, who nevertheless furnished me with a line of introduction to the care-taker of this precious farm, and further indicated the route in a very friendly manner.

" Caravan to Baltinglass, and car to Ballycragmorris," said he, following me to the hall-door, on opening which a gust of wind rushed into the hall, and for the first time I perceived that the learned Dennis had not yet invested his nether man with the most indispensable parts of dress, and apropos to mountains and mountaineers, shewed a pair of brown knees to the public, and the select boarding-school girls who marched past the door, while an ill-suppressed titter escaped even from the sour-visaged governess, who affected to hide her blushes under a faded parasol held sideways, from that magnus Apollo of Mountjoy, square Dennis M‘Gwiggan, solicitor.

Following that gentleman's advice, I started at twelve o'clock for Baltinglass, supporting the inconvenience and misery of being wedged into the caravan, a hearse-like machine, with eleven unhappy bipeds, not including four squallers, held upon the knees of four nurses, returning from a certain respectable institution, laden with fresh proofs of the anti-Malthusian spirit of the good people of Dublin. I bore all this, I say, and more than this, with the fortitude of Pizarro, or any other ancient Spaniard traversing unknown lands with El Dorado in his mind's eye. Ballycragmorris, and Potosi as connected therewith, sustained me in the midst of my woes, even when the exuberant nurse on my right requested me " to hould the child," and, suiting the act to the word, placed the screaming bantling in my arms, while she made sundry arrangements in her habiliments which no pen can describe. We did not arrive at Baltinglass till evening, and so far I was disappointed, having calculated on reaching the hill farm-house, where M'Gwiggan assured me I would find at least a well-aired bed.

I slept that night at Baltinglass, and started next morning betimes for the hills, upon an outside car, "*selon l'usage du pays.*" Dennis M'Gwiggan had spoken about the great military road, and I frequently stopped my charioteer in the midst of a glowing description of a tithe sale he had lately witnessed in Carlow, to inquire where the great military road was to be found, hinting that he had mistaken the direction received from my host at Baltinglass.

" Let me alone—I could find the way blindfold," replied the whip; " and if your honour will only look straight before you, you'll see something like a dirty white ribbon wandering down the side of a brown feather bed—that's the great military road."

And in process of time we toiled up the hills on foot, seeing that the horse was fairly blown in the midst of his vigorous efforts to tug the car through the ruts, holes, stones, and mire, dignified with the high-sounding title of the Great Military Road. The aspect of the country was most desolate: trees were out of the question, and, notwithstanding all that has been said and sung about the green hills of Erin, gray or brown would have been nearer the mark. To be sure, hills-look green at a distance, saith the proverb; and, summoning philosophy to aid me through the Slough of Despond, I had left my equipage far behind, when the shouts of the charioteer arrested my progress.

"Holloa! stop, and come back, your honour."

"What's the matter, my good fellow?" said I, returning to my charioteer.

"Why, nothing very extraordinary," said he; "only as I heard you were going to see Ballycragmorris, I thought it a 'quare' thing to see your honour walk through the middle of it without looking right or left."

"You must be mistaken," said I; "I understand there are some houses on the property. Nay, the very name of the place, Bally, signifying a small town, supports my argument."

"Then maybe it's joking your honour's after—to talk of towns up here."

"Come, come," said I, sternly regarding a list of names in the locale of Ballycragmorris; "where is Doyle Street? answer me that question. Who ever heard of streets, ballys, and places, in a spot like this?"

"There is Doyle Street," replied my man, pointing to a bleak and desolate mountain; "and, as I said before, this is Ballycragmorris; and if your honour wont believe me, ask this man walking up the road."

The man corroborated my whip's evidence, and further assured me that he was the care-taker and herd of Ballycragmorris; and moreover advised the carman to unyoke his beast, leave the car by the road-side, and follow said care-taker and herd, who would be happy to pilot us to the mountain lodge. Leaving the car in the ditch, we followed the herd— a broad-shouldered, clean-limbed, strapping fellow,

whose patched velveteen shooting-jacket and short
leather gaiters declared him to be " an idle man," as
every country fellow, no matter what his occupation
may be, is called, if he is not doomed to dig and delve
the soil from morning till night. We soon arrived at
the shooting-box, which was so judiciously concealed
in a ravine, that it might have served as the model
of a bear-trap, deer-trap, or man-trap; for should any
of the aforesaid animals wandering that way be given
to star-gazing, they would indubitably be taken in the
capacious chimney of the mountain lodge. It was,
nevertheless, substantially built, slated, glazed, and
doored in a most suitable manner; a high stone wall
enclosed the yard at one side, and below this a feeble
attempt at cultivation appeared—one acre of a wet
swampy valley being planted with potatoes and cabbages, and dignified with the name of the garden. The
horse was soon stowed in a cow-shed, my jarvey loaded
his pipe and sat down by the fire, while I sallied forth
with the herd to view the premises. The herd led the
way across the mountain to shew me the grazing stock,
and every step he took seemed to be more difficult to
imitate, till at last I called a halt, in the midst of a bog
that seemed to have been rent asunder in every
direction by an earthquake; in fact, we stood upon
masses of trembling turf, surrounded with deep and
horrible chasms—talk of the crevices of the " Mer de
Glace !"

" There are the cattle," said the herd, pointing to
sundry light-bodied cows and tiny calves, and some
sheep and goats browsing among the sedge and
heath. " We are paid so much a head for them," said
he, " and I have hard work to keep them in bounds,

especially the ramblers. I once followed a bit of a heifer to the top of Sugar-loaf, the highest mountain in Wicklow."

" Sugar-loaf! what a name for a mountain !" thought I. " But, my good fellow, where is this famous *gold mine ?*"

The herd looked askant at me over his shoulder, and I repeated the question.

" Do you think you'll be able to follow me, sir ?" said he.

" Certainly," said I ; " lead the way to the gold mine directly."

" O, very well," said the herd, very deliberately taking off his shoes and gaiters ; " now, sir, keep your eye upon me," said he, bounding from tuft to tuft, rock to bank, over sinking moss and rugged furze-brake, like an Indian, while I, filled with golden visions of Peru, Potosi, and El Dorado, made exertions to keep up with my leader that not only surprised that hardy mountaineer but myself also ; it wants but the will to accomplish the deed——yes, even encumbered with boots and an umbrella. But I must not boast of my feats too soon. The herd at last stopped at the bottom of a valley, through which a small mountain stream threaded its way. He began looking about among the gravel, and taking up a handful of it, presented it to me, demanding if I saw anything like *goold* in that. Of course I did not perceive the slightest vestige of the precious metal, at the same time expressing a wish to follow the streamlet to its source.

" By the bones of St. Patrick that will take you some time, then," said the guide ; " and you must step out a little faster than you did a while ago."

" Why," said I, " I thought the head of the stream issued from a mountain on this property."

" Och, listen to this!" replied the herd with a laugh; " why everybody knows the stream can be traced up to the black lough in the hills, and that's five miles from this."

In fact, I had been grossly deceived by M'Gwiggan ; the grains of gold found in the stream may have been washed from a mine somewhere in the bowels of the Wicklow mountains, or the aforesaid black lough ; and as to hunting for a mine in such an impracticable out of the way place as Ballycragmorris, I resigned the glorious prospect without a sigh, and now was only most anxious to get back again to Dublin ; but it was ordained I should not escape from Ballycragmorris scot free. Returning to the mountain lodge, we were caught in a storm—and such a storm !—the clouds of night seemed to descend from the hill tops.

" Run, run, run, sir !" bawled the herd, as he scampered before me; " we'll be *cotched* and drenched like rats."

Run I did, and, perspiring at every pore, looked back at the dense dark cloud rolling along the ground after us ; a broad flash of lightning quivered round us, and " Vargin protect us !" cried the herd, as he threw himself upon his face in the heath. A tremendous clap of thunder shook the ground under my feet, and I was fain to follow the herd's example. Down came the hail and rain in sheets ; my umbrella was shivered in a moment ; and though we were within one hundred paces of the lodge, we could not stir till the storm rushed over our drenched bodies, and we crawled into the lodge more dead than alive.

" El Dorado, adieu !" I groaned, as I remounted

the car on the road-side, and had the mortification to find the cushions wet as the recent storm could make them. " Farewell, Potosi; catch me treasure-seeking again!" said I, digging the hail-stones out of the pockets of my pea-jacket, and relieving my boots of the super-abundant bog mould with a slate.

" You have had a hard day's work of it," said the driver; " but there's one satisfaction."

" And what's that?" said I.

" Why we have the fall of the hill with us, going home; and that's what I call satisfaction," said he, chirrupping to his hack, and urging him into a gallop down the execrable road, over which we rattled at the risk of our necks, towards the pretty little town of Baltinglass once more.

Having made a short and agreeable tour in the county Wicklow, and admired everything worthy of admiration, I returned leisurely towards the city. Indeed, my car-man, whose services and equipage I had secured at —— per diem, seemed to regard our final separation (which was to take place in Dublin) with horror; he endeavoured to beguile me to the mountains again; then, finding I was obstinately bent on proceeding to Dublin, he volunteered to remain with me while I stayed in that city, and afterwards " drass me round Ireland" upon his car. Indeed, the poor fellow seemed to have had quite enough of the charms of Baltinglass, which he did not scruple to denounce as a " beggarly hole."

" What the devil are they looking for?" said my charioteer, as we descended from the Dublin mountains at a quick pace. " What can they have lost?" he exclaimed, pointing down the slope of a hill, towards which we soon approached near enough to discover at least a score and a half well-dressed men, scattered up and down the valley and hill-side, evidently seeking for something with much earnestness."

"If your honour will hold the reins, I'll go and inquire what they have lost," said Mallowney, briskly jumping off the car, burning with curiosity which I did not permit him to gratify, having a lively remembrance of the way in which he had behaved a few days ago. Passing a farm-house, I had seen a remarkably well-shaped cob standing in the bawn or yard in front of the house; the moment Mallowney heard me praise the horse, he said he was sure and certain the farmer would be very happy to sell it. Supposing such to be the fact, I permitted him to inquire the price of the horse.

Mallowney soon found the farmer, and seeing him in deep conversation with the man, I drove on quietly, as I had not the slightest intention of encumbering myself with an additional horse. A tremendous shout, followed by a tumultuous outcry, soon caused me to pull up, and looking back, I beheld Mallowney rushing after me at full speed, minus his hat, and blood upon his cheek, while the farmer and three men with sticks pursued him for a short distance, hooting like bedlamites. Mallowney soon jumped upon the car, and belaboured his back into a gallop. It was some time before he informed me about his mishap—it seemed to me to be all his own fault. He had begun by asking the farmer sundry knowing questions about his horse—how old he was?—how long the farmer had been " *his master ?*" and ended by saying he had once a horse the very picture of the one in question, but that it had been stolen from him.

This roundabout way of ascertaining the horse's price roused the farmer's honest indignation. He told Mallowney the horse was born and reared upon his own ground, as every man in the parish could swear. An altercation ensued—Mallowney raised his whip, the farmer's sons rushed to his help, and my charioteer narrowly escaped being well thrashed for his temerity; as it was, he received a thump in the face and lost his hat. But *revenons à nos moutons.*

"No, Mr. Mallowney," said I, "mind your equipage while I offer my assistance to those gentlemen seekers."

No sooner had I entered the field than one of the aforesaid men assumed his perpendicular; he was a big-boned, awkward-looking gentleman, turned fifty, dressed in seedy black; he stood up, and waving one hand in the air in a very triumphant manner, raised a small tin tube or penny trumpet with the other, and inflating his cheeks, he blew a blast through the penny trumpet that might have been mistaken for the goat-like bleating of a jack-snipe, poised in mid air, over a wild heath on a hot summer's day. I had hardly recovered from the surprise into which the solemn trumpeter and his trumpet had thrown me, when all the rest came scampering towards the trumpeter, who still continued to sound the charge till the stragglers came in, and a gallant band of grave and some gay-looking men rallied round him.

"Brethren and fellow-labourers, friends and lovers," said the solemn trumpeter, looking round him, and then pointing to his feet, "I hasten to introduce a rare Hycoperdon to your notice—same time, another of the Lychen family—both belonging to the class

F

Cryptogamia, both worthy of our admiration and regard."

By this time the attention of the brethren was directed to myself, and observing this I would have retired, but the great trumpeter advanced towards me with extended hand.

"Stay, my good sir, if you are seeking for knowledge, and have followed the steps of the brethren hither, hoping to glean ——"

I begged to interrupt the sapient trumpeter—assured him I had not followed himself or his disciples—my coming among them was purely accidental. "Much as I admire botany as a ——"

"He admires botany, my friends!" exclaimed the trumpeter.

"Botany for ever!" exclaimed several voices.

I replied that I certainly had attended some botanical lectures; but after six lectures, finding the lecturer still harping upon the fibre of a leaf, I despaired of ever getting to the top of the tree, and had given up the pursuit, not being blessed with perseverance and patience.

"But if you attended our lectures," said a fresh-looking, sanguine youth, "and heard this learned professor, the doctor, who, simple as he stands here with a little tin trumpet in his hand, is—"

"Forbear! Peduncles," cried the doctor, repressing the zeal of his young disciple; "and if I am an herb of no common growth, I glory not in the sunshine of flattery—no, rather let my sensitive heart recoil, shrink, wither in the shade, than—"

Tootle — tootle — too-too-to-to, bleated a trumpet in the corner of a field.

" Hello—hello ! what hast thou found ?" exclaimed the doctor, rushing towards the fresh trumpeter, while the brethren followed their leader across the fields as fast as they could scamper.

I brought up the rear, and began to enter into the spirit of the thing.

" One fool makes many,
But the old fool's worse than any,"

saith the proverb; not that I mean to say it is at all applicable to the learned doctor, who wiped the perspiration from his brow, as he mildly rebuked a long-faced wag called Sweet Scabious, for sounding the alarm over a mere leontodon, vulgarly called dandelion, or ———.

I now discovered that every man was possessed of a tin trumpet, which it was his duty to sound whenever he discovered a rare plant, herb, or weed; and, moreover, each member of the society rejoiced in some botanical *nom de guerre.* I was introduced to Mr. Secretary Sinapis, Messrs. Fumaria, Marrubrium, Papaver, Boletus, Plantago, and all the rest of the worshipful company; who one and all insisted I should stay and partake of an humble repast which they purposed to enjoy *al fresco* upon the grass, beside a brawling stream; and the labours of the day being declared at an end, each man shouldered his herbal, slung his trumpet behind him, and hastened to the spot where sundry hampers, baskets, jars, and bottles were piled. Two carmen were busily employed arranging some plates, knives, forks, and tea-cups, upon a level bit of ground, close to the ravine through which the aforesaid streamlet babbled; and the contents of the hampers and baskets being turned out rather un-

F 2

ceremoniously, a capital round of beef took the liberty
of running down the slope, and plunging its thirsty
sides into the water, from which, however, it was
quickly fished up again; and having merely picked
up an additional seasoning of thorns and gravel, it
occupied its original place at the *fête champetre*, and
formed a capital *piece de resistance;* hams, tongues,
cold chickens, pigeon-pies, and tartlets, vanished in
double quick time before the hungry botanists; while
the quick and rolling fire of the corks from long and
short necked bottles proved that the society were not
tea-totallers, though they drank out of tea-cups—the
cup or calyx being more classical and less liable to be
broken than glass; several toasts and sentiments being
drunk with all the honours, my friend the doctor,
who, being seated upon a basket as president, filled
the basket with great dignity of deportment, tempered
with the genial affability of a *bon vivant*—the president, I say, rose and proposed a brimming nectarium
to the health of our guest, passing a very unmerited
encomium upon a wandering disciple of Linnæus, as
he was pleased to call my unworthy self. I got upon
my legs to return thanks, and was received with three
distinct cheers. By the way, this getting upon one's
legs is a matter of such easy performance, that many a
man is induced to do so, and being upon his legs,
wish that he was off them again; suffice to say, after
looking like a fool for the usual time, stammering and
talking in the usual incoherent way, I broke down in
a treble parenthesis, and was rejoiced to find myself
seated upon the herbage once more, amidst cheers
mingled with Kentish fire, and an ironical jingling of
knives, forks, and platters. Several of the members
followed my example; their speeches were filled with

apt quotations, pithy remarks, and adorned with a superfluity of flowers, roots, leaves, branches, and technical terms, used upon such occasions by botanists. Songs were sung, and Acrostichum being loudly called for, a sentimental swain, with some dwarf ferns in his hatband, declared he was not in voice, nor yet in mirthful mood.

"No matter; you must sing or pay the penalty," roared a dozen voices; while the youth, seeing the impossibility of resistance, sang the following words to a well-known Irish air, assisted by four of the brethren, who joined in the chorus:—

SONG OF THE BEE.

I sing the song of the humble bee,
  Who, with Aurora rising,
Unfolds her wings right merrilie,
  And goes out botanizing.
Away, away o'er brake and brae,
  O'er woodland, hill, and hollow;
To win the first bright flower of May,
  Who'll follow—follow—follow?

CHORUS.

And here's a health to the humble bee,
  And soon may she fill her bag, sir—
Success to the sons of botany,
  And every comical wag, sir.

In hawthorn bush we'll wake the thrush,
  Our fairy bugles sounding;
In ferny dells touch wild heath-bells,
  And set the red deer bounding.
And we'll pass by each gay catch-fly,
  To where the blushing roses
Unfold to view the mountain dew,
  In which we'll dip our noses.

CHORUS.

And here's a health to the humble bee, &c.

On beds of thyme anon we'll climb,
  At Bella Donnas winking,
And many a smile reward us while
  On balmy pillows sinking.
Then up—away—from flowery spray—
  From heart's-ease and plantago,
Lest, loitering long upon flowers of song,
  We catch for our pains a lumbago.

CHORUS.

And here's a health to the humble bee, &c.

While the last notes of this harmonious song quavered upon our ears, the welcome strain of the hunting chorus in Der Freischutz cheered our sinking spirits, and, lifting up our heads, we perceived several gentlemen in black wending their way down the glen, some singing, and others beating time upon the rocks and stones, *en passant,* with their hammers. Sundry knowing winks were exchanged by the botanists when the party on the opposite side of the ravine halted, and began to holla out—

" Who are ye, holding on by the ground to keep yourselves from falling ?"

" The Dublin Royal Botanical Society," responded my party, with one voice.

" O ye asses—ye Nebuchadnezzarites—ye wolves in sheeps' skins, seeking to browze with the lambkins ye devour."

" And who are ye, who talk so big and look so little ?" roared our potent president, rising from the basket, like another Telamon Ajax.

" We are the Royal Dublin Geological Society, returning in triumph from the hills," responded our antagonists.

" O ye stone-breakers — ye miserable plodders, doomed to grovel in the crust of the earth," bellowed our champion, " hide your diminished heads, while we bask in the sunshine, and riot upon beds of flowers."

" Go home, go home with ye, ye weed-diggers—ye bluebottles and unclean · flies, clapping your disastrous feet upon the fairest flowers, and nipping vegetation in the bud like locusts!" screamed a thin, wiry little man, in reply to our last: but ere our champion could reply, Sweet Scabious, starting up, requested permission to answer that scurrilous atom in his own lingo, and the parol being granted—

" Hello, ye skinflints—answer me, ye marble-crackers. After all your delving in the ' bowels of the harmless earth,' what have ye found to comfort the mind of man? and are ye not plunged into the quagmires of doubt, into which ye would fain drag the unwary passenger who extendeth his hand to relieve ye ?"

" Silence, ye chuckle-heads — ye ignoramuses, standing for ever between your bundle of weeds, without strength of mind sufficient to turn right or left," retorted our opponents. " Ay, if ye were thrown, one and all, upon a desolate island, ye could not discriminate cabbages from scutchgrass.

" Desolate islands produce not cabbages," thundered our president, " and thus ye publish your imbecile, futile, and groundless assertions to the world."

" Pounded ! pounded ! pounded !" bellowed our party ; while the geniuses on the opposite side being, like ourselves, *Bacchi pleni,* were filled with such zeal for the cause, that they would fain have crossed the stream, and renewed the battle at close quarters. Our party were also well inclined to charge the foe, and fortunately the brawling stream still separated the belligerents, who seemed to have a very whole-

some dread of cold water.   Three rounds of Billings-
gate were discharged between the high contending
parties, when they regained their first position, and
the geologists, being worsted, began to wreak their
vengeance upon the ground, knocking sparks out of
the stones with their hammers, and kicking up the
dust on every side like pugnacious tom-cats: while
we, I mean my party, lifted up our tin trumpets, and
with one consent sent forth such a combination of
soul-rending sounds, breathing all our scorn, contempt, satire, ire, and derision in one long blast,
which the geologists, having no trumpets to return
"blast for blast," were either unable or unwilling to
hear, and plunging their fingers into their ears, they
abandoned their position, and made a hasty and inglorious retreat down the valley.   The evening was
far advanced, when several carmen, who had not been
inattentive observers of what was going forward,
hinted that we had better think of breaking up our
classical entertainment; and accordingly the hampers,
baskets, books, and herbarium, were transferred to
a long string of jaunting-cars, my own amongst the
rest, drawn up by the road-side, and we were soon
seated upon our jingles, and galloping right merrily
towards the metropolis.   We had barely rode a mile
when we overtook another string of outside cars, con-
veying the discomfited geologicals from the scene of
action.   And now begun a scene which I own I am
unable to describe, not being possessed of the ready
pen of a special reporter.   Wit glanced through the
clouds of dust that surrounded our cars, and thunders
of applause rose like the salutation of hostile fleets
upon running alongside of each other.   Our charioteers
had caught up a little of the spirit of the day; there

was opposition and hostility in their movements—
" the devil take the hindmost" was the cry, and away
we went at full speed, racing jaunting-car against
jaunting-car. Woe worth the day to the luckless
goose, hen, pig, or dog, that crossed our reckless
course!

" Take care of your limestone," hollaed the president's whip, as the step of his car brushed close to the
knees of the four geologists.

" Turnip, turnip, turno!" bawled one of the geological carmen, as he succeeded in turning one of our
cars into a ditch.

" Freestone, rotten stone," echoed one of our jarvies,
having performed a like neighbourly office.

The Dublin cries were duly bawled by the charioteers, as they passed and repassed each other.

" There goes my herbal," bawled one of the botanists.

" I'll pick it up," cried one of the hostile carmen in
our wake, guiding his wheel neatly over the leather
case, while our charioteer, in like manner, helped to
macadamize the road with the bag of specimens which
had fallen from the geologist *en avant.*

" There goes my hammer," cried one.

" And my hat," cried another.

" And my cloak," roared a third.

" Never mind," screamed a fourth; "depend upon
it, they

> " Will soon be here,
> They are upon the road."

And more than hats and wigs were presently spilt
upon the road, when we entered Dublin pell-mell, and
encountered a royal mail-coach, galloping out of town
as fast as our royal (society) cars where whirling into it.

" Breakers a-head," hollaed some of our party, as the leading car-load of geologists went smash against the wheels of the mail.

" Shoot them for falling, guard," bawled the mail-coachman, as he pulled up his tits, and looked down upon the *debris* of the first jaunting-car, and hopeless state of the second, which had only been upset upon the first.

The discomfited gentlemen were speedily extricated, all parties vieing to lend them assistance in this emergency. It was now discovered that the great capsized had escaped most miraculously with merely a few bruises, scratches, torn coats, and rent continuations. I was, moreover, rejoiced to see the late belligerent parties cordially shake hands, and congratulate each other upon their safe return from the perils and dangers which beset them in their recent campaign, and unite in raising a loud laugh when the mail-coachman pithily observed, as he drove off—

" Well, it's an old saying and a true one, ' God takes care of drunken men and children.' "

Here I took leave of my hospitable entertainers; and having declined a warm invitation to sup with them in some classic corner of Trinity College, called Botany Bay, I returned to my hotel to dream about " broad lands" totally unconnected with, and ascertained to be free from mines, minerals, El Dorado, Potosi, Ballycragmorris, and though last not least, from the humbug and brass of Dennis M'Gwiggan, solicitor, land-louper, or attorney-at-law.

———

Our letter of congratulation to the captain has been read, and he has returned thanks in a neat and appropriate speech; hopes he may always meet with such

agreeable passengers—thanks us for our forbearance
—compliments us upon our fortitude—hopes we may
all meet again, (in a better world, I suppose.)   Three
cheers, and one cheer more for the captain, proposed
as usual by the Baltimore lawyer, whose zeal vents
itself in whooping and holloaing at the termination of
every momentous affair like the present; indeed he
relates an anecdote of himself very *naïvely*, of the
misery he endured when on a visit with a very quiet
and pious family, who spoke in *sotto voce* and whispers,
till he could contain himself no longer, and requested
the master of the house to shew him into an empty
room or garret, in which he might halloo out and relieve his pent-up soul.

Off Sandy Hook, burning blue lights, sending up
rockets, firing the gun, till the pilot in his splendid
cutter runs alongside, and comes aboard.   This slim
dandified pilot serves us out like the blue-nose, runs
the Queen on a shoal, and here we stick fast for the
night, till the next tide serves.   In reply to the captain's angry remonstrance, the pilot coolly answered,
our situation was not singular, same time pointed to
a large three-masted vessel run aground by a pilot not
very far from us.   Fortunately it is a fine starlight
night, and we may turn in with all safety.

Roused from our slumbers at an early hour this
morning, huddle on our pea-jackets, and find, to our
inexpressible delight, we are close to New York, and
in five minutes our gallant ship is moored to a wharf
opposite a large gloomy building, called the Tobacco
Inspection.   Thus, after a voyage of twenty-five days,
during which we experienced one of the severest
storms ever witnessed by the oldest sailor on board
our steamer, and in the midst of which we were more

than once rolling at the mercy of the waves, considering our crippled condition in the midst of the
Atlantic, we may consider our landing here, in the
good city of New York, little short of a miracle.

And now the odious and hateful bustle of landing
began.   The post-office agent, a heavy swell, takes
charge of the letter bags with great pomp and circumstance, hastens to carry them ashore, but he is brought
up all standing by (Goddess of Liberty!) a dirty
swaggering fellow, who stands in the gangway with a
cudgel, the very incarnation of a vulgar Irish pig-
driver.   He tells the man of letters to stand back,
swears he has charge of the ship; in fact, he is a low
tide-waiter, connected with the custom house.   But
the agent says he is an officer, and is determined to
land the mails.

" And so am I an officer!" retorts the other, " and
a superior officer, you see, for I'll not permit a *sub-
althern* like you to land out of this vessel.   Push me—
push me! do—it's all I want."

" Throw him overboard!" said a voice.

The post-office swell vapoured up to the tide waiter,
and endeavoured to bully him, but it would not do.

" You think you're a great man," said the tide-
waiter, because you have a bit of lace on your cap,
and have your blue frock coat buttoned up to your
throat.   Arrah, man, I knew your father before you
were born—a labouring man in his shirt sleeves,
(loud laughter;) and I knew your mother too, as decent a woman as ever washed a basket of potatoes in
the Bowery.   You think very little of me!   Oh, I'm
not dressed out for company—I don't want to show
off before the foreigners."   And thus did the tide-
waiter continue to abuse, insult, gall, and harass the

poor agent or officer, till the custom-house officer came on board, and permitted the mails to be landed. The examination of our baggage was a mere form, compared with the ransacking and searching I have witnessed elsewhere; and forthwith we transfer our baggage to the jarvies, rush ashore, and rattle merrily over the stones, in cabs, coaches, and buggy wagons, to the crowded doors of the Broadway hotels.

CHAPTER VII.

New York hotels — Broadway—The planter's opinions— Peel's
Museum—Animal magnetism—Lady magnetized—Philadelphia
—Funeral pageant for the late president — Ferry-house hotel —
John of the rat, and the new bridegroom.

IT has been ever and aye my earnest desire to pass
through the highways of life quietly, without the
fracas, bustle, and ostentatious turmoil in which the
greater portion of the travelling public seem to delight. Arrived at New York, I consult with a fellow
voyageur as to the possibility of getting into a quiet
house ; he enters into my view at once, is well acquainted with the Broadway hotels, and I gladly
follow in his wake, and we make our public entry
through Broadway, and all the fine clothes, bright
eyes, severe, gay, grave, and quizzical faces of the
New Yorkers.

"They are going to church," said my companion,
Mr. Yellowley. This portly gentleman, who declares
he hates a crowd just as much as I do, will not permit
the carriage to stop at Astor House, and we are set
down at —— Hotel. At first I thought the whip
had made a mistake, and had driven to the doors of a
meeting house or conventicle ; but the black waiters
in white jackets, pouncing upon our baggage, speedily

undeceived me, while my companion elbowed his way through the dense crowd of gentlemen in black, sitting and standing about the doors, in the hall, in the porch, up to an elevated desk, upon which we found a large dirty book, flanked with pens and ink bottles, entered our names, and Yellowley was hailed directly by some old familiar faces, and again and again did he repeat, *pro bono publico*, the story of our hair-breadth 'scapes and the perils and dangers of our voyage. The curiosity of the crowd being somewhat appeased, we are permitted to clamber after our baggage, up to the top of the house, and enjoy the tranquillity of a garret. If this be Mr. Yellowley's quiet house, thought I, what must the hotels down South be.

We dine at half-past one, the boarders being summoned by the roar of a huge gong. Upwards of one hundred men, women, and children, sit down to soup, with a regiment of black waiters drawn up in firm array behind our chairs. The blacks perform their evolutions with mechanical precision — thus, fifty dishes are set down on the table with a loud clank— again fifty covers are whipped off, and the dinner proceeds amidst an awful clatter of knives and forks; every man, working away with resolution and haste, fills and empties his plate, regardless of his neighbour's wants. "Help yourself, and your friends will like you the better," is the motto here; a truce to conversation, also, while the all important business of eating is being gone through. Very little wine was drank, and whenever a man filled his skin, he rose up from the table and retreated down to the bar, there lounged about, smoking cigars, sipping brandy and water, chewing tobacco, glancing at the newspapers fastened on desks in the reading rooms, or seated close to door or win-

dows staring at the passengers in the street. There
is a restlessness, an uneasy shifting of positions, a sort
of perpetual motion about the men, coupled with an
anxious expression of countenance, and fierce frowning
brows bent upon strangers, which does not make a very
agreeable impression upon my mind, even though I
am prepared to admire the Americans.

"You must not judge of us by what you see here,"
said Mr. Yellowley. "The New Yorkers are all men
of business, they are citizens of the world; you must
go South and West to see the genuine American in
his true colours."

Stroll up and down the sunny side of Broadway—
meet several of our late fellow passengers, all in rap-
tures with the splendid weather, good accommodation,
beauty of the ladies, and intelligence of the men of New
York. I never saw such transparent complexions, said
one—such brilliant eyes, said another—such feet and
ancles, such bu—*adieu, mes amis, au revoir.*   But Mr.
Yellowley and his discreet son are not so much en-
raptured as the rest.

"I see nothing natural in the gait, in the walk of
those ladies," said the dignified planter, looking up
and down the pavé at the glittering ranks of fair
ladies, slowly sailing before the store windows, to see
and to be seen. "The odious custom of wearing pan-
taloons——"

"Pantalets, I believe, Mr. Yellowley," said I.

"Well, then, pantalets. I have no objection,"
continued he, "to see little girls—children, disporting
upon green lawns and sofas, wear pantalets — but
look there, sir, behold that venerable matron dressed
like a Parisian grisette, waist à la wasp or à la Psyche
—her flowers, her feathers, her chains, her flounced

pantalets. I ask you, sir, what can that old woman mean by affecting such infantine simplicity, twirling a parasol not bigger than a supper plate before her mahogany features?"

" You are severe, Mr. Yellowley," said I.

" I am determined to be so," said that gentleman; " I am resolved to discountenance every thing of the sort."

Placards at every corner inform us that a lady will be magnetized this evening at Peel's Museum, admission twenty-five cents only; and at eight o'clock we march into the Museum, and admire a fusty collection of stuffed beasts, birds, and fishes, and a live tiger-cat, more playful than pleasant, till the learned doctor arrives, and is recognised as an old acquaintance by one of our party.

" Why, G——," exclaimed our friend, addressing the doctor by a name not to be found in the affiche or programme—" why, G——, haven't we met before?"

" Very likely, sir," said the doctor, drily, arranging his spectacles; " as a public lecturer and professional man, I meet with fresh faces every day."

" Why, hang it, doctor, don't you remember me, Bob F——, your old comrade down South? But how comes it to pass you look so much older than I do? Why, man, you are as grey as a badger."

" I think, sir," retorted the doctor, " your comrade down South was a few years younger than I am," cutting the dialogue short by informing us that the *lady* was waiting in the theatre, a convenient lecture room, which was soon filled with ladies and gentlemen anxious to witness the performance. The lady soon slipped from behind a red curtain, and made a side-long inclination towards the company, while the gallant

little Doctor led her to an arm-chair, in which she was
presently adjusted, her head being thrown back, arms
hanging down, like a patient in a dentist's fauteuil;
she was a stout, blooming dame, verging to thirty,
good-looking withal, blushing like any rose.

The Doctor now briefly addressed us upon the
theory and practice of animal magnetism, declares he
is only a young beginner himself, requests our patience, turns up the cuffs of his coat, and goes to work
in a masterly manner, rubbing down the quiescent
lady in the chair with both hands, from the crown of
her head downwards, towards the tip of her fingers,
while we look on as grave as church mice, and preserve
a decent silence.   The Doctor, pausing in his labour,
asks the lady how she feels, and receiving no reply, he
steps forward on the stage, and declares she is now in
the magnetic state.   A black board is set up at one
side of the stage, and the Doctor requests any lady or
gentleman present to write any question and command thereon with chalk, and mark the result—half
a dozen young men spring forward, and we have
several questions and commands written on the board,
and rubbed out again, before the Doctor is satisfied.
"*Will her to raise her right arm,*"—the Doctor slowly
raises his right arm behind the sleeping beauty, and
she raises her right arm also; and her arm being once
in the air, the Doctor declares she has no power to
let it drop again, till he *wills it*—(loud applause)—
the lady still asleep, with her arm sticking out, like
the handle of a pump.   Mr. Yellowley here expresses
his unbelief.   He says it is all a hoax—that the lady
can bend her arm if she pleases; and Mr. Yellowley is
invited by the Doctor to mount the stage—" for," says
the Doctor, jocosely, " seeing is believing, but feeling

hath no fellow." Mr. Yellowley mounts the stage, and endeavours to bend the lady's arm—is cautioned by the Doctor to beware of breaking it—and our friend returns much perplexed, his example being followed by half the audience. The stage is crowded for ten minutes, during which time the poor woman's arm remained as before, nor did she seem to be at all conscious of being surrounded by a crowd. Several commands of a similar nature being obeyed, the Doctor began to write upon the black board himself. I'll tickle my ear with this pen—a new experiment; tickles his ear—the lady shakes her head, puts her finger into her ear. (Loud applause.) Doctor writes again. "Will any lady or gentleman lend me a snuff-box?" —a bottle of smelling salts is handed to him—Doctor smells it aside, and makes most diabolical faces and grimaces—the lady in the chair sneezes outright. (Thunders of applause, and cries of " Encore! encore!") Emboldened by his success, the Doctor declares that, as a final and convincing proof of the power of the magnetised, he will permit half a dozen gentlemen to write their names on a card, and one at a time mount the stage and read over the list of names to the lady, who will tell the reader of the list which is his own. Mr. Yellowley and others write down their names, and that gentleman mounts the stage and reads the names pencilled on a card to her, in a loud voice. " Now, what is my name?" said he, pausing at the end of the list. " Jones," said the lady, in a feeble voice. " Guess again," said he. " Martin," said the lady. Here the Doctor interposed, and requested Mr. Y. to return, and permit the rest of the gentlemen to read their names. They read, and read in vain; the poor lady did not succeed in naming one of the six aright.

" Now, gentlemen," said the Doctor, " you need not grumble ; and, before you condemn, answer me, candidly—' Did any of you actually wish and will the lady to pronounce your name ?' " Mr. Yellowley could not now remember what he wished the lady to do ; and of the six gentlemen, not one of them could say what he was thinking about when he took the lady's hand ; and being laughed at for their pains, the Doctor retires with the lady, amidst loud cheers. The Doctor soon returns, and politely offers to magnetize any lady present. No lady is fool enough to submit to his manipulation, but several gentlemen volunteer their persons to be magnetized, but the Doctor objects. '· It is extremely difficult to magnetize a man." A slender foppish youth having frequently disturbed the peace of the audience, rises, and boldly declares his unbelief ; notwithstanding all he has seen, he is convinced that there exists a secret understanding between the Doctor and the lady. The little Doctor's eyes flashed fire, and, in a fit of virtuous indignation—" Come up here, sirrah !" cried he, like an angry pedagogue addressing an arrant dunce, about to receive the reward of his stupidity. The young fellow was soon seated in the magnetic chair, and the Doctor, rubbing him down with might and main, amidst the laughter of the audience — " Now," said he, pausing to take breath — " now, sir, how do you feel ?" " Pretty well, I thank you," said the other. " Men," said the Doctor, addressing us, " have not always the power of magnetizing men. Come forth, Miss P———, and have the goodness to magnetize this gentleman." Miss P———, who had quite recovered from her magnetic fit, came forward, and was received with cheers, as she proceeded to rub down the unbelieving swain in the chair. " He's going !" said the Doctor, aside, to us—" he's nearly off !" said he, beginning to adjust the black board. " Well, sir, why don't you laugh now ?" said Miss P——. " Because I see nothing to laugh at," said the chairman. " Well, keep quiet," said she ; and another rubbing match ensued, during which the Doctor decided, by the cold feel of the man's hands, that he was sufficiently magnetized. " Well, how do you feel now ?" said the Doctor. " Rather sleepy," said the youth, with a yawn ; " and, as it is after bed-time, I'll bid you all good night." This was the signal for a general breaking-up, the young fellow shewing he was not in the magnetic state, by jumping off the stage, though the Doctor protested he would soon have been magnetized to sleep, and invited us to return and witness his miraculous performance another night.

Weary of the noise, bustle, and hubbub of my caravansary, I sallied out in quest of private lodgings— a severe pursuit,—what with clambering up steep flights of stairs, and being cross-examined as to your pursuits and intentions by cross old women and crusty old men, before they can make up their changeable minds as to whether they can let you into their fusty chambers without a reference and a month's rent in advance. Three days I toiled through Broadway in vain—all the good apartments were occupied—the dear and dirty would not suit—the weather grew most abominably cold—hail, rain, and snow, drove the gay promenaders from Broadway. I jumped into a railway car, and arrived at Philadelphia almost in time to assist at the funeral procession or melancholy pageant got up for the late president—the lamented Harrison. Having already witnessed a similar procession on a far grander scale at New York, I did not court the honour of swelling the ranks of the odd fellows, democratic young men, and strangers bringing up the rear of the procession. But, according to the rule laid down in my uncle's book—" Stick to your baggage," I followed my portmanteau and the creaking wheelbarrow of the black porter up Chestnut Street, vainly attempting to enter sundry hotels, the doors and windows of which were so closely packed with civilians—visitors from the neighbouring town—ladies, children, flags, urns, crape, and everlasting flowers, that the shadow of a straw could not find ingress, much less myself and wheelbarrowful of baggage. Seeing how matters stood, I was glad to retrace my steps to the river side, and consign my baggage to the care of a waiter in the bar-room of a small hotel, called " The Ferry House."

In the oyster-room, attached to this establishment, I found a group of country gentlemen, their wives, and daughters, admiring a huge rat, chained by the leg upon a high desk, and fed with sugar plums and nuts by the visitors. This rat had been recently captured by the proprietor of the house : he met him rambling along the wharfs, and declares he would not part with him for any money ; he says this is the biggest rat in America, calls him his pet, and actually puts the disgusting animal into his bosom. As the evening turned out wet and cold, I was constrained to sit in this oyster room, listening to the learned harangues of my host and an eccentric loafer, called John, a privileged sort of hanger-on about the house, who said and did every thing that came into his head. I soon discovered there was a sort of rivalry, a jealousy, between John and my host, respecting this rat—John pretending to a share in the vermin, as he had assisted in its capture, while the host takes all the merit and glory of the chase to himself.

"Pa," said a little boy, eyeing the rat—"pa, don't you think it is a shaved 'coon."

"No, my son," responded the father, "it is a Guinea rat."

"My, what a long tail!" exclaimed a young lady.

"I think it is a marmoset," said another.

"How tame it is!" said an old lady, venturing to pat the animal's back, a piece of familiarity the rat resented with a squeak, biting at the old damsel's fingers, and sending the whole party to the rightabout with a loud scream, as he leaped at them as far as his chain would allow.

Putting on my old cloak, I sauntered about the streets of the largest city in the Union till the lamps were lighted. The procession, "like the baseless fabric of a vision," had disappeared; the streets were, comparatively speaking, deserted; the shops had been shut at an early hour, and a gloomy impression hung dismally about my mind as I returned to the Ferry House, cold, cheerless, and disappointed. I found that long-bodied, duck-legged swaggerer, John of the rat, strutting about the bar-room—he had been drinking, and the effect of his potations lighted up his long kite-shaped countenance with a variety of unamiable expressions. He wore his high-crowned, sugar-loaf-shaped hat, firmly fixed on the back of his head, his hands thrust into the side pockets of a sailor's jacket, the collar of which sustained a pair of large red ears and a goodly sheaf of foxy hair; the nether man of this Adonis was encased in tight drab continuations, and old boots turned up at the toes in the Chinese fashion. A few boarders and a stray waterman still lingered about the stove, the bar-keeper smoked his cigar, and the host sat with his heels elevated against the stove pipe, pretending to read an old newspaper, and converse with a Dutchman beside him at the same time.   John was on his legs, making an oration upon what he called the present predicament, the awkward position of the *varsal world*, the death of the president, the downfall of the whigs, the rise of the locofocoes, capture of Mac Leod, and war with *Great Britting;* he had long watched the encroachments of *Great Britting* with a jealous eye; she wants a war—she seeks a whipping again, and there are men in Philadelphi can turn her up.   Here John, growing somewhat husky, ordered another gin sling—" Zay, a gin sling."

" No !" responded the bar-keeper—" you have had enough, and more than is good for you already."

" How do you know what's good for me, plebeian ?" said John, fiercely—"but I'll address myself to a higher quarter," speaking to the host.   " *Zay,* command that soaplock at the bar to attend to his business, and present me with my gin sling directly."

" Speaking to me, John ?" said the host, coolly lighting a cigar.

" I have already wasted my words upon you," said John—"I have thrown pearls before swine ; you turn a deaf ear to the stanch supporters of your house, you take to your bosom, and admit to your private ear, that son of a brasscap—yes, his father was a German brasscap, a man who fought through thick and thin for Great Britting, then deserted to the winning party."

" John, for shame !" said the host ; " you should not revile my friends."

" I'll not spare the guilty no way you can fix it," retorted John.   " Friends, indeed !—why should I be ashamed ?—I'll castigate the town,"

" Give him a cigar," said the host; " it will stop his mouth."

" I have cigars enough and to spare," said John, pulling out a handful of half-smoked, broken cigars.

" Well now, John, I have given you a great deal of liquor to-day—partly on account of your exertions about the rat, partly because it was a holiday—but I'll not permit you to make a beast of yourself."

" As to that rat," said John, moderating his ire—" that rat that you make such a rout about, it's a mere rat, a queer chicken, poor concern, mean affair, for a man like you to *bust* about; the rat is beneath my notice, and I know something about him some folks would be glad to know."

" What is it?—come, let me hear it, John," said the host, at the same time ordering the bar-keeper to prepare a brandy cocktail.

" I'll tell you," said John, smacking his lips and eyeing the tumbler in which the brandy cocktail was concocting—" I'll tell you that secret; I found it out to my cost, to-day: he'll bite if you touch his tail, he cannot abide any one as meddles with his tail."

" Pshaw! is that all?" said the host. " Why we all know that—hand me the tumbler." And the host swilled the inspiring mixture with great gusto.

" That is a regular Yankee trick," said John, looking as fierce and red as an angry turkey-cock; " first learn all you can, then cry sucked, and guzzle your liquor. I took you for a man, but I find you're a hog a hog—hog—hog!" and John strode up and down in great indignation.

Here a gentleman and two ladies, with whom I had travelled from New York, drove up to the door, and passed through the bar-room, with considerable fracas and banging of doors as they were ushered up stairs to their chamber by the waiter.

" A new married couple !" said the host, as he returned to the bar-room and resumed his seat.

" He's a smart man, I guess," said the Dutchman.

" And she is a fine woman," said the host.

" He's as pretty a man as ever sat to a table," said a black waiter; " I helped him to oysters and——" And the bridegroom entered the bar-room in his ecstatic way, commanded a sherry cobbler, and seeing the thirsty John leaning with lack-lustre countenance on the counter, politely invited him to join. John did not require much pressing. The bridegroom soon discovered he was a sort of privileged fool, and began to display his wit, at John's expense, to the great amusement of the host and dreamers round the stove.

" Take a chair, sir, I insist," said the bridegroom, with mock ceremony.

" After you, sir," said John; and with some difficulty the pair sat down together, face to face. The bridegroom paid John some very fulsome compliments, told him he perceived he was a man of parts— a genius—a literary character ; wished to be benefited by his conversation, begged his opinions upon affairs in general, and the wonderful rat in particular.

" Let us retire to a private room, sir," said John, " where we may converse apart from those jeering loafers." But the bridegroom declined the proposition, and John seemed displeased. Drawing his chair closer to the bridegroom, he began to catechise that gentleman. " Who are you, sir?—what is your profession ?"

The bridegroom, taken by surprise, responded that he was in the mercan*teel* line.

" Tile, sir, tile—mercantile, not *mercanteel*—*tile* is the word," said John. " Now, sir, you think because you're a merchant (and you may be a broken merchant for all I know) you may turn me into ridicule, make me a laughing-stock before those rowdies, soaplocks, and loafers."

The bridegroom still carried on the joke, though John was getting serious.   He protested that he had not the remotest idea of such a thing; he thought every man in the room had a right to seek information from the sapient John, because, as a public character, he was, like all great men, public property.

" Who calls me public property?" said John. " Take care, sir, how you attack my character.   You respect neither feelings nor morals."

A gin-sling served to close the breach which was fast widening between this comical pair; and John was induced to make an oration upon the present predicament and awkward position of the varsal world, &c. &c.; his audience being swelled by the arrival of sundry cab-men, one of them frequently interrupting John's speech with boisterous exclamations and shouts of laughter.

" Yes, sir, as a mercantile man, you will suffer," said John; " as a mercantile people we will suffer in this war with Great Britting. There is only a rope between us and a bloody war; we hang Mac Leod and take the Canadas, therefore, I say, there is only a rope between us——"

" And the gallows !" interrupted the cabman.

" You'll come to that soon !" said John, and then continued.   " We all know what Washington said when he ordered that Britisher officer to execution, with tears in his eyes. With tears in his eyes Washington said, 'I dined with this very man on a sweet potato in a tamarak swamp, but I'll do my duty; take him away,' said he; 'though he was my brother, or my father, he, I say, he should be hanged.'"

"Who—who, John?" bawled the cabman.

"Look in your history," replied John.

"Look yourself, John," cried the cabman; "you don't know the officer's name."

John, rising up with great indignation, "Begone, you rowdy! I'll kick you into the middle of next week if you dare interrupt me again."

"Go on, go on, sir, I beg," said the bridegroom; "don't mind him, he's beneath your notice."

"He is," said John, resuming his seat, "a vile, barking, coon-tree cur! As I was saying, that long, low, black schooner, off New Orleans, and her piratical crew of slave-dealers——"

"I beg your pardon, you were speaking about Washington and an historical event," said the bridegroom.

"Well, sir, I'll change my subject when I please," said John; "I'll not harp on about Washington to please you or any other man, no way you can fix it. Banking, sir, banking and the sub-treasury bill engross my thoughts. I have given up much of my serious attention to banking."

"Canals, John, or railroads!" bawled the cabman.

Here John made a short run at his tormentor, who escaped from him through the street-door; and John was prevailed on to resume his seat.

"The question is," said John, "what's to be done with our surplus cash? Are we to hide our talents, like the Dutchmen, burying their hard dollars in their cabbage plots? or shall we invest it in the public funds, loan it to the banks, Nicholas Biddle, or———"

" Black Nancy is at the door, with the child in her arms; give her some of the cash, John," cried the cabman.

Here John's self-possession deserted him. Starting up, he made a short kick and a box at the cabman, pursued him three times round the room, chased him half way down the wharf, and returned, puffing and blowing like an angry walrus. He found the bridegroom laughing over a fresh brandy cocktail, and rebuked him with his selfish conduct.

" I have entertained you and instructed you— enlightened your weak mind," said John; "but the moment I turn my back, you get another glass for yourself. I took you for a man, but I find you're a hog—you're a hog, a hog, a hog,—hog !"

" John, John," cried the host, " for shame, John; after all the gentleman's kindness to you, you call him a hog."

" I do !" retorted John; "I call every selfish guttler and guzzler a hog. I call him a hog, and I call you another; but if he's a hog, you're a bigger hog !"

" Go the whole hog, John !" bawled the cabman, peeping in at the door. But some of that malicious wag's companions pushing him forward, he fell head foremost into John's clutches, and the pair rolled over a portmanteau into a basket of oyster shells, while the bridegroom and spectators rushed to separate the struggling foes. The ferryboat bell rang shrilly, and a shoal of passengers pouring into our bar-room, announced that the New York mail had just arrived; the bridegroom ran to look for his bride; I hunted

out my baggage, paid my score, and as I stepped into
a cab, saw John emerge from behind the bar-counter,
with his hat knocked and crushed all out of shape,
as he shook hands with one of the fresh arrivals, a
most comical smile and frown playing about his
glowing visage the while.

"Good night, John!" exclaimed the cabman, as he
thrust my portmanteau into his cab, then plied his
whip, and the next moment we were rattling over the
stones to the Baltimore railway station.

CHAPTER VIII.

Tarry town—Washington Irving's dog—Caldwell—Uncle Sammy and his friends—Saratoga springs—Boarding-house acquaintances—A printer on the road—Barrister versus boatman—Stray damsel of the woods—Episcopalians and Universalists.

I HAD walked four or five miles from Dobbs' Ferry, under the broiling rays of a June sun ; a war of extermination had been carried on against the trees, till, at last, not so much as a sheltering gooseberry bush dare flourish a leaf near the public way. Gladly diverging from the dusty road, I entered a shady lane, which seemed to lead to the river—I was not disappointed. Passing through a quiet, sequestered ravine, I found a pretty little *bijou* of a Dutch cottage, with its picturesque gable ends and grotesque outoffices peering through the cool green foliage of the surrounding groves ; and, turning a corner, the broad sunny waters of the Hudson lay before me. Two labourers were slowly removing some sticks and stones from a little boat pier, lading a cart sustained by a team of heavy oxen, standing knee-deep in the water, quietly chewing the cud of contentment. Seating myself upon a stump on the sandy shore, I enjoyed the cool air and bright prospect before me, now counting the white sails glimmering about the Tappanzee, anon glancing after some gay leviathan of a steamer booming up the river, strains of wild music rising from her crowded deck as she proceeded on her voyage to Albany. Lifting my vision to the Rockland Hills, I longed for some of the cool ice which the deep mountain lake in their rugged bosoms furnishes forth to the parched citizens of New York. A large black-and-white Newfoundland dog, followed by a bandy-legged, red-skinned cur, with a sharp black eye and cocked ear, jumped out of a plantation and made up to me. I took the Newfoundland familiarly by the ear, he thrust his cold nose into my hand, and having exchanged tokens of confidence and friendship, he took a dip in the river and swam about to cool himself. The cur hung aloof, but I soon discovered that he was free from the waspish and worrying disposition of curs in general. I snapped my fingers, he danced about, trotted to a little fountain in the bankside and slaked his thirst at a little bason, while I enjoyed a reviving draught from the sparkling rill, as it leaped from its pebbly bed.

" Who lives in this cottage, my man ?" said I to one of the labourers.

" Washington Irving," was the reply. Another answer sufficed, " Washington Irving had started for New York this morning."

" There is a tide in the affairs of men," thought I, as I began to retrace my steps ; " two or three hours earlier I might have seen him."

Pausing at the little wooden gate, I looked in upon the quiet porch and unassuming front—the house of the far-famed author. A bonnet and parasol emerged from the hall door, and angry with myself for being caught lounging about the premises, gratifying an idle curiosity, I retreated, and had almost reached the high road again, when the Newfoundland dog jumped out of a grove before me, and plainly as dog could explain himself, urged me to follow him — jumping into the grove and looking back several times. I climbed after him, whereat he seemed greatly delighted, and began to whisk towards the cottage again, but finding he could not prevail on me to return home with him, he walked moodily after me till I reached the high road side. Travellers were approaching, and I shook off my friendly follower somewhat rudely, and sent him back, lest, haply, I should be accused of stealing or attempting to steal Washington Irving's dog. Seated on the stoop of the quiet little inn at Caldwell, I waited patiently till some of the Albany steamers would condescend to take in passengers at our solitary station. The host reminded me of one of the old Dutch skippers so faithfully described in Knickerbocker's New York; nathless, Uncle Sammy, though Dutch built, was far from being a Dutchman ; he had a kind word, a jovial salutation, and cordial welcome in store for every strange and familiar face, friend or foe, brought over from Peekskill in the little steam ferry-boat. His acquaintance with the denizens of the banks of the Hudson and the floating craft upon its broad bosom seemed unlimited. The weather was oppressively hot, Uncle Sammy seemed melting away in his shirt sleeves, his red and carbuncled nose seemed to hiss as the perspiration coursed down from his brows, enveloped in a red night-cap, while his eyes seemed stewing under his bushy eyebrows, glancing and gleaming from seas of rheum, liquidity, and tobacco smoke, like a pair of mud volcanoes. Uncle Sammy generally recog-

nised one or two of the passengers from Peekskill
with a sort of view holloa. " Ha, ha! here you are
again!" he would exclaim, extending his hand to some
smart sailor or son of brown labour.   " Ah! man, you
are from Peekskill ? (pronounced Pigskill.)

" I guess not, Uncle Sam ; I'm from Tappan."

" So you are, so you are; you're an Underdunk, I
know it."

" No, Uncle Sam, I'm a Vandunker."

" I knew it, I knew it—an Underdunk or a Vandunker all the same ; let's liquor upon it."   And
Uncle Sam and his friend would retire to the bar.
The quantity of whisky and strong waters Uncle
Sam imbibed with those flying visitors surprised me ;
to be sure, his conversation became rambling and ex-
cursive towards evening, but otherwise I did not perceive any change in his outward man.   His " You're
from Pigskill" sounded as cheerfully as ever, and
shrewd guess, an Underdunk or a Vandunker followed
quite naturally.   His wrath was as easily excited and
awakened as " a lion sleeping near a source" by a tall,
boorish-looking old farmer in a long smock frock, an
unshaven anxious looking hanger-on about the establishment, called Joel. This man Uncle Sammy called a
milksop, loafing about in the shades instead of looking
after the cow.   Joel protested he had sought for the
cow for miles and miles round ; " but she is an arrant
wanderer and fence-breaker," said Joel.

" Then there is a pair of ye," retorted Sam.

" I'll bell her the next time I catch her," said Joel.
And in the midst of the conversation the cow marched
up to a barn-door.

" I knew she would come home to be salted, Uncle
Sammy."

" Now then, get the bell," cried Sam. And we drove the cow into a shed, and secured her, Uncle Sammy holding on by one horn, a fisherman by the other, while Joel came along with a cow-bell and a strap, which he attempted to put round the cow's neck ; the cow resisted, Uncle Sam's pipe was knocked out of his mouth, the fisherman's nether garment fell down about his heels, and an idle old dog, who had hitherto divided his attention between snapping at the flies and scratching his ears, scoured down from the stoop, and fastening his teeth in the bushy hair at the end of the cow's tail, lent his aid to distract the cow, amidst the torrent of abuse, oaths, and threats, poured upon his head by Uncle Sammy, struggling backwards and forwards with the cow's head under his arm, till by a sudden jerk he was pitched on his beam ends on a dunghill, and the cow broke loose from all save her canine appendage ; that zealous hanger-on being either unable or unwilling to extricate his teeth, swung round and round in the air, to the great delight of a knot of little boys collected in the vicinity of a well-laden cherry-tree in the garden. But Joel, willing to retain his position in Uncle Sammy's good graces, kicked the dog off, and throwing himself upon the cow, bravely took her by the horns, and the bell was once more produced. The strap was too short. " What must be done ?" said Uncle Sam ; " there is not another bit of leather in the place."

" There is nothing like independence, Uncle Sammy," said Joel, as, stooping down, he pulled a long leather boot-lace from his short boot, and secured the strap and bell round the cow's neck.

" Nothing like independence, as you say," said the fisherman, as he tucked in his skirts.

" Come, boys, let's liquor upon it," quoth Uncle
Sammy; and the trio adjourned to the bar.

The season had just begun—that is to say, the
hotels and boarding-houses were airing, repairing,
painting, and glazing, for the reception of visitors at
Saratoga Springs when I arrived at this far-famed
watering place.

" You will find it rather dull just now," said a railroad companion, " Congress Hall and the Pavilion
empty."

" Try my private boarding-house, sir," said a respectable looking old man, touching his hat.

" I don't care if I do," said I; and followed my
leader to the outskirts of the town, to the white stoops
and unpretending front of his boarding-house, with
its little martin-house perched over the rose-em-
bowered windows.

" You may please yourself, and choose any room
you like," said my host, as he led me through the
house; " we have very few boarders just now."

I soon fixed upon a quiet little chamber, opening
on the veranda or stoop, and made myself quite at
home.   We dined at two o'clock—a plain and homely
meal, of which the host and about a dozen boarders
partook, while four nice girls, his daughters, waited at
table; judging from the appearance of the boarders
that they were invalids, I inquired of an austere-look-
ing man who sat next me how the waters agreed with
him; he answered with some embarrassment, and
took his departure without satisfying me on that head.
This man I afterwards discovered to be a carpenter,
particularly sensitive as to his position in society; being
originally intended for the church, and not having
the gift of the gab, he was what the Scotch call a

sticked minister, and now honourably supported himself as a journeyman carpenter. A lawyer's lady, and her sister and daughter, from Albany, acknowledged they had received much benefit from the Iodine.

" Give me the Highrock," said a dark-complexioned youth, the wag of the party, a young barrister, who sat at the foot of the table; " try the Highrock spring, sir; it is famous for sharpening one's appetite."

I verily believe the Americans are the most sensitive people on the face of the earth. A stranger attributes their silence to pride and melancholy; I attribute it to *mauvaise honte* in the men, and beshrew me if I know what in the women. Took a delightful stroll through the pine-groves at the back of our house; there is something exhilarating in the air wafted through a pine grove.

" Light, bad land, this," said one visitor to another, as they marched over the stumps, discussing the qualities of the soil.

Returning to the house, I overtook one of our boarders, a tall, good-looking man, in the everlasting black coat and continuations, and attempted to enter into conversation with him. He seemed in rude health, but fancied he was very ill indeed, and drank prodigious quantities of water. He was from Massachusetts, and was one of the most reserved men I have ever met with. One day, I found him fainting on a sofa in the parlour, and one of our kind-hearted ladies fanning him and supporting his head. I proposed that he should be carried to bed, and a doctor sent for ; but, opening his great black eyes, he protested against receiving any assistance with great vehemence, begged that a basin might be set beside him, and that he might be left alone. But the ladies having gathered

about him, I lingered at the window, while our venerable hostess kindly inquired into his ailments.

"I have been drinking five tumblers at the Congress, two at the Pavilion, and one at the Iodine,"
murmured the patient.   "Oh! those waters will be
the death of me!" he groaned; "instead of soothing
my tortured stomach, those sharp and chilling waters
have scourged my entrails."

"Oh! Mr. —— ! my! Mr. —— !"   "Oh!" and
"my!" ejaculated the ladies, as they retreated, and
left the victim of the spas to the care of the old hostess
and myself.   He became so ill that we had to put
him to bed, and send for a doctor after all.

"He has been quacking himself," said the doctor, as
he descended from the invalid's chamber; "he has
been drinking the waters without medical advice—
wrong, wrong, very wrong, to drink the waters without first consulting a medical man."

Sallied out before breakfast with the barrister, took
a sip at every one of the springs from the Congress
to the Highrock, clambered up the ricketty wooden
steps at the last, and retraced our steps through the
shabby wooden houses occupied by the renegade
Canadian French, to the upper end of Broadway, and
sat down to breakfast as voracious as hungry wolves.
The road in front of our house was repairing; and sundry citizens, obedient to the law, were working at it with
their own hands very leisurely.   Tradesmen cut a very
poor figure as out-door labourers.   One of them, a
short, squab little fellow, with a snub nose, wide
mouth, and blear eyes, wore a very high black stock,
hat almost as long as his body, and a new pair of
high-heeled Wellingtons; he had thrown his coat
upon the branch of a tree; he grasped an iron crow-

bar almost as long as himself, sometimes supporting himself upon it, then niggling a little round a stone, while his tongue rattled away ; and his fellow labourers followed his example, leaning on their shovels, spades, and crow-bars, while they listened to his eloquence or responded to his questions.

" We may safely call this a beaten track of life, my friends," said the squab labourer. " I find it almost impervious to the point of the Dotor's crowbar."

" The bar wants to be newly pointed, I guess," said a tall man with a stoop, a long skyblue frock coat, and a very bad pair of old shoes."

" It would cost five cents to get it pointed," replied the other. " Five cents, let me tell you, is not to be thrown away upon a loaned crowbar ; and though five cents is not worth the notice of a boot and shoe maker like you—by the way, I wish you had not made those boots so inquisitorially tight across the instep."

" Boots ! indeed ; why, do you wear boots on the road ? Look at my feet !" said the shoemaker.

" It's a singular fact," said the squab fellow, leaning on his bar, " and indeed I think I'll insert in our next week's paper, this question—'Who ever saw a shoemaker with a good pair of shoes, or a new pair of boots on his feet ?' I never did, for one. Hollo, squire !" exclaimed this genius to our host, "come down here, and take a turn at the bar ; you'll shine at it, man, like a parlour poker."

" No, no, no thank you, master printer. Why don't you work like a man when you are at it ? Fitter for you to send a substitute, I say, and mind your own business."

" There we differ *in toto*," said the printer. " I like to fulfil the law to a letter ; no shirking for me ;

no paltry substitute, no backing out. It is for example's sake, and to set the democratic young men a bright example, that I wield this unwieldy implement of husbandry. Look at my hands, all in blisters, for the good of society, and the benefit of the community. Talking is dry work—send me down a pitcher of hard cider."

" There is a pitcher of the Pavilion water at the back of the house, if you like to drink," responded our host, quietly.

The printer declined the cooling draught, and directed our host's attention to a stone in the road. " Squire, do you think it expedient for me to remove this here geological specimen ?"

" To be sure; why should it be left a stumbling-block before my door ?" replied the host.

" Very well; since you wish it to be transplanted, furnish forth four or five charges of gunpowder," said the printer. " I tell you plainly, I mean to blast it in a new and scientific way."

" Ay, and break my windows," said the host.

" That is your look out," said the printer; " or, rather, if you are looking out, you may chance to get your nose curtailed of its unseemly length by a flying splinter."

" Your own nose cannot be made much shorter, at all events," said the host; and the rest of the labourers gathering round the stone, tore it from the road, and cut short the printer's conversation.

Sitting in the parlour with the rest of the boarders, on Sunday morning, before church, we were favoured with the look in of a visitor, an old damsel, whose antediluvian appearance excited our interest and attention. This lady wore a short-waisted, short-sleeved gown, of faded brocade; her bonnet, "well saved, a world too wide," resembled an antiquated coal-box; her face, *malgré* the rude embraces of time, looked as round and hale as a last year's apple preserved in sand; round her throat she wore a necklace of very large gilt Venetian beads; long faded gloves almost covered her skinny arms. She flounced into the parlour, *sans ceremonie,* sat down on a sofa, divested herself of shawl and bonnet, and made herself quite at home. Thinking she was a relative, or friend of the family, the ladies and gentlemen did not speak to the visitor. At last the bells began to ring, and the host and his family marched off to their respective houses of worship; the ladies prepared to follow their example.

" My dear," said our strange visitor, rising up and approaching a little West Indian girl who was reading a tract, " My dear, do you use glasses ?"

The little girl replied in the negative, in no small confusion.

" Old woman! ma'am!—say, ma'am! can you loan me your glasses?" persevered our visitor, turning to a Scotch lady, who was reading.

The Scotch dame said she was sorry it was not in her power, as indeed she could not read without spectacles herself.

" Well, what's to be done ?" said our visitor. " I have forgotten my own glasses to home, and the bells are ringing."

" Perhaps, madam," said I, " we can send for your glasses, if you tell us where."

" Well, now," interrupted the lady, " I guess you think yourself considerable smart. You want to find out where I live."

I protested I had only intended to serve her.

" Well, loan me a pair of glasses, young man."

I regretted I could not accommodate her nose, but I had a telescope, which was very much at her service."

" Well, I guess I'll be going to the meeting, for I see I'll do no good here," said the lady, and resuming her bonnet and shawl, away she went.

Went to the episcopalian church, or school-house, in which divine service was performed by an Englishman. The windows of this building were thrown open with such rashness, that a current of air and dust was constantly streaming in upon the devoted heads of the congregation. Having sustained the draught for some time with the patience of Job, until I began to feel shooting pains in the ears, I retreated, and entered the new church of the universalists. The congregation was not as large as I expected, from the number of waggons and buggies about the building, and horses browsing about the road, or tied to the neighbouring fences. The preacher was a young man of sanguine temperament. He did not dwell upon the particular tenets of the universalists, but spoke of some recent conversion to the comfortable doctrines of his church. He related a conversation he had had with a certain man in the congregation then present, who declared he would give up his team and waggon if he could believe what the preacher told him—viz., that no man was born to be d——d to all eternity. This reminded me of an anecdote I had heard of an Irish priest who had quarrelled with his bishop, and set up a chapel on his own account. Getting into sundry scrapes and a riot, he was brought to trial at the assizes, and acquitted of the charges brought against him. Before he left the court-house, he entered into conversation with an influential magistrate respecting his reformed chapel, and his improvement on the old church of Rome. " We have got rid of holy water, sir," said he. " I am glad to hear it," said the magistrate. " And we can dispense with fasting also." " So much the better," was the reply. " And we have got rid of purgatory." " And I wish you could get rid of another very hot place," said the magistrate. This universalist minister would have suited that Irish magistrate, for he went a step further than the persecuted Father Crotty, and got rid of the infernal regions very much to his own satisfaction.

The harmony of our little society was somewhat ruffled this evening by a New England minister, or clergyman, who pays an annual visit to the springs, and a doctor who visits a patient in our house. Religion and infidelity the theme and bone of contention about which they fell together by the ears, while the lawyer stirred up the flame whenever he found it beginning to flag. All the sects, the shaking quakers, methodists, universalists, &c., were turned into ridicule by the doctor, who thought himself a very clever fellow. He exposed the humbug and the folly of the Mormon leader, Joe Smith, who had drawn together a tribe of fanatics in the west, by his book and pretended revelations; yet strange to say, continued he, a wealthy farmer not far from this has turned Mormon, and speaks of setting off, bag and baggage, to the city of Nauvoo, on the Missisippi.

" Better to believe in Joe Smith than nothing," said the minister, pointedly; " for if he deceives, upon his head let it rest."

" Ay, that's your trade," said the doctor. " You

would support a man like Joe Smith, or any other self-dubbed prophet, merely to support priestcraft."

The minister replied with more zeal and warmth than the doctor expected. He denied that he was an infidel; same time, in his professional career, he had seen many a Christian die in agonies of doubt and fear, and many an unbeliever, soldier, and sinner, shuffle off his mortal coil as coolly and calmly as if he was changing his clothes.

The minister rose up in great indignation, and said he would not hold conversation with any man who held such opinions. I was sorry to see the good man give way, as there were several young people listening to the conversation, who looked upon the minister's retreat as little short of defeat.

Rode to Saratoga Lake with the barrister, put up our horse and buggy at the hotel, and descended to the lake in quest of a boat—found one stuck in the mud, which we could not launch, and espying another south side of the lake, we looked about for its owner, but finding none, took the liberty of rowing up the lake in it. Presently a man began hallooing after us; but, as my learned friend observed, the fellow was on the opposite side of the lake from that which we had taken the boat, and ergo, the boat did not belong to him. Resting on our oars, however, we heard his voice denouncing us loud and clear, for having presumed to take the ferry-boat. My learned friend rose up in the boat and responded, giving his opinion, gratis, that the appellant might terminate his doleful days with a rope, *felo-de-lac* or *felo-de-se*, before he would get the boat from us; and by the way of shewing a *non sequitur*, we resumed the oars, and pulled vigorously up the lake. Shoals of little fishes played round us; and we admired the wooded banks of the lake, a round wooded hill especially. The flies soon became very troublesome, and we returned slowly towards the spot from whence we had taken the boat; but the man who had hailed us from the shore, now made his appearance in another boat, which he pulled towards us with great speed; we pulled our oars and arrived at the landing-place before him. "Now let us make a strait coat tail for the buggy!" said my legal friend. I was not disposed to run, and advised a parley. Meantime the ferry-man approached us, and reproached us with having made away with his boat, and finally demanded half a dollar damages.

" Half a dollar!—half a dollar, indeed!" exclaimed my friend, slapping his brow—" who ever heard of such an extravagant demand?—well, after that I find you are deaf to reason. I'll not argue with you." And my friend marched off into the bush, and deliberately took off his clothes, entered the lake, and began to swim about.

" Well, stranger," said the angry boatman, turning to me, " I guess you must pay me for the boat."

" Extortion!" bawled the barrister, as he sputtered along through the water.

" You'd best be civil, my chap," said the boatman; " if it wasn't for your darn'd imperence to me when you took the boat I'd not have looked for a cent."

" Don't mind him, sir," bawled the barrister; " let him take an action and recover by law. If he recovers at the court of Saratoga, we can appeal, and take our position in the higher courts at Albany, and laugh at his beard. Hurrah! If you had known how warm and pleasant the water feels, you might have joined me, and we could have swam round the lake, without tugging his heavy old boat along."

"I'm not going to argue law with you now," said the ferryman, walking into the bush; "and as you took possession of my boat without asking, I'll take possession of your clothes until I'm paid."

This *coup de main* swamped the barrister. How could he return to Saratoga in a state of nudity; but to be outwitted by a clown was most inglorious. He protested and exclaimed against the barbarian in vain, and finally I was obliged to pay him and send him about his business, grumbling against the barrister for his *tarnation tongue.*

Returning home, we found a large land-tortoise trudging along the dusty road; I captured him, and presented him to the ladies at home. They screamed out that it would bite them, and I consigned him to the garden, from which he soon made his escape.

My friend the barrister related a history of our adventure on the lake to the ladies after tea, and raised a laugh at my expense, when he told them of how cleverly he had left me to pay the angry boatman: but I soon turned the tables on him, and by particular request the barrister was urged to spout a poem for the ladies, after the manner of a celebrated ventriloquist and orator. He chose Campbell's beautiful poem—"A Chieftain to the Highlands bound," and bestriding a chair, took the liberty of putting his arm round Miss or Mrs. Eola Thrempley's waist; elevating his voice, he shouted like a man in a storm—

" Boatman, do not tarry—
    I'll give to you a siller pound to row us o'er the ferry."

Then sinking his voice to a deep hoarse growl—

> " Oh, wha be ye wad cross Lough Gyle,
>   That dark and stormy water."

Then replying in the chief's voice, anon in the old ferryman's, till the ladies became excited and interested; but when he came to the doleful lamentation of the father, and groaned and moaned—" My daughter! oh, (oh—ho! oh—ah!) my daughter!" the ladies had recourse to their handkerchiefs, and the eldest of our young ladies *boohoo'd* outright, which terminated, somewhat abruptly, my friend's eloquent entreaties, and oratorical display.

CHAPTER IX.

Troy—Boys and bull-dog—Railroad—Canal—Accident—Mistake
—Whitehall—Bishop—A learned leech—Lake Champlain—
Fine steamer—Burlington—American kindness—St. John's—
Montreal—St. Lawrence—Irish immigrants—The Bishop and
his men—Kingston—Pleasant hotel—The new House of As-
sembly—Stormy debate—Toronto.

SAUNTERING about the streets of Troy in quest of
lions, my progress was somewhat impeded near a
church-yard, (full of tomb-stones, almost concealed by
tall hemlocks,) by a merry group of young Trojans,
running in a ring, hand in hand, round a hat belonging to one of the party, the object and fun of the
game being to make one of the crew trample upon it;
and if a merry wight could be made to dance on
his own *chapeau de paille*, their happiness would be
complete. Close to this merry group sprawled a huge
bull-dog; he seemed to enjoy the sport quite as much
as the boys, and though he did not join in the dance
round the hat, he had got hold of a huge round
paving-stone, which he tossed as a kitten would a
ball of worsted, between the fore paws, biting it with
the sides of his mouth, then lifting up his huge round
head, " Ev'n for joy he barkit wi 'em."

Knowing the savage and morose nature of the bull-dog, I was much amused at his playfulness. A cart-horse broke loose, came galloping down the street, the boys ran out of his way, the bull-dog's ire was roused at this interruption; he made an abortive effort to seize the horse by the nose; the horse kicked at him, *en passant*; the bull-dog pursued him in a rage; the boys pursued them both, crying, " Go it, Ty ! Hurra, Ty !" &c., and the whole pack of them vanished round a corner. I turned towards the grave-yard, from which a vagrant wind wafted the loathsome, rank, and abominable smell of hemlock, henbane, and ratsbane. I fled the pestilential air, and wished the Trojans would prove their Eastern origin by weeding their fathers' graves, and planting flowers thereon. A grave-yard, take it what way you will, is an unpleasing spot to find in the midst of a city, but a neglected grave-yard, breathing of aceldama, in such a situation, is a stain upon the breast of humanity.

Took the railway to Borough. In the same car, sat a very fat and facetious gentleman, in great good humour with all men, especially the government men—he had just received a civil commission of some importance; even the sun shone out so gloriously upon him, that he was fain to hoist an umbrella out of the window, to protect his honoured head from a *coup de soleil*; but the conducteur, or clerk of the check, made our stout gentleman draw in his umbrella, and, shortly after, I resigned my seat to the melting swain. Got into the canal-boat, in which, for the novelty of the thing, I wished to take a short voyage; the captain, or master, of the boat soon made his appearance on deck, and bade the passengers look out for bridges. The track-line was soon fastened to the horses, and

H

away we splashed, as fast as two good nags could tug us, through the water.   The captain, a tall Dominie Sampson looking man, with a stoop in his shoulders, and a bald pate—for, though in the prime of life, he had got rid of his hair, probably by rubbing his head against the ceiling of the boat and the bridges.   He began, pen in hand, to take down our names, a matter of easy performance, the passengers being only seven in all—a great big behemoth in black was called the episcopal Bishop of Vermont—a silent wight; he read the papers, from first to last, advertisements, and births, deaths, and marriages; a certain sprightly lady, who declared, aloud, her abhorrence of the English, who did not dare persecute any other nation, save the Chinese, reminded of the fact, by being asked to make tea at breakfast; her companions, thin laths of students, enlivened us by reading, alternately, the sermons of Dow, jun.   The captain entered this lady's name in such a singular orthography, that I copied it; "Miss—Thigh—Ersa—Lee." Then came a little busy spry-looking man, hopping about his wife, a flauntingly-dressed old woman, who sat with great dignity in the ladies' cabin, while her good genius proceeded, with singular zeal and many demonstrations of joy, to set before her, upon a spider table, what I took to be a great stone, but, on closer inspection, proved to be only a sponge—and why, or wherefore, I could not divine.   This man afterwards rebuked me with ingratitude, very much to my surprise, as I had never had the felicity of seeing him before.   We spoke about the Brandiwine ship-of-war; she had just returned from the Mediterranean, where I had seen her and boarded her, one fine day, at Toulon.   "You forget who placed you on board that frigate, sir," said the little gentleman, looking at me very disdainfully. "I received little assistance," I replied; "in fact I did not need any, for the hand-ropes and ladder were let down—and—" "Ah, gratitude! gratitude!" sighed the old gentleman. And well he might sigh and groan, having mistaken me for a middy, who got a snug berth on board the crack frigate through this diplomatic agent's assistance. I found this gentleman more agreeable and intelligent afterwards. He had a farm near Whitehall, upon which he was retiring to spend the rest of his days, far from the busy hum-drum of life. Speaking of agriculture and manure, he said he remembered the time when all the manure in Troy and Albany was thrown into the river, the wiseacres not knowing how to dispose of it in any other way.

The number of low wooden bridges on this canal render it particularly unsafe and unpleasant, especially as there is no alternative between sitting cooped up in the cabin, or running the risk of having one's brains knocked out on deck; but even the ladies prefer the post of danger, and there is a perpetual ducking of heads, and sprawling about on all fours, while the man at the helm, or the captain, keeps singing out—" Bridge!—mind the bridge!" We had just passed by a poor helpless labourer, lying on his face on the track-way, and the boatmen, taking it for granted that he was *drunk, and an Irishman,* began pelting him with potatoes, one of which struck the poor wretch in the side, and he threw up his arm with a convulsive motion. I called out to the men to desist, and the steersman's reply was unique: "Zay, when you find me drunk on the road, you may pelt me with stones and potatoes."

While this conversation was going on, I was on my

legs on the deck, and the next moment lay sprawling upon it, as helpless and insensible as the man on the shore ; in short, I had received a " tarnation tunk on the head," as one of the boatmen said, as he tendered his assistance, while the bishop, who had been astride his travelling bag, kept on exclaiming—" Not seriously hurt by the bridge—not seriously hurt ?" his aid and advice being confined to that query.

We did not arrive at Whitehall till eleven at night, and every house, save the large rambling hotel, we stopped at, being shut up, I passed a wretched night, without receiving any medical aid. Next morning, procured the attendance of a learned leech, who made sundry abortive efforts to apply cupping glasses to my head, and finally bled me in the arm, and advised me to go a-head to Burlington, and get leeches, and apply them to the temples ; and, being assured there was no fracture, I went on board the splendid steamer, " Burlington"—arm in a sling, head tied up, and in doleful dumps. Just as we were leaving the wharf, my fat railroad officer rushed down the wharf, bag in hand, and stepping upon the foot-plank, plunged down into the water, and disappeared. The engine was stopped, and the poor gentleman rescued from his perilous situation. He had caught hold of the paddle-wheel, and narrowly escaped being broken to pieces ; his hat and private correspondence were found floating aft ; and when he was dressed in the captain's clothes, he waxed merry again, saying he had been " wetting his commission." Our meeting on deck was singular enough. A few hours past—but yesterday—we had parted in high health and spirits, journeying in different directions; now we met upon the deck of the steamer *streaked* enough, having barely escaped with our lives, and only wanting a Methodist preacher to *improve* upon the occasion. The situation of Whitehall, surrounded with swamps, must be particularly unwholesome, though, from a height above the town, the view of the lake is said to be exceedingly picturesque. Verily I shall not forget Whitehall, and the canal and the bridge as connected therewith, for some time.

The Burlington is fitted up like a pleasure-boat—everything in apple-pie order; the captain's office uniquely adorned with coloured French prints of the "Loves and Graces," mirrors, and varnish glass door handles, bell-pulls, buhl, ormolu, and *marquetiere par tout;* then the captain's private sitting-room, upon the promenade deck, with its light summer curtains, festooned about the windows, its luxurious rocking-chair and crimson sofas; even the spit-boxes were ornamental and useful, being converted into flower-pots, half filled with clay, and a young growth of mignionette and tongue-grass. The weather was delightful, and the shores of the lake extremely picturesque.

Burlington.—Here I quit the boat for the town; the shore seems all in a bustle, the militia and volunteers, and their bands, crashing away, much to my confusion, as I calculated upon resting a few days in sweet tranquillity in this town; but independence, eve and day, must be celebrated with a vast deal of noise, it seems, even here. Drive up to the principal hotel and secure a good bed-room—sally forth to look for leeches, and find but one in the whole town—buy that one, and apply him to my right temple—call upon a certain medico, called Hatch. The good man cupped me upon the back of the neck two or three times, and I feel much better, *Dieu merci;* so, please the fates, I'll disappoint the rats a little longer, *malgré*

the shouting of the boys, the blowing of horns, and
explosion of pop-guns and petards in the square
before our door.   Being cut down a good deal with
bleeding, and cupping, and leeching, as I sat in my
window, with "spirit sinking," a gentle tap at the door,
and the next moment a tall, very tall gentleman stood
before me.   He said his ladies insisted he should call
and see the sick stranger, and offer any assistance in
their power. I thanked him, &c., and compliments being
passed, he retired.   That evening I received sundry
bottles of essences, and perfumes, and restoratives
from this amiable family, and in the morning, what I
valued more, some fresh flowers ; but it is only those
who have been smitten down upon the bed of sickness in a strange land can appreciate such gifts.   On
receiving those flowers, I waked, as it were, from a
lethargic dream, my heart was so full, and my head so
busy, with one thought—" How shall I return thanks
to this amiable family ?"—that I seemed to have forgotten I was an invalid, and forbid to walk, advised
to stay in my room, in a recumbent position, by my
leech. I donned my clothes, and sallied forth, walked
right up the hill to the college, entered a meadow,
looked down upon the lovely little town, the sunset
lake, eyed the dim shadows and lofty peaks of the New
York mountains on the opposite side, towering away
into the clear blue sky ; and twilight grey " had in her
sober livery all things clad," ere I returned to mine
inn, steady as a rock and hungry as a hunter.

Burlington is decidedly the prettiest American
town I have seen. Rows of locust trees in the streets,
and flowering shrubs and flowers before the doors of
the houses—light stoops and fancy colonnades, and an
air of quiet neatness about everything, speaks of hap-

piness and contentment. A farewell visit to my kind
friend, who accompanies me down to the steam-boat;
he has been sojourning at Burlington with his family,
and returns to Boston, his native city, in a few days.
Leave Burlington with regret; the people of the
hotel have been exceedingly kind and attentive.
Embark in the Whitehall steamer for St. John's,
where we arrive at seven in the morning. The
British fort at the head of the lake, with the sentries
stalking backwards and forwards, has a singular effect,
and one is inclined to exclaim—"What, in the name
of fate, is worth guarding so closely in the desolate
swamps and underwood of all the region round about
St. John's?"—the custom-house officers declare we
are once more on the soil of our sovereign lady the
Queen; and truly a more wretched, miserable town in
a swamp, is not to be found in the British dominions.

Breakfast, and start for Montreal, by railroad and
steam-boat, and arrived at that venerable old town in
the midst of a storm of hail, rain, and wind, such as
one might expect to find in Nova Zembla in April,
rather than in Montreal in July.

Start in a coach, followed and preceded by a "caval-
cade of coaches," to La Chine. Embark on board a
steamer, and mount the St. Lawrence, against wind
and tide; my fellow-passengers are lumberers, gentlemen, who have just returned from Quebec, where they
have disposed of their rafts for less than the cost of the
labour, not to speak of risk and loss of time piloting
said rafts down the rapids. They say there is a glut
of timber in the market, and the timber is perfectly
unsaleable. So much for lumbering. The harsh
and sour conversation of those gentlemen betokened
disappointment, and timber, sticks, logs, and blocks.

frequently supported their arguments. One would wager a deal plank to a pine log; another, three deal boards, delivered at the mouth of some jaw-breaking creek; and long before we reached Prescott, whole rafts were pending upon obstinate opinions. I observed a party of Irish emigrants crawling aft in earnest admiration of a small steamer in our wake. Upon her deck stood several priests and clericos, their heads adorned with the venerable bonnets *des prêtres*, and their long, black vestments streaming in the wind.

" It is his lordship the bishop," said a tall, severe-looking gentleman in black, upon whose brazen, beetling brow, well-shaved blue chin, dim, brick-dusty coloured cheek, and close, lipless mouth, the word Jesuit was as easily read as though it had been stamped in burning letters in the flesh——" his lordship the bishop; he is going to the Caledonia springs for the benefit of his health," said this lofty and pompous clerico, to the admiring group of men, women, and children; while they expressed their admiration and surprise, turning up their eyes, like ducks in thunder, and sending forth a variety of singular sounds, such as our coachmen cheer on the nags with.

" It's a real bishop entirely," said one devout old woman.

" Jick, jick, jick!" echoed the rest of the men, women, and children. " The heavenly man, with his hair streaming, like a hank of yarn, over his shoulders, in the wind, and his whistments furling about his precious limbs."

" Oh, mother, mother!—look at his red stockings!" exclaimed a boy.

" Whisht—whisht, you blackguard, ridiculing the garments of your clargy and the holy man. See how condescendingly he waves his arm, turning to his deacons and coadjutors, from right to left. (Omnus, ' Jick, jick, jick! Thisk, thisk, thisk!') Now they present him with the book; he's going to *do his office* before the wide world, on the bare deck—(here the party devoutly cross themselves)—but the wind, bad manners to it! turns over the leaves faster than he can read; he must go below to do his office, more is the pity. He returns the book, and now the coadjutor with the long nose presents his superior with a round box, and the superior presents the box to the bishop, making a curtshey at the same time. The bishop receives it."

" Why does he rap the box with his knuckles, mother?"

" What's that to you—don't be exposing your ignorance af the saremonies of your church! Now he opens the lid, the wind whisks something into the dear man's eye. The bishop sneezes; the coadjutor sneezes; the pious man with the book sneezes; the holy man with the green bag sneezes; the tall father with the big umbrella sneezes; the devout disciple in the cloak and green spectacles sneezes; the man at the wheel lets out his hoult, and sneezes. God bless them all—(' Thisk, thisk, thisk!')—and may they have a pleasant passage up the Ottawa. Thisk, thisk, thisk! Amen."

Again we scramble out of the steam-boat into the coaches, and jolt along the picturesque banks of the St. Lawrence, catching glimpses of the famous rapids. Meet a coach laden with passengers downwards bound, and the stiff clerico who has seated himself in our coach recognises some friends; to one of these, a smart old gentleman, our clerico particularly addresses himself, telling him that he should recollect that he was the father of a family.

" You are going to visit a city—take care, sir: and always remember you have now a wife and family at home ;" but he altered his tune when a light, sprightly little damsel put her foot on the step of the coach-door, and shook his reverend hand, while his reverence, modulating his voice like a sucking dove, begged to know—" When do you return to us, my dear ?" " Not for a month—a long, long month"—" Ah, don't say so, my dear girl, you are going to a city," &c.

The coachmen cut this billing and cooing short— and once more, *en route* to the forte at Coteau. Here we see several cannons (great guns too) serving as curb-stones by the road-side ; arms broken off, and rendered unfit for service by the valiant commander of this fort during the late disturbance in Canada. This brave man caused several guns and other stores to be thrown into the rapids below the fort, for which meritorious action I hope he has been justly rewarded.

Coteau-de-Lac: here we get into the steam-boat again, and steam up Lake St. Francis, against a bitter cold wind; find the people belonging to the steam-boat remarkably uncivil to the passengers, and the tone of hostility assumed truly disgusting; for my own part, I always carry with me a pass-par-tout, and, once established in good quarters, sally forth, and go to and fro, in steam-boat or hotel, on land or water, making my own observations very quietly; and though I seldom or ever interfere in what does not concern me, felt inclined to espouse the cause of two Canadian girls, who had unwittingly broken through some of the many rules and regulations placarded about the boat, such as " Deck-passengers not permitted aft of the shaft," " Gentlemen will walk this way," " Deck-passengers beware," &c. Those confounded steamers always remind me of enormous rat-traps, in which even the lords of the creation may be caught, and " done for," even if they escape blowing up, and par-boiling.

Coaches again. What a horrible jolting and truly fatiguing day's journey we have had, and now proceed, at a snail's gallop, to Dickenson's Landing, a miserable, bleak, wretched spot, where we huddled on board a steamer *encore*, and tumbled into our berths under the wholesome impression that our steamer is safely moored by the swampy bank for the remainder of the night.

Brockville: I like the appearance of this little town passing well. The church and chapel bells were ringing, and the good folks marching devoutly to divine service. I had some thoughts of following their good example, when the shrill ringing of the steam-boat bell recalled me. I rushed to the shore, and *malgré* my haste, was within a rope's end of being left behind with the good people of Brockville. And now we threaded our course through the lake of 1000 Isles, of every shape and size, some heavily timbered, others affording pasture to herds of cows and horses; while ever and anon, the white front of a settler's house peered out of the dark woods on the right bank of the lake shore; and at last the fort and ruined barracks of Kingston or Cataraqui became visible, and we were soon gladly jumping on the wharf or steam-boat landing-place of the new capital of the two Canadas.

The appearance of Kingston, with its permanent stone houses, treeless streets, and narrow lanes, reminded me of an Irish town in the vicinity of a good stone quarry; the small doors and windows, and close, confined fronts of the houses, give the streets a gloomy appearance even in summer; and the sun shining out, at last, I fagged through the broiling streets, seeking an hotel, or boarding-house. The best hotel was full of Members of the House of Assembly; and the second best could only afford me a bed in a double-bedded room. Moreover, the porter who carried my baggage was a stranger in the place, though he pretended he was well acquainted "with every hole and corner in Kingston." At all events, he seemed determined to make me acquainted with every out-of-the-way corner in the place, till at last, losing patience, I made him deposit my baggage at the corner of the square, before the eyes of several loungers and loafers, and appealing to the by-standers for information, was directed to an inn, or public-house, kept by an Italian. Mounting some high, stone steps, I was greeted at the door by a dark-eyed little Venus, with a child in her arms, for such she seemed to be when she said I could have a bed-room all to myself. I hastened to send for my baggage, and was soon installed in a very tolerable apartment, commanding a view of the pigs, dogs, and chickens in the back yard; three old sleighs, a goodly pile of firewood, and a pent house at each corner. Feeling feverish and fatigued, I turned in at once and slept like a watchman, till the aforesaid little maiden knocked at my door and inquired if I meant to sleep all day. I assured her I did not; jumped up, looked at my watch, and found I had been in the arms of Morpheus much longer than I supposed. Breakfast was over, and while another tea-pot and chop were preparing, I walked into the parlour, or sitting-room, scantily furnished with broken sofas, cracked chairs, and a fragment of dubious-looking carpet; two country gentlemen, farmers, sat close to the window, watching the singular motions, and attending to the sayings and doings of a little man with a very red, brick-dusty coloured face—sweeping profile, reminding me of that of George the Third, as still seen upon venerable halfpence—while his body, at variance with the royal pomp of his face, tapered away down to the heels in a vast, green, Newmarket coat, with brass buttons, almost concealing the tight nankeen continuations that covered his shrunken shanks; and his feet, lost in a pair of long-heeled, yellow slippers, seemed to be pinned loosely to the tail of his coat. At a little distance, he looked like a kingfisher; in his hand he twirled playfully a staff, like the handle of a sweeping-brush—at one end of which, dangled a key of no small dimensions. This prudent gentleman, thought I, is resolved to carry the key of his bed-room door attached to his walking-stick, or mayhap he is grand chamberlain to the Governor, or carries the key in his office as grand——"

" Do you want this, sir?" said the kingfisher, presenting his staff and key to me, with a bow.

I declined the offer with much surprise, and the honourable member, for such I soon discovered him to be, wearied with perambulating the room, sat down between the two farmers.

" You want to hear the debates, you do; well, I'll post ye convenient to the reporthers." (Here the farmers return their hearty thanks for the honour &c.) " Never mind, don't thank me, don't say another word; sure it's my duty to accommodate my constituents. You have accommodated me, so I must accommodate you."

" And you'll vote for the new road ?" said one of the constituents.

" And get us a bridge ?" said the other.

" Easy—be easy !" said the honourable knight of the staff and key, whose speech betrayed his Milesian extraction. " Let me alone." (Puts his finger to his nose, and winks.) " I'll road and bridge ye." (Many protestations of thanks and external regard.) " I'm the boy for *log rolling*."

While this conversation was carrying on, I observed a round, little man, in a blouse, and broad-leafed, palm hat, hurrying to and fro about the hall, with a bundle of old newspapers under his arm, and exclaiming, as he looked into holes and corners——

" Où est il—Diable, où est il ! Sacre bleu, où est il allé. Nom de Dieu, où est il—sacre nom de Dieu, où est il !"

At last one of the constituents insinuated to the honourable member, that the Frenchman was looking for something that the said member had in his possession.

" Let him look for it," replied the little M.P., disdainfully; " he belongs to the noisy opposition."

But the member of the noisy opposition soon entered the parlour, and forthwith made a hasty exit, with the staff and key which the Kingfisher member presented to him, coolly observing, " I see what you are polling for—I believe you are looking for this."

Sally forth to view the town, cross the clumsy wooden bridge, (paying a heavy toll), ascend the black and barren hill, from which the old fort and ruined barrack seemed to grin defiance at the town ; but the view of the lake and the shipping-wharfs, dock-yards, bridge, flag-staffs, and distant woods, fill up the

picture, well worth clambering the walls of the fort
to look upon.

The seat of government having been recently removed to Kingston, Messieurs, the speculators, have
set to work—" *lots have risen*"—and carpenters', stone-
masons', and tradesmen's hammers make the welkin
ring. Indeed, the stone-masons and their men render
walking through the streets not merely unpleasant,
but dangerous—fragments of stone and splinters flying
about in every direction.

Visit the house of Assembly : a large, airy building
at some distance from the town, commanding a fine
view of the lake, and admirably situated for an hos-
pital ; for such it was built and occupied, until the government, in its wisdom, converted it into a House of
Assembly, sending the invalids to the right-about.
It is said the house is occupied by the legislature *pro
tem.*, and the good people of Kingston have not time
to be sick, now the tide of statesmen, civil officers, and
hangers-on have been poured upon them. Ascending
the stairs I entered the lobby of the house and strangers' gallery—a portion of the house railed off for
strangers and the press. The honourable members,
particularly the noisy opposition, mustered strong ,
the debate was both warm and interesting, as it concerned the elections, and affected the seats of several
members, against whom petitions had been presented
—some of the petitions being sent up too late, others
too early. The speaker or chairman had a hard card
to play—indeed he looked exceedingly uncomfortable
in his gown and white gloves. As the debate progressed,
his face became flushed, and he looked, as some one near
me remarked, "sharp and excited." Sir Allan M'N—b,
with his shrewd Scotch face, and shining bald pate,

sustained the bitterness of both parties, as he sat at the table with some noisy brawlers, attempting to form a third party, I suppose, or *juste milieu*.   The French-men seem sadly put out by the new regulation, that all speeches in that house must be delivered in the Queen's English ; and several honourable gentlemen from the lower province laboured very hard to make themselves intelligible and ridiculous—especially old Monsieur Viger, who seemed to be eternally on his legs—convenient to the speaker's ear—taking imposing positions, like an old *maître de danse* moving a minuet, superb gesticulation assisting his meagre stock of English, an occasional escape of French saving his boiling breast from a blow-up, as, like an impatient Indian pony harnessed to a superb old cabriolet, he laboured to bring his splendid notion before the house, —Aylwin, and others of the opposition, having laboured to assist their leader.   The gentlemen of the Trea-sury benches began to dole forth their doleful replies. One bald-pated man said something in an unknown tongue, and order and silence was repeatedly bawled out ; another slender gentleman, in light yellow whis-kers, followed, and naïvely assured us his was a maiden speech (*malgré* yellow whiskers)—he went on hesitating and stammering, broke down in a quadruple parenthesis, got up again with a trope, threw himself on the compassion of the house, and sunk down in a musical and third-handed simile, in a transport of awkwardness.

"Par Dieu," said a Canadian near me, " dis English must be one langue fort dificule—de English cannot speak it demselves, and dey say de French must speak it for dem."

Anon, we had another oratorical display—the noisy

Billy Jonstone, clamouring against Sir Allan and the opposition; his rough wit and sledge-hammer eloquence smiting both friend and foe at random. Another backwoodsman followed this learned member's steps, he attempted to imitate Jonstone, lost the thread of his argument, got into a quagmire of doubt, floundered about, got back to the original stump from which he started, and kept on hallooing that "the majority should be protected from the minority," till his hearers became, like himself, confused with listening to such bullfrogish balderdash, and many, like myself, cut and run before midnight.

During the debate, I observed the honourable M.P. of the staff and key : he pretended to be very busy, whisking about the house, whispering to the members, calling out "order," and "hear—hear—hear," like an old hunter who smelt a fox. He had *posted* his constituents where they might have posted themselves—among the strangers. I thought he was both noisy and idle, though perhaps he was busily employed, *log*-rolling the while, for his constituents.

This morning at breakfast I heard sundry surmises, doubts, and fears, concerning last night's debate, and a brawl or uproar that had broken out somewhere in the rear of our hotel—our slumber had been broken at the "dead of night," by cries of "Help! rascals! murder!" &c. No one knew from whence those cries proceeded, or where the row had taken place, save the honourable Mr. Kingfisher. He had nearly finished his meal in solemn silence, was coquetting with his fourth egg and some white fish, when, clearing his voice, he gave us to understand that the brawl occurred just as he returned from the House of Assembly, fatigued, and over-laden with the cares of state.

" Then, perhaps, sir," said a young fellow, winking at another, " you had the good fortune, the felicity, to witness, and perhaps assist, at that row yourself."

" What do you mean, sir," retorted the little member, angrily.   " Is it me, you mean to say, helped to kick up a row—a row that, I believe, originated in that low *quentoon* in the lane, at ———."   A shout of laughter interrupted the little member's lame explanation, during which he got upon his legs, and shuffled out of the room, his face glowing like a red-hot fire-shovel.

This splendid day I took a long walk with a Scotchman, recently arrived from the land o' cakes ; he is in quest of a brewery.   He says the people of Kingston ought to drink good wholesome beer and ale, instead of the vile trash put off upon them for pure malt and hops.   The first brewery we entered, seemed to be a very shy concern, yet here we met with a sour rebuke.

" Sir," said the Scot, to the brewer, " I understand you want to dispose of your brewery ?"   " Sir," replied the brewer, " when I do, I'll let you know ;" and off he marched in high dudgeon.   " The devil take Carmano," said the Scot ; " it was he that put me on the wrong scent."   We visited other brewers, with the same success ; save and excepting that some of the brewers were a little more complaisant, though one of them told me, he believed I was no friend to the brewer, because I could not swallow some of his heavy-wet.   The land about Kingston is both light and bad ; and skirting the lake, it is little better than a pine barren.   The governor's house is nicely located on the lake, convenient to the penitentiary.

Fell in with a lot of Irish and Scotch emigrants ; they had just completed some bright deal board houses.

The men were employed by the government, and the women were washing their clothes and children. I asked several of them if they had bought any land; they said they had not, and betrayed most lamentable ignorance, not one of the lot knowing the name of the vast lake before them. But this did not surprise me much, as we have a wealthy Yorkshireman and his wife at our hotel, as ignorant of the country as the babes in the wood. They bore us to death with stupid and unmeaning questions. They expect to find shingle palaces in the woods, and sugar trees, and apple trees, and peaches, and all sorts of fruit trees, and Indian corn, growing wild; and wild turkeys as easily caught as tame ones, and, I verily believe, if a Yankee told them it rained " striped pig" in the back settlements, they would believe him—voyons, voyons.

Visited the dock-yard and the House of Assembly once more, where the debate seems as hot as ever; return to the hotel, and find my host and the Scott disputing about the brewery question. Signor Carmano insists he never told the Scot that Mr. —— had a brewery to sell, while the Scot accuses him of a treacherous memory, and offers to make a bet about it, and, finally, both agree to settle the matter, by *tossing* up a coin of the realm for a bottle of porter. The Scot wins it—and our host produces the London stout, grumbling at his ill-luck. He says he has been a soldier, and fought under Wellington at the Peninsular War. By birth he is a Sicilian, and by what turn of the wheel of fortune he was set down here, on the wilds of Canada, I could not learn, though he undertook to relate his history, and in such a variety of tongues and garbled and unconnected way—one moment charging the French — then reverting to the gran disgracia of his marriage with a termagant — anon clambering up Vesuvius—then bringing in Nelson by the neck and heels—dancing a fandango with an Andalusian maid—telling us about the perfidy of his friend and dear companion—his brave comrade, who basely robbed him of his hard-earned cash—ran away to Buffalo—became a great man—where "he walk about the coffé rooms"—"smoke him pipe"—"light him segar"—while I,—I, the pride of our regiment— the povoro diavolo—I am the poor devil now—work, work, work, in my dirty old shirt sleeves, not time to shave—per bacco, caracco, caramba, cospetto." And here our host indulged in a torrent of strange oaths; he had already taken the lion's share of the porter, and now regaled himself with whiskey, which melted his obdurate soul, so that, when he tramped, by accident, upon one of the dogs, he caught him up in his arms, hugged him, and calling him by all the endearing names, in the four languages, presented the filthy, old, half-blind, bloated cur to the Scot, as his lamb, his sheep, his fanciula, &c.; related the dog's history—he had belonged to a renowned captain, who boarded and lodged chez Carmano. This captain knew the value of the dog, and yet what did he, when he heard that Carmano loved him? Presented his dog to his host, in lieu of paying his bill, on leaving the hotel. Another cur was, in like manner, praised; he was lame of a leg, and had been scalded in the kitchen; but, considering that he was a present from another friend of the house, he was allowed to dwindle out his miserable days on a sofa, instead of being shot, and put out of pain. Another dog was intruded to our notice—a black pointer, whose precise value our host had not exactly determined; he was a present also from a country gentleman, who had spent a winter very agreeably chez Carmano. "I dare say he can set a leg o' mutton verra weel, when it's roasting at the fire?" said the Scot. Our host now became so noisy, that we thought it prudent to retire, especially as he insisted that we should join him in a barcarolle, in which the dogs joined chorus, while their master, bottle in hand, attempted to dance el bolero.

This morning the whole house seems to be turned topsy-turvy, what between the screaming of women and children, shouting and laughter of the men, howl-ing of dogs, and smashing of glass and crockery. Leap-ing from my bed, I threw on my clothes as hastily as if the house was on fire, and rushed down stairs. I found everything in confusion, the floor of the *salle à manger* strewn with the *debris* of cups and platters, glasses, trays, and egg, chairs and tables, &c. But the affray, or row, was over; and I heard with regret that all the disturbance was occasioned by the host himself, who had taken it into his head to be jealous of his wife. He began by ringing the dinner bell till he broke that noisy alarum, and having collected a goodly assemblage of his boarders about him to learn the cause of his ringing the bell in that furious manner, he accused some of them, and abused others, finally assaulted them all, and sent the whole posse to flight. Their flight was to him a proof of their delinquency, and being barricadoed out of Flanders by his wife, he dealt his daughter a blow with a trayful of tea-cups, and laid waste the breakfast-table ; meeting the king-fisher member with a blow of an egg upon the nose that sent him flying out of the house, and an honour-able doctor, who for quietness' sake stood upon the steps before the door reading the newspaper, received a *tunk* under the ear with a loaf of bread that sent him sprawling into the middle of the street. At length, quite exhausted, our valiant host rushed into some hole in the lower regions, where for the present he lay in *perdu,* while his wife and daughter endeavoured to restore the house to order, and excited our sympathy as they went sobbing about the house. One of the boarders assured me that the host was really dangerous when those fits of jealousy seized him ; and not very long ago, a worthy magistrate was so grossly assaulted by him, that at his wife's request he sent for the police, and had him carried to the Penitentiary, where meeting with a man whom he had imprisoned for debt, Carmano gave him a full acquittance, and had him discharged forthwith, to the great delight of the debtor, and the dismay of Madame Carmano and his family.

Having little inducement to remain longer in the house of such an obstreperous wight, I took a farewell walk round Kingston, and embarked in the steamer for Toronto.

Port Hope.—Here we landed fifty or sixty Irish emigrants, bag and baggage. How these people intend to get along, I cannot divine, there are only two of the party can speak English—the rest holding sweet converse in the ancient Irish.

Toronto exhibits an imposing front to the lake ; the good people were all crowding along the shore in Sunday gear. Consigning my baggage to a stately nigger, I followed him to a very tolerable hotel fronting the lake. The day waxed very hot and oppressive, and the house was still as a convent—indeed, at first I doubted if any one resided in it at all, and felt the change from noise and uproar to peace and solitude so powerfully, that I sallied forth, even in the sun, to seek the " human face divine." There is a listlessness about this great overgrown town, that displeases me; even the plank footways cannot give elasticity to the step. One feels weighed down with the heavy air and drooping aspect of the people who have crowded into the streets and lanes of Toronto, and for what purpose I cannot divine, for there is little or no trade to induce such a swarm of people, rich and poor, to build up streets of two story houses here, instead of scattering themselves over the vast tracts of wild lands around them. They live huddled together; and now the seat of government is removed, the good people of Toronto look blank enough. "It cannot be concealed," said a tradesman, " the *city* has been seriously injured by that blow; but we must and will have the seat of government brought back again." Others pretend it is a great benefit that the seat of government has been taken away; for, say they, the clerks and *employés* bought up all the good town lots at exorbitant prices, but now things will find their level. Level enough, truly, thought I; for the whole town is built on a dead flat—flat as a pancake. Not even Young Street, with its rich country-seats and cockney villas, could induce me to live in Toronto or its vicinity. " I've got the ague here," said a tailor to me, as he took my measure; " my wife is ill of the fever and ague even now, and I occupy one of the best houses in the best street in Toronto." Bad enough! Nevertheless, the aguish tailor resolved that I should suffer also, for he spoiled a shooting jacket and continuations to match, so effectually that I could not wear them; and then had the impertinence to tell me

he was not particular as to the fit, because he took me
for a Yankee.

Perambulating through the town, I saw several
drunken men, at all hours.ᐧ The races were over, and
there are no public amusements to enliven the dull
scene. Our *table d'hôte* has dwindled down to one
veteran half-pay officer, a lank and melancholy lady,
and our host; the hostess prefers dining upstairs by
herself, and conversing with her noisy parrot. " Well,
if I had a wife who would not come down to dinner,"
said the old half-pay, " I would lock her up, and feed
her on dry toast and gruel, through the keyhole, till
she would beg to be let out." This piece of intelligence being conveyed to the hostess, through the
lank lady, she attacked the half-pay when he lounged
into her parlour at tea. She upbraided him with his
unkind, vile, and uncharitable remarks upon her absence from the dinner-table, and bid him begone about
his business. " But in truth, I don't know where to
go," said the luckless wight. " Polly, pretty polly!
How well the parrot looks to night, Mrs. P——."
" Never mind the parrot, sir—go, I say. Go and
smoke on the stoop, if you like, or drink in the bar,
but you are no ladies' man." " Now, my dear Mrs.
P——, be reasonable. Sit on the stoops, indeed!
drink in the bar!—I hate the thought." But the poor
devil was obliged to retreat, and I saw him walking
about in front of the house with a cigar in his mouth,
looking as melancholy as a cat.

The celebrated poet of Toronto called one day while
I was out, which I regretted, having been favoured
with a sight of a new edition of his poems, through
an admirer of his genius, his stanch supporter, the

clever and amiable Mr. W—d, of Mona's sea-girt isle.

Extracts from " Select Poems, by Sir John Smith, LL.D. and P.L., Toronto.

" TO THE MOST CELEBRATED CAPTAIN MARRYAT, ETC. ETC.*

" The most celebrated Captain Marryat
    Of our day stands unrivall'd as the sun,
Whose great fame all should wish to arrive at,
    And in his most transcendent course to run.

" High on the pinnacle of honour and fame
    Captain Marryat is now a soaring,
And great and exalted is his good name,
    And most widely through the world it does ring.

" Captain Marryat's fame shines most brilliantly,
    Giving light to the whole universe wide,
And all will remember continually
    And will look up to him as their guide."

Bravo! Sir John; now for another aspiration:—

" Our most dearly beloved brother, the Rev. William Case,
    Was the first person to sow the *good seed*
Among the Indian and the native race,
    And for it they were in very great need," &c. &c.

The chivalrous Sir John does not confine his muse; he permits her to laud captains and methodist preachers to the skies, and to march to the frontier like an Amazon—*en avant :*—

* Vide Captain Marryat's " Diary in America," for the poem upon the Ladies of Toronto.

I

" A POEM ON THE NORTH-EASTERN BOUNDARY QUESTION.

" The long disputed North-Eastern Boundary Line,
    That has excited Britannia and America,
    Now appears most hostile and like war a sure sign,
    For Britons will protect the claims of Britannia.

" I would advise Brother Jonathan to be careful
    Not to awaken the strong Lion of England,
    For the Lion will act and behave most fearful,
    And the Lion will always maintain his bold stand.

" Brother Jonathan will find that it will not do
    For him with the Lion to trifle and to play,
    For the Lion will sharply bite all that near him go,
    And are so foolish and silly to go in his way.

" Let Brother Jonathan let the Lion alone,
    For the strong, powerful, and the furious Lion
    Will make Brother Jonathan for his crime atone,
    And Brother Jonathan the Lion will ride upon ! ! !"

Editor's Note.—" *It is to be understood in the last line of the above poem, that the Lion will ride upon Brother Jonathan.*"

It is to be hoped the bard of Toronto will furnish a saddle for the occasion, to save Brother Jonathan's back from being galled during the Lion's rough riding,

      " And when he next doth ride abroad
      May I be there to see."

" A POEM UPON THE SEAT OF GOVERNMENT BEING REMOVED
FROM THE CITY OF TORONTO. BY THE SAME.

" Fellow citizens of the city of Toronto,
    You must not be frighten'd and alarm'd,
    And let your property for a little go,
    For I am resolved you shall not be harm'd.

" If the seat of government is taken away,
    My projected improvements will make this town grow ;
    When they are finished it will shine like a bright ray,
    And money in this town like a river will flow.

" My projected improvements are as follows—
   I mean in this town to bring the Don and Humber ;
When these improvements are made we will have no
      more sorrows,
   For our riches will increase beyond number.

" And also a railroad to the Balsam lake—
   From this city the distance is seventy mile ;
Then to go there from this town will a short time take,
   And from there to this city will take a short while."

Adieu ! Sir John — may your shadow never be less ; and if, by your " projected improvements," you can make Toronto livelier instead of larger, your " fellow citizens" should erect a pillar to your genius, return you member to the house at the next election, where your wit, eloquence, and " projected improvements," might convince—even the Honourable President of the Board of Works, that—

   " Money in this town like a river will flow."

CHAPTER X.

" BROCK's monument tottering to its fall!" exclaimed
one of my fellow travellers, as we toiled up a hill, at the
request of our coachman; "paying for a ride, and requested to walk," as another drily observed.

" It was poor spite to destroy a monument, fix it
any how you will," said a Buffalo man.

" This is the spot where Brock fell," said an old
lady, halting beneath a scrubby bush.

" Were you in the battle, miss?" inquired another
lady.

" No, miss; but my son was, and pointed out this
exact spot."

" Was your son a Britisher, miss?" demanded a
stern-looking wight.

" No; he was American born, sir," said the old
damsel, drawing herself up and eyeing the speaker
most disdainfully.

I was glad to hear my fellow voyagers (American
citizens) one and all reprobate the wanton and mis-
chievous act, though I was not a little surprised to

hear that Lett, the incendiary, escaped unscathed, and was still at large in the States. Passing through a rich, picturesque, and fertile country, a sound " like the rushing of many waters"—the roar of the Falls —was heard ; and presently, descending from our rickety conveyance at the door of the Clifton House, the far-famed Falls of Niagara were before us. At first sight, I was disappointed; for though the *coup d'œil* from Clifton House — embracing both the Horse-shoe fall and the American, and the wooded isle that seems to quake in the midst of the war of elements—is unrivalled, the height of the Falls is materially diminished, and consequently their effect is lost by viewing them from the banks of the river, which are on a level with the head of the Schute. It was only on crossing the river at the ferry that I became impressed with the awful grandeur of the scene, and the first impression destroyed. The books in which visitors incribe their names, &c., at the table-rock, or pavilion, deserve to be ranked amongst the curiosities of literature. I am sorry to say they are sadly mutilated, and sometimes whole pages torn out, by sacrilegious visitors. Here we find all sorts of effusions, for the noise and uproar of Falls beneath seem to inspire the visitors, and even the most stolid and Dutch, wax poetical ; during my visits to the table-rock, I took the liberty to transcribe some of those bleatings into my note book.

Extract from the Visitors' Book, 1841.—*Table Rock House :*—

" Here I record the startling fact—
I've been beneath the cataract:
Bid Niagara's fairest daughter
Bring me a glass of gin and water;

' What have you seen beneath that fall,'
Let shrinking clerks and spinsters squall ;
Naiads and muses, one and all,
Apollo, and ye sacred nine,
Inspire me to write something fine.
Yon soaplock darts a hungry look,
He's dying to devour my book.
That fairy-footed child of song
Murmurs ' He keeps the book too long.'
While this dear creature, growing bolder,
Reads what I scribble, o'er my shoulder.
Gin sling—gin sling, ye gods and fishes,
A sherry cobbler, be propitious ;
A brandy cocktail, waiter—fellow—
The cataract I must outbellow.
Pegasus rears—he's in a hurry,
My Charon swears he'll cross the ferry ;
Without an Obolus I find
It will not do to stay behind ;
And having bravely battled so far,
' Fly round an Independent loafer.'

                                "SAM SLICK."

" Babbler, forbear ; in silence go thy ways,
And in oblivion end thy doleful days—
My holy awe is turn'd to shame and rage,
To find such nonsense scribbled on this page.

                                "EZRA TIBBS."

" By my troth, Arcades Ambo,
            Blackguards both,
    What think you, Massa Sambo?

                                "ADAM SMYTH."

" I've seen the falls of Terni,
    The lakes of sweet Killarney ;
    This waterfall it beats them all
    Without a bit of blarney.
            It need no further journey.

" I've seen.a burning mountain,
  And wonders past all counting ;
  Have taken *tay* over the way,
  Beside a burning fountain.

" The only thing I wish is,
  I may escape the fishes,
  And safely spy old Ireland's eye,
  For I am not ambitious ;
      I need no further journey.

" My love, my life, my cara,
  Shall hear of Niagara ;
  When, without fuss, she gives a buss,
  To her own T. O'Mara.
      I need no further journey."

———

" Where is the red man, where the tameless child—
  Soul of the desert, monarch of the scene ?
  He stood unblench'd and heedless in the midst
  Of warring elements, the direful jar
  Of riven rocks and mountains rent in twain ;
  While crashing forests of the sturdy oak,
  The giant pine, and dwarfish tamarack
  Glanced wildly by, like leaflets in the blast,
  When Erie, rising in his pearly shroud,
  Leap'd like a billow from the vasty deep,
  Pursued by Huron, chased by Michigan,
  Impell'd to burst his bonds by Superior ———,
  What barrier could stay that band of brothers ?
  The mighty ravine opens, and a peal
  Of stunning thunder bids the earth recoil,
  Ere the unbridled waters madly sweep,
  And crested Erie took his fearful leap
  Down Niagara to Ontario.
                            "EUMIKA THRUMS."

———

" Where is the red man ? where is the white man ?
  Where is the black man ? all right—good night, man.
                            "PETER PARLE."

" C'est trop—c'est trop, mon ami,
    Trop difficile d'écrire.
Je ne puis pas vous exprimiez,
    Tous ce que ce lieu m'inspire—
        Jamais—Jamais—Jamais !

" Niagara est unique,
    La chûte, la plus grand, la plus belle,
Superb—sublime—magnifique !
    Enfin, c'est—pretty well.
                        " DE JOINVILLE."

" When God speaks, let man hold his tongue.
                        " ICHABOD CRANE."

" The above was loan'd, stolen, or stray'd, from John Bunnion
or Doctor Watts.
                " SY. BAGGS, M. O. U., Missouri."

" Sy Baggs,
    Father of Wags,
    Who the devil are you ?
    Take Bunnion and Watts,
    And tinker your pots,
    In M. O. U.
                " J. BARLOW, Boston."

" What a glorious water power is here; fully sufficient to drive
all the mill wheels in the Union, I calculate.
                " J. HOBBS, Ramsbottom."

" My ! what an almighty plan for washing sheep.
                " L. HOOSIER, Miss."

Here follows a long rigmarole in Dutch, savouring
of Scheidam and the Zuyder Zee; and another effu-

sion in the Eurika Thrums style, which I skip over, and conclude my elegant extracts with—

> " Here in the balcony,
>   Basking ' like any fly,'
> I slantindicular sit in my chair,
>   Whiffing a light cigar
>   Over this water war,
> All at my ease, with my heels in the air.
>
>   " Fly round, my tulips,
>   Bring me mint julips,
> Iced to a miracle—fix'd with a straw—
>   Wooing the eager lip
>   Deeper to suck and sip,
> Rich as a bottom in sweet Arkansaw.
>
>   " Writing and rhyming,
>   And all this tall climbing,
> Tickles my fancy, though all in my eye—
>   Boy with a corn cob,
>   Lightly my shoulders rub,
> Ecstasy—ecstasy—now let me die !
>
> " N. P. WILLIS."

" Take off every stitch of your clothes, lock them up in this drawer, put on this here red shirt, duck pants, straw hat, and slippers," said the host of the pavilion, to whom I signified my intention to visit that delectable grotto under the horse-shoe fall.

I obeyed, with certain reservations, as I did not at all admire the damp flimsy habiliments tendered for my outward man ; and followed the guide down steep flights of slippery stairs and steps to the water's edge. Here, pausing a moment to view the terrible yet magnificent scene, we pushed on to the table rock, drenched with spray and mist, *en avant.* The guide laid hold on a penny cord, nailed into the trembling rocks ; he disappeared under the broad sheet. Holding my light hat with one hand, and the cord with the other, I plunged after him, and in a moment was thoroughly wet to the skin; violent gusts of wind dashed the water in my eyes, while I groped my way under the cataract.

"We can go no further," hallooed the guide. So here, in this misty shower bath, we set our backs to the streaming wall, and contemplated the roaring waters round us. Receiving a smart slap on my shoulder, I turned, and beheld an eel cut in twain slide down to my feet; picked him up, together with some slippery stones, and hurried after my guide, who had already retreated from under the broad sheet. As long as the overhanging rocks hold their place there is no danger, but beshrew me if I trust my neck under that superb shower-bath again. *Le jeu ne vaut pas le chandelle*, and one dollar is quite enough to pay for being thoroughly drenched, with permission to get your head broken; and your body made food for fishes by a single false step, or a slippery stone.

Returning to the stairs, we were greeted with the cheers and laughter of a merry group of "fair women and brown men," from the American side. One or two of the party were disguised in oil-skin dresses, but my guide assured me that a number of visitors content themselves with a good splashing, without the broad sheet, few having nerve enough to venture under it. This being intended as a compliment, I swallowed it "*cum grano salis*," shook off the reeking garments, and received my certificate; upon which the following lines are inscribed:—

WRITTEN DIRECTLY AFTER GOING "WITHIN THE VEIL" OF NIAGARA; BY GRENVILLE MELLEN.

"O God! my prayer is to thee, amid sounds
That rock the world!—I've seen thy Majesty

> Within the veil!—I've heard the anthem-shout
> Of a great ocean as it leapt in mist
> About my thunder-shaken path.   Thy voice—
> As centuries have heard it in the rush
> And roar of waters!   I have bent my brow
> Within thy rainbow—and have lifted up
> My spirit 'mid these vast cadenas !   I've seen
> What is the wonder of Eternity—
> And what this vision'd nothingness of man."

The only benefit I experienced from that severe drenching under the falls, was the complete cure of rheumatic pains in my shoulders, contracted by sleeping on a damp stone floor, in Spain, and lost, I sincerely hope, for ever, under the falls of Niagara.

The plan of erecting a new city on the Canada side has been abandoned.   Even the sole and only hotel here seems quite deserted.   The young American lady and her husband have taken their departure, the piano sleeps ; and the airy Salon no longer echoes back the sweet songs of that heavenly little woman in black, who, without all that circumbendential humbug and mendicant entreaty, sat down to the instrument, and enchanted us all.   Looked into Barnett's museum ; it contains upwards of five thousand interesting specimens, a great portion of which were collected in the immediate vicinity—that is to say, below the falls. Wolves, catumonts, cats, and badgers—yea, fish and fowl, being slain in their last leap, it being gone-goose with them the moment they get into the rapids ; three or four living rattle-snakes are likewise here made rattle their tails, for the company.   Descend to the ferry, where the Yankees stare very hard at the red coats and bright muskets of a sergeant's guard ; posted there expressly, I hear, to cut off deserters, and intercept contraband goods.   Found the soldiers inspecting one of the largest fresh-water fishes I ever saw; his back was broken, but life was not extinct. Toil up the wooden stairs on the American side, and get installed in a good room, six feet by ten, at the Cataract House—walk over the wooden bridges to Goat Island, the freedom of which I obtain by paying twenty-five cents.   Here I fell in with a severe-looking missionary, who had just returned from China. He had a very singular-looking lad with him, an oblique-eyed Chinese, who spoke English tolerably well, and took off his shoes as he approached the horse-shoe fall, either to secure his footing, or from some superstitious feeling.   Entered into conversation with some amiable young ladies seated on a bench, waiting for their father and friends, who had descended some ladder to enjoy the waterfall on the American side; presently a very gentlemanly old fellow tumbled up the stairs, and declared that Mrs. W—— had fainted below, and that her husband and others were carrying her slowly up again.   "This is the second time she has fainted to-day," said he; "but her spirit is indomitable.   She fainted at the bottom of the whirlpool steps; she was taken ill upon the Canada side, and now she would insist on going down that steep and dangerous place.   But her spirit is indomitable, my dear!"   I was happy to see this high-spirited woman soon after supported to a seat, where she revived; and, having regained her strength, her indomitable spirit began to soar, and she signified her intention to ascend to the top of the tower beside the falls.

The stick and cane-sellers drive a pretty considerable trade here: every visitor feeling himself called on to present himself and his friends with Goat Island hickory twigs, of all sorts and shapes, varying from the grotesque and gnarled, to the smooth and varnished.

Return to Cataract House, and get seated, with some difficulty, at the crowded tables—every railway car setting down fresh visitors at our door, till the house is so crowded, that I rejoice even in my closet. Marry, the window or green jealousy opens upon the balcony, which the ladies seem to appropriate to their own use, and thus I am constrained to hear more than is agreeable. "Did you see that Canadian on the stoop, with his grey clothes?" (meaning me,) "my! how shabby!—mean economy, Miss; keeps his good coat for Sundays, I guess—the Canadians are all close-fisted, Miss." Not wishing to hear any more, I strode out into the balcony, even in my grey suit of Tweeds, while the young ladies tittered audibly, and the words—*exclusion* and *intrusion*, went in at one ear, and out at the other. Fatigued with walking all day, I felt little inclined to sit, inhaling other men's tobacco smoke, in the bar, and, fetching a chair, sat down in the balcony—a piece of audacity the young ladies did not expect a man in grey could be guilty of, and they walked up and down, holding their heads very high, as if they doubted the purity of my intentions.

Visit the whirlpool with Mons. S——n, the *maitre de ballet* and Zephyr of Mdlle. Fanny Ellsler, and a rich Southerner and his little swarthy son; *en route,* this magnate began to boast of his wealth. He found it no easy matter to spend his money in this cheap country, he said; then directed our attention to his coat, his vest, his pants, his boots, all made by his own nigger—a slave, of course—so that the making of clothes cost him merely the keep of his nigger; anon, he expatiated upon the beauty of his plantation in

South Alabama, and cross-examined poor little S——n about Mdlle. Fanny, and the rest of the loves and graces behind the curtain. To examine the whirlpool, we descended several hundred rude steps, and down slippery places to the water's edge. Contrary to my expectation, the water in the midst of the pool seemed elevated higher than our heads, instead of looking down into a boiling vortex; we saw enormous logs and beams of timber mingled with other *debris* whirling round and crashing together with astounding rapidity.

"Three deserters from the British," said our guide, (who, by-the-bye, I suspected to be a deserter himself;) "three deserters tried to swim over the river last night; one got safe over, and the others were swept down to the whirlpool. Do you see anything white floating in it?" said he, mounting a rock and peering into the wild waters. "I once saw the bodies of seven deserters in it," continued he; "and the people used to come from a distance to look at them, bobbing round and round like babbies, till at last the timber smashed them to pieces." He then told us how one of the ferrymen was carried into the whirlpool; his boat was dashed to pieces, and the man got on a log, and went whirling round and round, while hundreds of people looked on, unable to assist him; when—miraculous to relate!—the log upon which the ferryman rode was driven into the bank at the Canada side, and the man was saved.

Visited Schlosser, the place where the "Caroline" was cut out and sent adrift over the Falls. The wooden and rickety building beside the wharf looked like a barn; it is a lonely, bleak-looking spot, and the solitary public house in the rear does not look very inviting. While sketching the barn, &c., a 'little steamer arrived from the Canada side, took the mails on board, and as the rain began to fall in torrents, I embarked also. Taking a wide sweep with the stream, we beat up against the current to the celebrated Navy Island. It is heavily timbered, and large enough to hide an army of desperadoes still ; indeed, I marvel the Canadians did not cut down the trees upon the island when it was evacuated by the sympathizers.—Land at Chippewa, and march down the banks to the Falls, cross the ferry below them once more, bid adieu to the cataract house, and whirl away to Buffalo in the railway cars. Hang up my hat in the American, the best hotel I have met with this side the Atlantic. Looking for the last Nickerbocker, I was directed to the agent by the bookseller—entered a cabinet-maker's, and inquired for the agent.

" He is up stairs, I guess," replied one of the workmen ; and I mounted the ladder, passed through a loft full of carpenters and shavings, mounted another loft, and found Mr. Childs, the agent, a strapping young fellow, with his shirt sleeves rolled up, planeing away at the leg of a chair. He said he had not the Nickerbockers by him, and asked me if I was a subscriber. I said I was not. " Then," said he, " I am sorry to say I cannot let you have a number ; but if you wish to read the work, or any particular article, call at my house up town, or, if you prefer it, call in at the Young Men's Association Reading Rooms."

Mr. Childs resumed his work, and I went my way to the aforesaid reading rooms, where I found periodicals and newspapers, both new and old, of home and foreign manufacture. Buffalo, being the " mustering mead" of emigrants from the Old World and New

England states westward bound, exhibits a rare medley of enterprising, determined, plodding, desperate, and anxious countenances. When the old country emigrants get thus far, they are generally pretty well awakened from their pastoral and sylvan dreams; it is too late for them to retrace their steps, and the sturdy Englishman grunts, " In for a penny, in for a pound ;" the Irishman throws up his hat, and roars, " The devil may care ;" the canny Scot thinks he may " as weel go a bittock further;" the Frenchman shrugs up his shoulders with " *a pis aller ;*" while the spry New Englander drawls " come along" and "go a-head," as he pushes his way through gaping crowds of Dutch, Germans, and Swiss, sets down his pack full of Yankee notions on the deck of a western leviathan, and squats himself down, as cool as a cucumber, beside a high-pressure boiler.

Embarked on board the Bunker-hill steamer—a vile, nasty boat as ever I set my foot on ; and off we go, spluttering and splashing through the sunny waters of the Erie, while the harsh coughing and booming of the steam reminds us that, though eating boiled and roast one minute, we may be boiled, roast, barbecued, and served up to the clouds, upon cast metal platters, the next minute.

Cleveland : here we are safely moored to the wharf, with carpenter and smith sledging away at the broken paddle-wheel ; the captain is laid up a-bed with the ague, attended by his wife and daughter, while the passengers are loafing about the streets and lanes of this fine town. Sauntered through the west end of Cleveland, sat down under a nut-wood tree in front of a very fine house; the cool shrubbery around it, high French windows, Venetian blinds, pilasters and architraves of cool stone colour, were pleasant to look upon; and presently a blind flew up, and revealed (a beautiful young girl in her teens?—not at all,) a swarthy old gentleman, seated in his library, reading a handsomely-bound book; a red damask curtain half concealed a pillar over against him, and in the background gleamed the gilt backs of many books, and a bust peeped in the corner. The yellow-faced gentleman in black sat as steadily as if he wanted some passing artist to take his portrait, or win the heart of some fair passenger, to whom the devil himself would be irresistible in such a garniture and goodly frame. The shrill ringing of the steamboat bell caused me to start from my reverie, and leaving the literary gentleman alone in his glory, I rushed on board the Bunker-hill. Enter into conversation with two Baptist preachers; they say Michigan is very unhealthy—that every new comer into that country must count upon getting fever and ague—a pleasant prospect, no doubt. One of them said he lived near Mrs. Clavers, the author of Montacute; he said her book might be relied on. Went ashore again with the Baptists; we marched up to the lighthouse, followed by the first beggar I have seen for some time—a ragged youth, the picture of indolence and indigence; he begged for money to go to Michigan, where he said his mother dwelt, and was a very respectable woman.

" Name—her name, sir?" said one of the Baptists, sharply.

The youth told the name, and the Baptists gave him good advice but no money. " Now, hark'ee, sir—begging's a bad trade. I know your mother, and her friends are respectable. How came you down here?"

The youth said he had been bound apprentice to a shoemaker in Detroit—said shoemaker took him to Buffalo, where he beat and starved him, and so he ran away.

" Now, hark'ee, sir; how came you to run away from your master? Go right on board the Bunker-hill, sir, and work a passage to Detroit—yes, sir, work till the sweat runs down your nose, sir; better far do that than go begging a-head to Michigan. If you do, you'll meet many hard-faced chaps between this and that, sir." Thus advised the baptists, and the boy went away.

" It's a hard case—a hard case, sir," said they, as we returned back again to our steamer, but could not find our beggar carrying wood aboard the boat.

The boiler deck is occupied by Dutch emigrants from the old country; they carry their beds and bedding along—pots, pans, and kettles—genuine campers out. The women, round and strong, dressed in good homespun linsey-woolsey, as happy as the day is long. Not so the English emigrants forward; they have neither beds nor bedding, nor cooking apparatus, nor utensils—to be sure they seem to have some heavy chests and trunks, but their baggage is all roped and nailed down as if they were never to be opened again, while the women, in light printed calico dresses and tight stays, looked washy and discontented. One young couple, from Lincolnshire, said they did not fear the ague as they had both of them had the " hager" at home in the fens; another poor woman, from Somersetshire, had actually brought out her seven children, the eldest of them a girl of fourteen or fifteen, the rest young and feeble. She said she was going to join her husband, who was a stonemason in good business at Madison, in Wisconsin.

I asked her if she knew whereabouts Madison was; she answered, "Close to Lake Michigan, and near Chicago." Having purchased a map of Wisconsin, I soon undeceived her, and pointed out the nearest road to Madison, which is at least seventy miles inland from Lake Michigan; I was glad to find this poor woman profited by the hint, as I afterwards met her with her family at Madison.

Detroit: here I took leave of the Baptists; they pressed me very much to go home with them, saying they would give me plenty of the best their land afforded; butter and honey, corn, bread, and pork—everything but money. Notwithstanding all this, I was not to be tempted, and the good men went their ways to the railroad, while I sauntered down to the steam-boat wharf, to witness the departure of the splendid steamer Illinois, and the Bunker-hill as she went booming up the St. Clair with the rest of the passengers. The Illinois is decidedly the finest steamer on the lakes, and the rough old master, Captain Blake, is a general favourite. Seated upon a pile of pine-logs, I enjoyed the fresh evening air, after the close, hot breath of the steamer. Carriages and waggons were hurrying down to the wharf, porters, passengers, emigrants, and sailors, bustling to and fro; and a troop of the U. N. S. artillery and waggon train boarding the Illinois, added not a little to the confusion—the horses rearing and plunging on the forward deck, arms gleaming in the gorgeous sunset, flags and banners streaming gaily aloft from every taut line fore and aft the Illinois, even the figure head of a fine Indian warrior seemed to "grin horribly a ghastly smile," while ever and anon the pent-up steam burst out with a wild roar, and the cables strained and groaned as the pad-

dles beat up the water, like an impatient war-horse
pawing up the spray.   Tiny steamers cut up and down
the Detroit, and a solitary Indian or two might be
discerned strutting about in their blankets on the
Canadian side, while the merry rub-dub-dub-dub of
an English drum, and the shrill squeaking of a "wry-
necked fife," was distinctly heard as a company of red-
coats marched along the frontier road—now lost, now
seen, amidst clumps of trees, and the white-walled
houses of *les habitants.*   My attention was presently
engaged by a singular group at the end of the long
pine logs upon which I was seated.   A huge old German boar-hound had laid himself down, in sphinx-like
fashion, watching a stout dun-coloured Indian pony,
which stood ready saddled and bridled, between the
Argus-eyed old boar-hound and a splendid black Newfoundland or Labrador dog.   A prying and spry race
of little boys, aspiring to mount a horse under such
favourable circumstances, hung aloof when they saw
the boar hound's white tusks; and the hair rose on his
back if an idle cur presumed to approach his charge.
Not so the Newfoundland, he was evidently an arrant
loafer, changing his position every minute; now rising
up, now throwing himself down, anon basking at full
length, wistfully eyeing the passenger dogs and men—
willing, if he dared, to enter upon a game of romps,
even with the pony, for want of a better play-
fellow.   At last a bear was pulled along by one of the
artillerymen, and the Newfoundland could no longer
restrain his curiosity: he rose up, and followed the
rough gentleman almost on board the boat, where
having received a good thwack from a sailor, he returned back to his first position, followed by a brisk
little terrier, as shaggy as a door mat, wide awake, and

full as restless as a bag of fleas. This cur hung about our logs most perseveringly—his object, to induce the Newfoundland to desert his post again, and have a game at rough and tumble with him. He played all sorts of tricks, scampered backwards and forwards, kicking up the dust, pursued his stump of a tail round and round, like a kitten, scraped up the earth beside a stone, as if he had found a rat hole, and being exhausted, lay sprawling before us, chewing a dry chip with great gusto. Hitherto his pranks had almost escaped the Newfoundland's notice, but now he got up with a deep pant; erecting his magnificent tail, he looked merrily and wistfully at the terrier. The terrier stood up, with his chip sticking whimsically on one side of his mouth, while his merry little eye seemed to say, " Come, take it if you dare." " Have at you, master," seemed to escape from the " gentleman and scholar," as he gave chase, and pursued the terrier; and they doubled, they ran, they rolled, tossed and tumbled together, splashed into the water, wiped their coats in a heap of ashes, and resumed their gambols on the green. The steamer with her flags, her band, pink parasols and white jackets aft; blue, green, and grey jackets, and snorting horses forward; the bear perched on one paddle-box, Blake on the other, took a wide sweep towards the Canada side, and dashed bravely down the river. The crowd about the wharf began to disperse, and the plaintive whinings of a dog smote my ear. I looked, and behold a thick-set, remorseless, red-haired German, in top-boots and jockey coat, stood over the Newfoundland. There he lay, all covered with mire and dust, panting, on his back, with his paws up as if supplicating for mercy.

" Ha, ha! you tink I not see you, my friend," exclaimed the angry German, as with a short whip he chastised the dog. " I gib you my boney to mind while I go in steam-ship, I durn my pack; why you no stay mit Caspar—Caspar my own coot hund? Coot Caspar, vatch min pferd. Ha, ha! you von idle rascal; take·dis and dis."

Here I interposed in behalf of the Newfoundland, explained how sorely he had been tempted by the terrier, turned the gentleman's attention to the said scamp of a terrier, sprawling in the dust at a very respectable distance from us, till the German sought for a stone, and chased him away with many strange oaths.

" Ya, ya! I know dat derrier well," cried he ; " he von mischief. I sold him long ago. Donner und blitzen, he von great rascal! Taught him many tricks —taught him to mind my wagon. Left him to mind my new buggy in dis ver spot von day. Now, sare, vot tink you he did? Chews de new silk lining of my buggy; takes out von new silk cushion in his mout, bites a great hole in it. Potsdend! I come back, I find him eating my cushion; chase him; he run away mit my seat in his mout; then lies down again, chews it before my two eyes: I run at him—I coax him to come back; he run round and round, tearing my seat to bits, I running after like von fool or mat-man. De people laugh and shout; I belt him mit stones; he run home. I sell him to any one— sell him to de butcher, but still he always loafs about my dogs."

Rejoiced to find the German's wrath turned against the terrier, I questioned him about his boar-hound. He had brought him from Wirtemburg, and said he was the prince of good dogs, that he could not live

without him, &c.   As to the Newfoundland, he said
he was young and silly, but he hoped he would one
day be above playing with curs.   This singular individual mounted his pony, and wishing me a good
night, cantered away, the boar-hound jumping before,
and the Newfoundland slinking behind, and throwing
furtive glances toward the retreating terrier, as he
rolled away, like a ball of dirty worsted, to his own
kennel.

CHAPTER XI.

" DEAR me, what a vast difference there is between
the cursed Yankee steamers and our own tight little
craft," said a round, rosy-cheeked little man, as he
rolled about the empty seats and benches in the cabin
of the steam-boat, Brothers.   " Room enough here,
sir," continued he, " to stretch one's legs."

I assented, same time attributing the " boasted
space unoccupied" to the absence of passengers—three
queer looking people being the first cabin passengers,
and half-a-dozen raw Scotchmen, and their beds and
bedding, all the deck passengers bound from Detroit
to Chatham on the Thames.

The rain soon drove the Scotchmen down, and
down they came, sweethearts and warm beds and bedding, into the cellar-like cabin, as damp, cold, and
cheerless a hole as ever I was pent up in.   Nathless,
being accommodated with a copy of the *Weekly Chatham Journal,* I copied verbatim the following paragraph from its veritable pages:—

" ' Hurrah ! there she goes ! how quick !' were the

cries that met our ears the other morning, as that beautiful boat Brothers started from the wharf. ' Well I declare !' said a stander by, ' there she is actually turning the point already.' And sure enough, when we turned again to look, all we could see was the tops of her tapering spars, and the dense volume of smoke that curled in her rear, mixed with the glittering spray, like the dust which the mettled steed, in his rapid course, flings in clouds behind him. We feel proud that our little town is able to send such a boat on the broad waters of our lakes. * * * Who has been on board the Brothers, and has seen the taste and elegance displayed in her fittings up, and viewed her cabin table groaning under the weight of savoury dishes and delicacies of every kind; but, above all, who that has feasted on the good things of that table, that will not join with us in the meed of praise to the jolly fellow who commands her?—one of the best little captains ' wot walks the plank.' There are very few boats on the western waters can compete with the Brothers in speed. She literally

' Walks the waters like a thing of life,' " &c.

Having read the paper through, I rubbed my eyes, and began to look about for the " taste and elegance displayed in her fittings up," which certainly had escaped my notice ; but in one thing I could not be deceived—namely, her speed and motion. Never in my life have I suffered more severely from the jolting, tossing, rolling, and heaving, save in a springless waggon on a corduroy road. Every nail in the boat seemed to quake in the straining timbers, during the six hours thus wretchedly spent crossing the Lake St. Clair; certes, we had some squally weather, but the wind was

K

all in our favour.   The engine at last ceased to groan,
and hastening on deck, I went forward to the bow of
the boat, and found one of the hands taking soundings
with a long stick.

" What water have you there ?" cried the captain.

" Four feet !" bawled the boy.

" Go ahead !" said the captain ; and we paddled
boldly on.

" Stop her—stop her !" was the next order, as sundry jerks, rubs, and scrapes informed us that we were
not very far from the bottom.

" What do you find there, sir ?" bawled the captain.

" Land, sir," responded the man with the long rod.

" Is it the bar ?" hallooed the captain.

" May be it is," responded the other.

" Hard or soft ?" was the next query.

" Soft sand or mud," was the rejoinder.

" Go on—go ahead !" was the command ; and presently we pushed and paddled through mud-banks
and sand-banks, into the renowned River Thames.

The danger, if any, fairly over, a dirty, curly-headed
negro boy, assisted by a greasy yellow man, began to
spread out the table-cloth, and arrange the festive
board.   There was a vast deal of clatter, and " much
ado about nothing"—the boy undoing what the man
did, the man finding fault with the boy's arrangement ;
both sleepy, cross, and lazy.   At last, the boy began
chopping up some greasy butter with a knife, putting
square bits upon sundry plates, turning the butter
round with his finger and thumb adroitly, then sucking his fingers with his blubber lips.   That done, he
scratched his head, and began to cut up a loaf of
bread expeditiously, while the yellow man set a savoury dish of fried pork and onions upon the board,

and began to pour out some very black tea, which he had brewed aside in a vast metal teapot. "Who that has feasted upon the good things of that table," thought I, and not been most vulgarly sick forthwith!

"You don't sup, sir?" said the captain, somewhat crossly, as I paced the deck.

I said something about want of appetite, and he went below, murmuring something about good sauce, and bad sailors. At last we arrived at our destination, as the clock chimed twelve—not the town clock indeed, but a house-clock, even that feeble bell being distinctly heard through the general stillness of the place; in fact, the good folk of Chatham had all gone to bed, and a thick mist hung over the river and town. We were behind time, to be sure, some three or four hours, having left Detroit at four in the afternoon, and arrived at Chatham at twelve; but the boat-owners and hotel-keepers might have afforded the passengers at least a guide, or porter, if, indeed, they expected the Brothers at all. "The jolly fellow" (or acid clerk) who commanded, refused to let any of his men pilot us to the hotel, and we walked up the slippery clay bank and dubious track into the main street. The whole town seemed wrapt in slumber—not a voice was heard; but a solitary dog barked and whined at a creeking branch somewhere in the woods. The Scotchmen and the rest of the passengers now began to thump at the rickety door of the hotel, and presently we were admitted by the burly Boniface in person.

"How many are ye?" said he, beginning to count on his fingers. "Well, I suppose I can accommodate ye, two and three in a bed."

K 2

" I want a single bed—a bed to myself, at all events;" said I.

The host seemed struck of a heap by this singular request, and he repeated, holding up his hog's-lard candle—" A bed all to yourself—a bed to yourself? You can't have a bed to yourself, sir. I cannot accommodate you."

Forth I sallied, and took the opposite side of the street, beginning with the first of a rickety row of wooden houses, of all sorts and sizes. Thump, thump, thump! went my good hickory against the door, till a voice sung out—" What do you want?"

" Lodgings, an't please you, for a single man."

" We don't take in no lodgers," was the response.

" Hope not; good night."

Then to the next house I addressed myself, and a shrill voice sung out—" Who are you?"

I responded to the sleepy beauty, and was told to " go to de debble—I vartuous young lady."

The devil you are, thought I, as I moved on, singing " Lubbly Dinah;" and was presently informed by a drowsy Hibernian, that if I " followed my nose" for a dozen perches further on I would find the new hotel, a decent house, " in which I would be hospitably treated at my own expense." A pole and swinging sign brought me up all standing in front of the new hotel, a vast, rambling, rickety, wooden concern, which soon resounded with kicks and blows, till a light gleamed from a window, and the front door being opened, a sturdy wight, with an axe in one hand and a candle in the other, demanded—

" What be in de vind now—que voulez vous faire, avec votre bruit d'enfer?"

" Restrain your choler, and put on your inexpressibles, cher Monsieur," said I; and I explained
my wants, while the host seemed to doubt his senses,
that a guest should ever find his way into his hotel, at
such a time of night too. It was a godsend worth
returning thanks about.

" Hello! Marie —Jean — Antoinette!—get up!"
bawled the host; " here is a gentleman wants a bed-
room all to himself! Tout, tout, tout—vite, vite, vite—
depechez vous, mes enfans." Then, leading the way into
his bar-room, this good fellow asked me to drink something, drank my health, and wished me prosperity; he
did more, even at that late hour, he pulled on his shoes,
and trudged down to the steamer for my baggage,
carried it up, on the top of his shoulder, shewed me
into a large, airy bed-room, and bid me good night.

This dreary, wet morning, sallied forth to look at
the town. A congregation of miserable houses of
all colours in the rainbow—blue, white, pink, and
grey, and not a few domiciles of bright boards inter-
spersed with rough loggeries, while stumps stood
boldly out of the earth on all sides, and the old abo-
riginal wood frowned dismally at the back of the yards
and enclosed gardens. Indeed, it is a matter of
great surprise to find so many houses, and streets, and
projected buildings, and improvements taken in hand
by the people of Chatham, before they had actually
cleared land enough about their town to support the
tithe of them. The streets are laid out with little
judgment—exceedingly narrow and crooked. The
barrack, built on the isthmus, or island, on the Thames,
enlivens the prospect. This is the " West End" of
Chatham, I suppose; and here, for the first time, I
saw the black regiment on drill. They are all run-

away slaves (barring the officers); they look fierce and
pompous enough; I dare say they would fight like
devils with the Yankees, rather than submit to go
back to the plantation again; same time, I think the
Canadas safe enough without a guard of darkees, and
was happy to hear they would soon be disbanded.
Find the country about Chatham remarkably flat; the
air oppressive; water bad; people poor, indolent, and
wretched-looking.   Such were my first impressions as
I returned to mine inn, and sat down with my host
in the bar.   He told me his simple history in a few
words.   He had been a lumberer on the Thames, till
one fine morning he saw the gentlemen and surveyors
marking out streets in this goodly town; when he saw
this, he said he could hardly believe they were in
earnest, but when lots were advertised for sale in
Chatham, the old habitants up and down the river
laughed aloud.   However, he had saved a little
money—some forty or fifty dollars—laid it out in lots
here; sold his lots some time ago, and was able to
buy this hotel; but he said the confinement did not
agree with him at all.   " Here I sit in the bar all
day, and few people call; and when they do, I
must drink with them—that's the rule.   I have a fine
large house now, but I am not half so happy as when
I had only a bit of a shanty and my axe in the woods,
with liberty to go where I liked."

Thus far did my host unbosom himself to me, expecting a like return.   Whereupon, I told him I had
some thoughts of buying land, and turning farmer in
the woods.   This piece of intelligence my host soon
conveyed to a constant customer at the bar—a boosey
painter and glazier, jack-of-all-trades, proprietor of
one of the grotesque fabrications down town, which,

like the owner, was almost empty. This genius, from " Paisley direct," reminded me of Balie Waft; nathless, he had not prospered as well as Waft had. Whisky was his bane—his rock a-head through life. His wife and children were almost naked, and without food, while he went gossiping about the public-houses, tippling here and there.

" You want a farm, you do," said this uneasy individual, hitching up his waistband, and endeavouring to look wise, severe, and consequential. " You want a farm, sir ! I am happy to hear it, because money is in greater request in this country than land, and what, sir, I say, signifies money without land—pshaw, it's here to-day, there to-morrow, gone the day after, God knows where ! But the land—the land, sir—the ancient soil of our forefathers—that is, I mean the—the terra firma of Great Britting,—that cannot fly away through the sarculating medium—that cannot slip through our fingers." And having concluded his oration, the painter tossed off the residue of a glass of whisky. Pleased with the deference I paid to his elocution, painter Waft told the host he would soon learn all about and the whereabouts of every farm for sale in the district, and off he went. At dinner, my hostess, a very pretty Canadian, apologized for the absence of other guests ; the poor woman had prepared dinner for a dozen, and actually had two servants to assist her to do the work of the house, and wait upon the boarders—myself and a sick man, who had crawled down to dinner, a most revolting object, his hair almost all gone, revealing his unfortunate, diseased pate ; he had fever and ague strong upon him, and even in this wretched state presumed to devour beef-steaks and potatoes. He said he had been attacked with the ague the fourth day after his arrival in Chatham, but I shrewdly suspect he brought the seeds of the disease with him. The hostess did not shew much tact in the *menage* of her establishment, and I question if the receipts would cover a tithe of the expenditure. Still she had her salon neatly furnished, and her pretty little daughters very neatly dressed, *a la Française*.

The painter Waft soon returned; he had in a short interval heard of more farms for sale than I could visit in a week. So many sweet spots, and delightful plans was his noddle filled with, that the host was obliged to send him about his business, to cobble up a broken window, for peace' sake.

The land-agent being from home, and the office shut up, I was glad to hire a gig, the only two-wheeled vehicle of the sort I had seen this side of the Atlantic. Seated in this old, rum concern, I rode some six miles down the river, to see the farm of a certain Tom Crow, and was directed to his house by a wayfaring man. It was an old Canadian fabric, close to the river. Tying my horse in the huge shed, I entered a small porch, and was met by the proprietor, a spry, smart-looking, fellow, very like a Yankee. He apologized for not asking me to walk in; the fact was, he had just opened a public-house, and his house was full of drunken people. "But I'll go and dress myself," said he, "and shew you my lands." I told him it would be a work of supererogation——he was dressed enough for my company; and without further palaver, we threw our legs over the high rails by the road-side, and strode into his farm. The value of the farm was said to be in its open and timberless state; it was part of the plains, or low, marshy land, which being drained and reclaimed by the old French settlers, offered no small inducement to new settlers in the wilderness. Mr. Crow's crops looked bad and backward enough; the cattle had trampled down his Indian corn and peas; and on closer examination, I found the soil worn out and exhausted, though close to his house I observed a mountain of manure, covered with rank weeds, which would have enriched the farm we were looking at. "But I have no time for that kind of work," said the proprietor. Further on we came to the original prairie, or marsh, covered with thick, sedgy grass, which Mr. Crow assured me made excellent hay; the soil, black loam. The proprietor frequently boasted that there were "no trees to trouble a man's head with, nor stumps to break his shins." "You have a few yonder," said I, pointing to some fine old oak and elms, standing in a field near the house. "They're girdled though; I girdled them," said he, with a sour grin of delight. I was sorry to find his words were true; he had spoiled the beauty of the farm, in his inveterate and ill-judged enmity to trees. He further said, he had a wood lot in the government woods, from which he cut fire-wood, and occasionally wood for the steamers, for which he received four dollars a cord. His hay, when saved in the barn, cost him two dollars a ton. He gets for his wheat, good and bad, bearded or not, five York shillings a bushel at the Chatham mills; sells his oats, also, for two York shillings a bushel. Calculates that he clears more than two dollars per acre by this farm, and modestly offers to sell it for twenty dollars an acre; says his nephew has another farm for sale, right opposite, on the other side of the river, and volunteers to shew it. "We are all Crows about

K 3

here," said Mr. Crow, as he introduced me to another
relative of that ilk, who ferried me over the river in
his log canoe. This farm was heavily timbered, a
strip of the river bank being badly cleared; and yet I
thought it more desirable than the other; *certes* both
together would make a nice farm for any man. The
wooded farm was much cheaper, being offered, with
its frontage to the Thames, and a block of two hundred
acres of hard wood, for four hundred dollars. Re-
crossed the river in the canoe, and wishing Mr. Crow
a very good evening, returned to Chatham.

Painter Waft and my host were surprised to hear
of Mr. Crow's exorbitant demand. " Let him keep
his farm," said Waft; " we have lands enough and to
spare. I mind the time (and it's not very long ago)
when I could have got as much of the plains and
woods as I could shake my stick at, for a gallon of
whisky."

" Why did you not avail yourself of the opportunity ?" said I.

" Because it was contrary to my principles," responded Mr. Waft, with dignity. " Gallons of
whisky, sir, would have been drank. What then—
debauchery followed—drunkenness stalked the land—
I set my face against drunkenness. A little drop like
this in my glass cannot harm any man; a genial glass
is requisite in this green country, sir ; but when it
comes to gallons, then, sir, I make my bow."

" Bah !" said the host, winking at me, while the
painter emptied his glass, and declared that he had a
very great mind to turn farmer himself, if he could be
spared by society. To this the host grunted assent,
and, from his manner, evidently wished the painter
far enough off.

"I love a farm dearly," said painter Waft—"I could work in a garden, morning, noon, and night."

"Sacré bleu," exclaimed the host, "you have a garden, as full of black stumps as your own jaw."

"Call you that wee bit of yard a garden?" said the painter, with a look of contempt. "He knows no better, sir; but we old country folks, we know what a garden should be;" and the poor wight (being piqued at the host's remark) went on to say he despised the town—"What's Chatham to me? I can do better without Chatham than Chatham can do without me—I'll shew you that, some fine morning. Yes, I'll go to Bear Creek—I have my eye upon a good location there—I'll go to Bear Creek, and I'll build me a loom."

I had heard of a man "building a bower" in the wilderness; the building of a loom demanded an explanation, but the painter vanished the moment his harangue was ended, leaving the host to explain that he guessed the *vaut rien* had been a weaver once.

A worshipful magistrate now introduced his unpleasant red phiz to my notice—a bustling, meddling, little man, just as fond of his glass as the painter. He began by lending me the well-thumbed newspaper, and following up this piece of civility with a host of questions; in short, he was a bore of the first water, without one spark of originality about him, and I shook him off at once. Notwithstanding the cold shoulder I turned to him, he still persevered, and finally took his departure, saying, "that he supposed I would consult him before I ventured to purchase any land in the vicinity."

The bar-room gradually filled with townsfolk; the painter also returned, but his fire was out, and he slunk down in a corner. The awful number of blacks gathered into Chatham was the subject of discussion on the tapis.

" It amounts to a grievance," said one.

" It amounts to a nuisance," said another.

" Why, man, the darkees carry all before them," said a third; "and those runaway niggers may be our masters before long."

" The black regiment emboldens them so," said a swarthy little smith.

" Like to see them keep the wall side in the States, as they do here," said an American.

" Never was more skeered in my life," chimed in painter Waft, " than I was last evening, on my way home. Turning a corner, gentlemen, tilt against me came three of the black sodgers—they swore awful at me, I tell you; and more than that, for though I reeled back from the planks to let them pass, one of them gives me a cut across the —— with his rattan."

A burst of indignation followed this detailed outrage; in the midst of which, the door opened, and entered a black man, spicily dressed in black. He had a hammer in one hand, and some placards in the other.

" Can you loan me a few small nails," said he to the host; " I want to put up one of these placards in the bar of your place ?"

" What is it all about ?" inquired the host, very gruffly.

" Oh, a dinner !—a public dinner that the coloured folks mean to give."

" Nails !" interrupted the host; " I have no nails; and if I had I would not permit my wall to be defaced by your blackguard placards."

" Brayvo !" cried painter Waft—" Well said, I say ;"

and the rest raised their voices, while the poor black slunk out, abashed.

"Eating and drinking, wooing and fiddling, and preaching, all the summer," said our host; "that's the way with the darkees; and starving and perishing all the winter."

"Hang me, if I subscribe one farthing for firewood for the blacks, next winter!" said the smith, sourly.

"It is money thrown away," said another; and again the door opens, and three tall black soldiers marched up to the bar.

"Please can we have some beer?" said they.

"No," said the host; "you can't have none."

"Brayvo, brayvo!" bawled the painter Waft, while the discomfited darkees retreated, muttering oaths deep and loud.

"I'll take a glass with you, captain, after that," said the Yankee.

"And so will I!" exclaimed the rest, and in the midst of this spirited boosing match, I retreated to bed.

This morning, at breakfast, my host informed me he had heard of a famous farm for sale; and having received the necessary directions and landmarks, I started on foot, through the New Wood road, full of stumps, and logs, and other little impediments. The air was oppressively close, and the dense woods on either side echoed with the buzzing of musquitoes and flies; the occasional shrill note of a woodpecker varying at intervals the dull hum-drum of the insects. By the time I had walked about four miles, I felt as weary and depressed as if I had marched thirty, and, allured "by the smoke that so gracefully curled," deviated from the rough-hewn track, and entered the brush and stumps of a new settler.

A short distance from the road I found a tall, gaunt, wild-looking man, presiding over or feeding, a huge fire of logs and brushwood. Exposed alike to the heat of the fire and the rays of the sun, the man's face seemed half baked, but it was easy to see he had not been always a labourer. There was an energy almost amounting to impatience in his movements, and firm and contemptuous curling of the upper lip, which spoke the rage of the inward man, at the purgatorial state it was doomed to before its time.

" You seem to have a fatiguing job, my friend," said I, sitting down on a log, *sans ceremonie*.

The burner muttered some reply, which was lost in the hissing and crackling of the flames, as with half-averted face he continued his labours. Again I opened my fire, and inquired if he knew where the H——'s lived; this drew a more reasonable reply, and I soon learned the history of the man before me.

He was an Old Country man, of course ; had been in affluent circumstances, married, outrun the constable—bankrupt. Creditors and friends raised a fund from the residue of his shattered fortunes, which enabled him to emigrate with his wife and six children—a disastrous voyage—delays at Quebec and Montreal—illness of his wife and children—arrival in the land of promise—capital all expended *en route*. Rented a house in the town, went into woods to look for his lot, got fever and ague, and finally got into the hands of a speculator, who rented or let him the same wood lot for four years—conditions hard enough, clearing land for another man in the midst of a wilderness, with permission to sell fire-wood to his neighbours ; to mend the matter, his log-house was burnt one night, and one of his children injured.

He pointed to a hovel which had escaped my notice ;
he said his family lay there at night—at present they
were " out in the woods, looking for berries to satisfy
their hunger," and concluded a chapter of accidents
by revealing a deep ulcer in one of his legs.   A tree
had fallen upon him when he first began to wield the
axe ; he was alone in the woods, and was jammed
down under the tree for the best part of a day, his leg
miserably crushed ; sores and ulcers formed, which he
could not heal.

" By my sole exertions I have built up another log-
house," said the poor fellow ; " the rude walls are
standing, but the most difficult part of the job, the
roofing-in, I despair of completing before the winter."

Pondering upon the hapless lot of this unhappy
man, I wended my way across a rough corduroy road
and rude attempt at a log-bridge, over a vile, stinking
pond or slough, redolent in marsh, miasma, and
putrid air, and swarms of flies.   A little beyond this
romantic piece of ornamental water, I found my
farm, or the sixty acres of clearing in woods, which
I had walked so far to see.   This farm had been
cleared by the united exertions of three brothers
—Old Country men, of course ; they had expended,
according to their own shewing, about one thousand
pounds already ; they had oxen, and farm-servants,
and horses, and cows, and a loggery and small
frame-house ; in short, it was easy to see how they
had expended their money.   As yet the ground was
as full of stumps as ever it could stick—beech, but-
ter-nut, oak, hemlock, and some pine.   They thought
they had done wonders ; for my own part, when I
looked at the dense wall of forest which surrounded
their little clearing, I thought by the time they had

cleared the half of their five hundred acres, they would sink, sore and sorry old men. They dug wells for water, once a week at least, and let their cattle live on browse in the woods.

All they asked for their land, cleared and uncleared, was six hundred pounds, with which they said they would move into the home district. They were bachelors to boot, and wanted wives.

"Why don't ye go into Chatham," said I, " and take wives from that flourishing little town."

"The Chatham girls look very high, and give themselves so many airs," said one.

"And they have no fortunes," said another.

"And the girls think they are fortunes in themselves in the country," said a third.

I wished these fortune-hunters good evening, and wished they might find young ladies with fortunes, romantic enough to prefer the solitude of their log-cabin, and log road, stump fields, and sweet piece of water, to the busy "hum of life," and a chance of sometimes seeing a new face, even in that outskirt of civilization—Chatham.

Having made an agreement with a Wiltshire lad, who had a horse and gig to let, we started away from Chatham, on the right bank of the Thames, the weather broiling hot. Five or six miles higher up, the river became narrow, and at times the banks picturesque. Here we got into some of the old French farms, which they had disposed of since the last disturbance; the gig also broke down, and we were fain to borrow a plank, and substitute it for the rickety seat, same time cutting a new linchpin from a green-wood tree. I was not a little surprised to find the axletree was hard wood also; in fact, what with ashen springs and oaken pins, the gig, or double sulky was a wooden concern peculiar to the country.

" Indians !" exclaimed my whip, pointing into the forest.

It was a Potta-wattomie bivouac ; half a dozen men, rolled up in dirty blankets, lay round the red embers of a fire, their feet turned towards it. On a rude sort of raised platform, covered with mats, snored the squaws and their papooses ; a few dogs and an Indian pony lounged in the rear ; the men raised their black heads as we passed, and shewed most villanous faces.

The Potta-wattomies have been driven out of these lands in the States, and bands of them have migrated into Canada. They are regarded with a jealous eye by the settled Indians and whites, who say they are arrant poachers and horse stealers ; be that as it may, they seem to be very like gipsies. Sixteen miles from Chatham, we halted upon the banks of the river, and forthwith walked through some well-cleared fields, backed by heavily timbered woods of black walnut and white oak. The fields of grass and weeds told a tale of misery and woe ; the proprietor of the farm had been compromised in the late troubles, had fled into Michigan. His farm lay neglected, and he wanted to sell it ; as the property was not actually confiscated, I thought it worth looking at. There were two good log houses on the premises, one of which had been very unceremoniously taken possession of by an Irish family, who, in the plenitude of laziness and power, were using up the adjacent barn for fuel ; besides the frontage to the Thames, this farm was well watered by a small creek running into the Thames through masses of fallen timber. The banks of the river were covered with wild gooseberry trees, laden with fruit,

of which we ate, together with wild currants, straw-
berries, and chokecherries.

"This is the spot for a man with some capital,"
said my whip, waxing eloquent as he satisfied his appetite with wild fruit. "This is the wholsome place—
far better than Chatham," continued he ; "and if you
really want a farm, you may speed farther and fare
worse. I would advise you, sir," said he, "to lose
no time about concluding the bargain, for, after all,
who knows but the owner may put it up to auction,
and then it will bring twice as much as he asks."

As it was getting late, I resolved to cross the river.
Descended the steep bank to the water's edge, when
the horse suddenly plunged in, and began to swill the
water, while my whip, espying a log canoe sticking
out of a nook higher up, went to fetch it, as he said
he was sure my carpet bag would be upset into the
river if he did not ferry it over in the canoe. The
water about the middle of the stream reached the
horse's shoulders, and I calculated on getting safely
over to the opposite side, when I observed my confounded whip bearing down upon me in a long
unwieldy log canoe, which he endeavoured to steer
through the rapid current with a long stick.

"Keep off—keep off!" I bawled in vain, for the
next moment the canoe came full tilt against the side
of the horse, a spirited old stager ; he reared and
plunged, turned his head down the stream, and away
he went, splashing, swimming, and scrambling through
the water, while my whip, laying hold of the back of
the gig, swung after, in his log canoe, shouting,
"We'll all be drowned." Not relishing the splashing,
I was receiving, I got a good pull on the reins, and,
aided by a snagg against one of the wheels, brought up

the startled horse, though he splashed and kicked off two of his shoes, and snorted as if he saw a catamount. The river being thus safely forded, we returned back to Freeman's Tavern, where we found a heavy, spring-less waggon, laden with feather beds and big boxes.

" It is the London mail," said my whip.

" Do you call this lumbering waggon the mail?" said I, same time pointing to a grand placard upon a barn door, announcing the fares and hours of departure of the royal mail, headed with a woodcut of a fine open coach, full of ladies and gentlemen, and drawn by horses at full gallop.

" Mail's ready to start," said the coachee, tucking up his long blouse; and, pulling out a tin trumpet, he favoured us with a whine, groan, and squeak, swinish enough to have roused all the pigs in the parish.

The host asked us into his parlour, and while his wife prepared dinner he served up a dish of personal adventures and hair-breadth 'scapes, not unfrequently met with in the backwoods. He was an American born, of an enterprising turn; had travelled far, been to the western country—the far west—spoke loudly about the flat-foot Indians, the crows, sauks, and foxes; passed lightly over that part of his eventful history that wafted him from the far side of the Mis-sisippi, with his wife and daughter, to his present location as tavern-keeper in Upper Canada. He merely rented the tavern and a few acres; the situa-tion was picturesque, and he had improved the place, —his garden, his melon patch, his Indian corn, his onions, his beans—everything seemed flourishing.

" Have you seen Prince since you arrived?" he in-quired of my whip.

" Noa," replied the whip; "but I hopes he's well."

" Come and see him," replied the host, as he led the way into a small yard, and lifting up his voice hallooed, "Prince, Prince, my Prince! come out, come out! and smile upon your humble visitors."

A grunt was the response, and presently forth marched a round corn-fed Berkshire boar, turning up his snout most disdainfully, while the host presented his majesty with a handful of green-corn cobs.

Notwithstanding the favourable appearance, considerable elevation above the Thames, and some old cleared farms in the vicinity, the host assured me the country was far from being healthy. "We have suffered more sickness since we have been here," said he, " than I ever experienced in the States. We have had fevers of all sorts—my eldest boy is only just recovering from a congestive fever. My wife and daughter have had fever and ague here; I myself, with all my partiality to this place," continued he, " have almost resolved to quit it. Every summer I am attacked with a fever, which hangs about me; and even now I am not free from it; the slightest scratch on the skin festers and becomes a sore immediately. Look at my foot: my great toe, chafed a little by a tight shoe, has swollen as big as my fist, and I am forced to limp about in this old slipper. You saw that young woman who attended you at dinner; I brought her here in rude health from Detroit, now she is sickly enough to be a burden, instead of help. Ho! Matildiana; how is your head, gal?"

" Better, sir," responded the maid.

" What are you doing, gal?"

" Lying down on the bed,—I felt pretty ugly just now."

" Well, stay quiet, gal, and I'll give you oil by and by—that will make you pretty smartish, I guess."

This dialogue between master and maid did not restore my confidence in the salubrity of the country. I turned into my downy bed with many misgivings, and lay panting and puffing for air like a porpoise all night.

This morning we pursued our journey at day-break, and halted to reconnoitre the ground on which the disastrous Battle of the Thames was fought. An old Indian had described the battle to my guide and whip, and he dealt it out second-hand to me. It was in this battle the celebrated warrior Tecumsch was shot, as the Americans say, by old Tippicanoe, the late General Harrisson. The battle at best must have been bush-fighting, for even at the present day the ground is heavily timbered. When the new road was being lately made, several skeletons were dug up, and also the debris of guns, buckles, swords, and caps. This fight was maintained by the Indians, long after Proctor ran away. If he had stood his ground, even with his handful of men, the Indians, would have rallied round him till the last man was slain. As it was, the Indians threw the American forces into confusion; and had not old Tecumsch been slain, the Americans would have had little to boast of. Further on, we found the site of an Indian village, which the Americans had destroyed, and the Indians never reoccupied. On the opposite side of the river I longed to visit a peaceful little village belonging to the Moravian Indians, but my whip did not approve of fording the river again. Here an Indian rode up to us with

two ponies; he led one, a very pretty black colt, with
a skin sleek as a mouse, small head, good shoulder,
long neck, and clean black legs.   He wanted to sell—
fifteen dollars was all he asked, and would take part of
the price in goods.   The Indian was well dressed in a
strong suit of grey jean, or fustian.   He was the son
of the Chief of the Moravian Indians, and, as Brant
said of a very fair Indian boy, looked " half missionary,
half Indian."   He was very reserved, his short com-
mentaries being confined to "yes" and " no," and a
short grunt.   The country now became more thickly
settled, but the land did not seem to be very good.
The settlers were chiefly Irish, as their houses and
farms bespoke. " The Indian root doctor !" exclaimed
my whip, as he pulled up, and entered into conversation with a tall old fellow, with a shrewd grey eye,
—" Well, Doctor; you never sent me no pills yet."
" Well, I haven't had time," responded the Doctor.
" You heard how they locked me up for a month, for
practising without a ' diplora,' though the people as
knows me, says I can do as much with my little finger,
as the whole body of tyrannical doctors can do with
their diploras."   He then informed us he had just
been " curing a man far gone in the black janders,"
" and I'm going right away to cure a woman with a
cancer in her nose."   He then boasted of his knowledge of herbs and simples.   " You ought to take
some of my powders, sir," said he to me—" I make
them up of Jesut's bark and gerreymanders."

" Where do you get the Jesuit's bark? " said I.

" In the wood, to be sure," replied the Doctor.

" Will you have the goodness to shew me the tree?"

" A dozen of them, if you like to follow me," said
the Doctor; and off we went into the bush.   The

tree was not so easily found, though at every step the Doctor either plucked or pointed out some herb or shrub, the sovereignest remedy for pains, aches, and all the ills that human flesh is heir to. " This is the dogmatic tree, from which the Jesut's bark is taken," said he, having led me a pretty dance through the wood and swamps, for nearly an hour.

" Why, this is a mountain ash !" said I.

" Put on your spectacles, sir," replied the Doctor. " Ash, indeed !—perhaps you can tell me the name of this tree, or this scrubby one, or this yarb in my hand ?"

I was obliged to plead ignorance.

" That's the way with the Old Country folk," exclaimed the Doctor ; " tell them a thing or two, and they'll cry out they knew it before. Now, I shew you a tree—a valuable tree, which you might have passed ten times a day without minding ; but the moment I point it out to you as a dogmatic, and very important bark—' Oh, you knew all about it—it's a common tree, not worth looking at !' "

" What tribe do you belong to ?" said I.

" How—tribe ! how—tribe !" inquired the Doctor.

" You say you are an Indian doctor ; what tribe of Indians do you belong to ?"

" I'm no Indian dog !" roared the medico. " This is the reward I get for my pains !"

I explained. I did not mean to insult the learned leech—had made a little mistake.

" But I tell you, I am no more an Indian than the Governor-General," bellowed the Doctor ; and we parted rather hastily.

" He is a rum-'un," said my whip ; to whom I explained this *contretemps ;* " and he cannot bear contradiction of any sort. I wonder ye had not a set-to in the bush; for he is very hot and sore since he was in prison and fined."

Halted at Brett's Tavern, to bait: here we found the Indian and his ponies; he had fallen a dollar in the price of his colt; but money was so scarce, that I question if he could get seven dollars for the best steed in his village in a day's ride. Finally, he put his colt into the stable, and left him in the hands of his good friend, the tavern-keeper, to sell him for him if he could, or, what is more likely, keep him for *his keep*, in a very short time. Having taken some tea and eggs for luncheon—this being all the hostess could set before us—we prepared to depart, when a horse-jockey came up to us, and said there was a friend of his lying very ill in the tavern. "He has been in a raging fever for some days," said he, "and now talks the greatest nonsense ever I heerd. I wish some one would go in and talk to him, for I find there is no use in my arguing with him any longer."

"I should think your arguments thrown away," said I. "The man is in a raging fever, you say— why don't you go for a doctor?"

"I sent for the doctor a few days ago, but he has so much to do."

"If you will tell me where the doctor lives, if it is not too far off, I dare say I can send him to your friend."

"Oh, for that part of the matter, I can ride over to his house in an hour!" replied the jockey.

I urged him to do so; and we pushed on, reflecting upon the many vicissitudes, ills, and ailments we are subject to in this remote and semi-barbarous region. Cross the wooden bridge, and halt for the night at Delaware, on the Thames. This is decidedly the prettiest spot I have yet seen in Canada. The village is in its infancy, and the land around it being held by absentees and speculators, there is no immediate prospect of the peace of the valley being disturbed by a needy horde of land-loupers. I found my host and hostess civil and very obliging persons; the former, in a brown study about a scrape he had been drawn into by the Indians, to whom, in an evil hour, he had sold some whisky. He said they were New York, or Tuscarora Indians; and, as they were dressed like ourselves, and spoke good English, he never thought of refusing them, whereupon, one of the party went and lodged information against him. He was summoned before the magistrates, was to attend the sessions next day, and be fined.

A waggon full of those said Tuscarora Indians now came up; the women with papooses in their carved cradles, and sporting men's hats, with bands of tin or silver lace round them, quite stylish; the men sported blue frock-coats and continuations. The party had been to London, buying furniture for their new settlement. The tribe had recently sold their lands in New York, and emigrated into Canada, where they have purchased upwards of three thousand acres of land from private individuals, and then leased it from the crown, so as to receive the usual presents, and be treated with the same indulgence as the Canada Indians.

Pushed on towards London, the country growing more hilly and picturesque every mile.

" My eyes, what a chance !" exclaimed my whip, as, jumping nimbly from his seat, he began to pick up sundry shillings and sixpenny pieces, lying on the road; and, with many demonstrations of joy and de-

L

light, he wiped the dust and dirt from the coins, and put them into his pouch. Shortly after, toiling up a hill, we met a neat one-horse phæton, in which sat a stout, round-faced man, a spare anxious-looking lady, two nurses, and children, all dressed in decent mourning.

"Do you know that man?" inquired my whip; "well, I dare say you have heard of him. That is Jones, the Indian preacher, who went over to England, and married a woman of fortune."

London at last, with its Gothic court-house, and white stoops and red coats, seemed to spring up, from the woods through which we were travelling, like an enchanted city in the wilderness; but the first appearance of London from the opposite side of the Thames is more prepossessing than, on closer inspection, I found it to be

CHAPTER XII.

" I KNEW he was a bad 'un," said my whip, looking fiercely after a stiff conceited clerico who had just cantered by upon his high horse without deigning to look down upon our shattered gig and sprawling gigster.

" Never mind him, my lad," said I ; " we can get on without his assistance." And we began to hammer up our old bone-setter again. I could not help smiling at my whip's honest indignation, for in a new country like this, it is expected that every man will lend his neighbour a hand in case of any accident or emergency; besides I had travelled with the stiff gentleman in black before, and had heard him volunteer his advice when it was not required. It was too late to think of returning to London, we therefore pushed on, leading the horse, in quest of some settler's house or tavern; fortunately, the road was in tolerable repair, and though the night was dark as pitch, after sundry mistakes and refusals, we halted at a tavern, which my whip discovered by the sign over the door, which he read thus, " The ox and sable," (aux sables.)

Having secured the horse in the stable *sans cere-monie*, we entered the log house, and were assailed by a sturdy mastiff. The kitchen, parlour, and hall, into which we made our *entré*, was much larger than I expected; we found two disastrous looking Irishmen standing up bravely before a huge fireplace and roaring fire; between them hung, or was suspended, a quarter of beef, red and raw, which they were weighing after their own fashion; a very dirty and uncouth woman nursed an infant in the chimney corner; two half-clad urchins peeped from behind her; three ragged boys occupied the other corner. And the weighing of the beef ended, and the dog turned out, with some difficulty, we were permitted to approach the fire; the men returned, as they said, to look after the horse; and presently we heard a noisy dispute about the beef.

" Twopence a pound—soo!—twopence a pound for that red meat, is it ?"

" Ay, and it's little enough for my labour, (let alone the loss,) dragging it through the woods for five or six miles."

" Be easy; you know very well it's little better than carrion—the cow died a natural death."

" I'd like to see the man dar say that but yourself. Died! I killed her with my own hand! The moment she began to droop, and her tongue became black, I killed her."

Here the conversation was carried on in whispers, and one of the men (our host) returned, and demanded if we would not eat some supper. " Plenty of beef here, gentlemen," said he. " We can roast a piece in five minutes."

If I had not overheard the conversation, I dare say

I would have gladly acceded to the proposition. My whip betrayed the same disgust more openly; and we determined to have some milk, which our lovely hostess proceeded to boil in a singular utensil, used for sundry purposes—baking bread, stewing meat, and now boiling milk to the consistency of sour curds and buttermilk. This delectable beverage was set before us in two basins, but it smacked so confoundedly of onions and grease, that I would not swallow a tithe of it; and finding the heavy wet-bread as sticky as beeswax, and about as eatable, I begged leave to retire, if our fair hostess could accommodate me with a bed.

" A bed between the pair of ye, I suppose," said she.

" A shake down anywhere by myself," said I; and after a deal of whispering we were shewn into a small room with three beds. The host, hostess and his children occupied the larger, and we were soon wrapped in the arms of Morpheus.

Waking up with the cold, some time during the night, I was surprised to see the room brilliantly illuminated by the silvery rays of moonlight streaming down upon our beds through numerous chinks in the roof and crannies in the wall. Truly, the Irish peasantry are behind all others in the comforts and necessaries of civilized life. I cannot say they make the best settlers in a new country; they expose themselves to cold, and heat, and damp, in the woods, just as freely as they do in their native wilds, and soon feel the bad effects of such rashness. Dear-bought experience comes too late, and when fever and ague has done its work, they lose all heart, and betake themselves to drink, or make tracks, as the Yankees say—plunge deeper into the wilds, and perish. The

Irish women are a careless set in the woods. Their ignorance of the art of cookery is a sad drawback to the happiness of their husbands and children. That they can boil a pot of potatoes, is allowed on all hands; but in Canada men require a more generous diet than potatoes. Since the schoolmaster is abroad, I don't see why the cook should stay at home. Dr. Bowring, or some of our practical men, should take this thing in hand—a measure of such vital importance ought not to be neglected. Government cooks should be sent out, and cookery schools ought to be established throughout Ireland. My midnight lucubrations were speedily brought to a close, when my eye rested upon a shining mass at the foot of my bed; stretching out my arm suddenly, I clutched (no " air-drawn dagger," but) a rib of the quarter of raw beef, which my host in the plenitude of his hospitality, had laid between our beds.

Still declining the beef, we breakfasted this morning upon a few eggs, the cow having carried off the milk into the woods; and while my whip put to our trusty roadster, I paid the score, which, by an effort of genius not at all rare, our host had discovered to be fifteen shillings, Halifax currency. I demurred, and as the fellow pretended to be a tavern-keeper, shewed him that I had not the least idea of being imposed on—demanded the items and dittos—set them down on a leaf of my note book, and by his own shewing, reduced his bill from fifteen shillings down to ten, which I paid him for the sour milk, bad bread, stale eggs, and mouthful of wild hay our horse had browsed on during the night, and started away from his tavern full as weary as when we entered it.

The road to Goderich is the least interesting I have

yet travelled, running through dismal forests, seldom enlivened with a settler's hut, and a few acres of clearing; the stillness and silence of the woods have a singularly depressing effect on the spirits, and as for birds, deer, or game of any sort, I can safely say I never saw a single tail or feather in my perigrinations from Chatham to Goderich. To be sure, in the vicinity of Chatham I have seen a few black squirrels and some red-headed woodpeckers, but such "small deer" cannot be called game, even in Canada.

We are now in the North American Land Company's territory. In some places the woods are not so heavily timbered, and considerable improvements have been made. The uniform price of the company's land is said to be three dollars per acre: the road is very good, and the air seems purer and clearer.

" Hello! what news about the contest?" bawled a man from an oak-clearing and barn, half a mile off. He soon came running down to hear our reply.

" What contest?" said I.

" Oh, the contested election," said he. " When did you meet the commissioners? They wanted to examine me, but I'm no politician."

" We are well met then, friend," said I. " Hang politics; I never trouble my head about them."

" I'll take a seat in your gig to Goderich," said this worthy axeman.

" Noa, you can't, man," replied the whip; " the gig's all in a smash, and I wont carry any more weights."

A mile further on we stopped to bait at a good frame cabin, with garden and clearing. The proprietor of this farm soon arrived from the woods: he had a team of oxen, cows, and hogs, a lot of two hundred

acres on either side of the road ; his wife and children
looked happy and contented, and the man himself was
a fine specimen of a pioneer.   He had already cleared
three farms—selling off, putting something to wind-
ward—pulling up stakes, as the Yankees say, and
marching afresh into the woods.

" I have now fifty or sixty acres of this farm cleared
and fenced," said he ; " I have two good barns, this
house, and other improvements made.   I'll sell you
this farm as it stands, and I'll be reasonable in my
price."

" And where will you go, if you sell your farm ?"
said I.

" Into the bush.   Perhaps alongside of you ; that is,
if you buy."

" I should always be happy to have so good a neighbour," said I.

" Come, then—will you make me an offer for the
farm ?" persisted the woodman.

I declined making any offer for the present, and pursued my journey to Goderich, where we arrived just
as the last rays of the sun went down, in Lake Huron.

The town of Goderich stands on a high bank,
above the lake ; it has a bleak and exposed appearance ; and, as at Chatham, I felt inclined to exclaim
against the building mania that seems to possess Old
Country people. Instead of establishing themselves in
the woods, they expend their capital upon houses and
stones in the town, and, so far from improving their
condition by emigration, they are frequently worse off
in those new colonial towns, than in the old established towns at home.   For my own part, I cannot
conceive what the people would be at—huddling
together, bag and baggage, into every bit of cleared

swamp, cut up, gridiron-wise, into streets and lanes, in which the poor devils purchasing lots are invited to build houses, and establish another thriving new town. If people must, and will live together like a swarm of bees in a hive, they ought to thrust themselves into the midst of Manchester, Birmingham, or London, where they may enjoy all the bustle of life, and be fooled to the top of their bent, without running the risk of crossing the Atlantic in a rotten vessel, and seeking society in the back woods of North America. The winters are said to be very severe here, especially when the winds sweep over the half-frozen lake. The harbour, at the mouth of a small river, called the Maitland, (by the way, a very dry name for a river,) is said to be secure; certes, the craft therein run little risk of being swamped, one very small boat, high and dry on the shore, and the little American steamer, being the only vessels I saw. To be sure, they say the fishing boats are all out at their stations, somewhere in Lake Huron; but, considering this is the only port on the Canada side of the lake, I expected to have seen something more.

Took leave of my whip. Poor fellow! he seemed very much cast down at the thought of returning to his home alone. "But needs must," said he; "if I could sell this old horse here, I would embark along with you, sir, and may be I would have a chance of seeing the Old Country once more."

Before I embarked, my stick and umbrella, which I had lost between London and Goderich, was restored, by an Irishman, who had picked them up, and now modestly demanded two dollars for his pains. I gave him half a dollar, and left him as happy as a king in the bar of my hotel.

The Canada Company pay the proprietors of the steamer a round sum in hard dollars for every visit said steamer pays to Goderich, though neither freight nor passengers from that port would pay the expense of the trip; and as it is, the captain assured me it was a losing concern.

We had in the first cabin two Americans from Virginia; they had saddle-bags and boxes full of geological specimens, which they had recently collected in their tour through Canada, and were agreeable and intelligent men. Our day's voyage on the lake was very monotonous, the heat very oppressive, and the view limited, owing to a white haze, which filled the air and affected the eyes. I have since heard that cases of ophthalmia are by no means rare in this region. Lay-to at Fort Gratiat, while a company of the U. N. S. artillery, and some prisoners came on board to be conveyed down to Detroit. I was amused at the sour looks and crabbed appearance of their dwarfish fifers and drummers. They struck up "Yankee Doodle," "Hail, Columbia," and other national airs, whenever we neared the Canada side. The soldiers seemed little satisfied at the nature of the service they were on the rout for, and four or five of them were under arrest for refractory conduct. The Florida war and the Indian rifles being little to the taste of the corps, though the majority of them belonged to the pugnacious natives, whose sons fight for fun and frolic, more than for wealth or glory. The officers and their wives seemed to have a little of the *esprit de corps* also; they seemed to think it "a pretty considerable bore" to be marched off to fight the Red Seminoles— Bill Jones, Tigertail, and Co.

Intending to wait the arrival of the Erie steamer,

I stopped at that most stupid of all stupid places, Detroit. The weather was most infamously close, damp, and hazy; everything seemed redolent of fever and ague. I tried the theatre—found it deserted; the very fiddlers refusing to play to empty benches; while a neighbouring store-keeper accounted for the absence of play-goers, by saying that the company was made up of all the "hard cases" in Michigan.

The bar-room of the American was the only place in which a newspaper could be seen for five minutes, and the general stillness and dulness of the place was only varied by the loud coughing of the steamers, as they paddled up and down the Detroit. A steam ferry-boat constantly plies from Detroit to Sandwich, which I visited twice during my sojourn at Detroit.

The land on the Canada side is held by French Canadians and Americans, and the farms have quite an Old Country look.

The non-appearance of the Erie steamer caused no small anxiety in the town. The bar-rooms of the American were crowded with townspeople, anxious to hear the news, (if any ;) and a variety of drinks, gin-slings, and sherry-cobblers, were hastily swallowed with every vague report, till at last the sad truth flashed upon us. The Erie, as all the world knows, was burnt on lake Erie, and an unknown number of souls sent to settle their last account. Hosts of townspeople gathered round every one who had later tidings, and the newspaper-offices were beset with crowds, seeking authentic information; but when the steamboat despatched from Detroit in search of survivors returned with only two—the captain and a boy— severely burnt, I never saw blacker despair, and mortification more deeply and suddenly stamped, than

upon the faces of some of the expectant crowd. Yet
not a word—not a murmur, escaped them; as every
man went quietly to his own place, to vent his grief
for the loss of friends and relatives, in private.

At last, I am rejoiced to say, I have got my foot
out of Detroit, and once more head up the St. Clair,
in the steamer of my choice, the gallant Illinois. In
the bar-room I found a tall, muscular young son of
brown labour, who had been rescued from the wreck
of the Erie steamer. Our captain, Blake, to his credit
be it spoken, gave him free passage, bed, board, and
drink, for nothing. He was, therefore, a sort of lion,
in his way, and told his "thrice-told tale" of all the
perils and dangers he had escaped, with a good grace.
He said the boiler-deck was very much crowded, and
the passage-money was not half paid, when the flame
burst out, with an explosion, from some oil and varnish
cans right over the boiler, whereupon the deck passengers rushed forward, with "a yell," and crowded
the deck so, that it was impossible to get back or forward. As the engines could not be stopped, the speed
of the boat was very great, and the wind (for it was
blowing a gale) soon blew up the flames to the hurri-
cane deck; "and then," said our informant, " the Swiss
and Germans began to jump overboard, like sheep, and
as fast as they got into the water, the paddle-wheels
made mash of them." He described the most heart-
rending scenes—women tying children round them—
young men and girls jumping overboard, hand-in-
hand. Finally, he scrambled upon part of the paddle-
box, and jumped into the water, so as to escape from
the wheel. Fortunately, he could swim; struck out
from the burning mass, and got hold of a floating
bench, on which he rested, while he saw the Erie, like

a floating volcano, wheel round in her mad career, and return in his direction. This he described as being the most horrible part of the affair. To avoid being run down and crushed, he was forced to abandon his plank, and swim, for a long time, till he found the boat keel, with several people clinging to it; he held on also, and saw the Erie sweep past, like a mass of fire, while shrieks, and groans, and yells, told that some miserable wretches were still alive. It is said, two hundred souls, men, women, and children, perished in this dreadful manner. The poor Swiss little calculated upon such a sad catastrophe, when they left their own wild hills and lovely lakes, enduring all the hardship and fatigue of a long sea voyage, to perish thus so miserably, in sight of their land of promise.

Makina, or Makinaw, with its antiquated French village and white-walled fort on the heights, is the most European-looking spot I have yet seen in this New World. This was one of the earliest, and I believe principal stations and rendezvous of the great fur-trading companies, servants, chasseurs, Indians, and mighty hunters; and at present it has all that stirring appearance of mimic war, owing to the sudden influx of Indians; a regular gathering of the Chippewas and Ottawas seems to have taken place, and their long rows of wigwams, fires, canoes, picturesque dresses, varying from the eternal blanket, to the docskin hunting coat, scarlet leggings, and ornamental moccasins of the Indian braves and warriors, as they strode up and down the lake shore, mingled with French fishermen (half-breed), squaws, smart grey uniform of the U. N. S. troops from the fort, and presently the pink, green, and yellow parasols of our lady passengers, escorted by our exquisites, in their

broad-leafed sombreros and white-sleeved round-
abouts, presented a *coup d'œil* from the promenade
deck of our dashing and gaily-pennoned steamer,
rarely to be met with in the midst of wild lakes and
desolate regions. Several of our deck-passengers,
traders and pedlers, went ashore, and quartered themselves in the village, their object being to trade away
their trumpery with the Indians whenever they were
paid. I regretted to find drunken Indians lying
about the lake shore in every direction. The poor
industrious squaws, who have all the labour and
misery on their backs, were busily employed cleaning
white fish, which their lords and masters presently
sold to the traders in that article, who, with their
workmen, were busily at work, barrelling up and
salting said fish; while others paid the Indians, in the
public-houses, with whisky. There was a perpetual
howling and monotonous groan and hum rising from
several of the wigwams, and some of the ladies expressed a desire to peep into one of them; we therefore surrounded one of those lodges, and looking in,
through the chinks of the mats, beheld about a dozen
men and women sprawling on the ground, some with
whisky bottles in their hands, chanting a most discordant and dirge-like song, which one of our party
said was a love-song, while a hoary-headed chief, a
very young squaw, and others, were wallowing together
in a state which decency forbids me to describe. Our
ladies, indeed, ran back to the steamer and hid their
blushes; for my own part, I was quite disgusted with
the scene of riot and debauchery I witnessed on every
side, and followed the ladies. We found a venerable
old chief of the Ottawas, attended by some very
respectable Indians, walking about the deck; he

neither could nor would speak English or French, though he seemed desirous to shew that he was very friendly. He had fought against the Americans in the last war, and, like many of the Indians congregated here for payment, contrived to get paid in Canada also. I observed the Indians very proudly displayed their English blankets, or any other article they possessed of English manufacture. Having taken in our supply of wood, we walked away from Mackinaw, and left the Indians in their glory. I remarked to some of my fellow-passengers, that I had not seen a single good-looking Indian woman among the motley crew on the island, and they had not been a whit more successful. The drudgery and misery of the Indian woman is stamped indelibly upon her broad, meek, melancholy face, while her pigeon-toed gait, and squab figure, declare her to be inured and doomed to slavery, from papoose to toothless squaw-hood.

While we made a splendid run through that deep, inland sea, Lake Michigan, I was amused with the versatile genius of one of the passengers, who had wooed the smiles of fortune, in every known trade and profession in the Union with little success, though now he seemed to have got to the top of the tree in his own estimation, for instead of regulating a bank, as director, or vetoing a bank bill, as president, he had invented a windmill suitable to the prairie—had actually gone to Washington and lodged his model windmill in the Patent Office. He had another model along with him, which he presently took from his deal chest, and hooked it together; it seemed to me to be a very complicated affair: a large horizontal wheel, with upright frames, like Venetian blinds, or jealousies, to catch the wind ; the speed of the mill to be regulated by the opening and shutting of said windows, by long wire hooks-and-eyes attached to the upright shaft. The model was certainly a very nice piece of workmanship. The mill-house and all the machinery, mill-stones, and bolting machine ready for work—— " Now then," said the great inventor, " I'll set her a-going ;" and sundry passengers lending a hand, this windmill was hoisted on the promenade-deck, when the ladies and exquisites crowded about to see its performance. The mill was adjusted on top of a flat skylight, and soon went merrily round, to the great delight of all, but unfortunately the wind was blowing fresh, and the inventor, attempting to regulate the speed of his mill, received a rap on the knuckles that made him sing out. He then attempted to stop it altogether. Stop it, indeed ! As well might he have attempted to stop the steamer by laying hold of the paddle-wheels. Round flew the windmill, while its owner, like Don Quixote, attempted to arrest its speed, which was playing the deuce with its machinery. He succeeded in loosening some long wires, which seemed to increase the velocity of the mill-wheels, and rendered it actually unsafe to approach it, as the long sharp wires and hooks spun round the edges of the wheel. Finally, the projector was obliged to leave his mill to the sport of winds and waves, and the next morning, when I mounted the deck, I found the poor windmill quiet enough, a melancholy wreck.

" Milwakee !" sung out sundry passengers, as we let off our steam, and made signals off a high, bold shore, on which a lighthouse and sundry white buildings, backed with dark woods, appeared. Presently a small steamer came out of the Milwakee river, and we were boarded by a crowd of anxious-looking people, inquiring after the fate of the Erie. They brought newspapers to us, and we left some of our passengers with them. I was so much struck with a leading article in one of those papers, that I transcribed it into my note-book, *sur le champ :*—

" Wisconsin is a young buffalo: and though in a minority, he roams over his beautiful prairies and reclines, in his pleasant groves, with all the buoyant feelings of an American freeman. He slakes his thirst at the purest fountains that gush from the adamantine base of his lovely soil, and bathes at pleasure in his limpid lakes, paved with agates and sapphires. He paws up lead with his hoofs; he ploughs up iron and zinc with his horns; and cultivates the richest soil the green earth affords. When John Bull talks of war, he stretches his muscular form on his elevated plains, and shaking his head, looks at the North East Boundary; then casting his eye at the Oregon, he bellows in thunder, his eyes flash in lightning; he whisks his tail in the whirlwind, shakes his mane in the tornado, and, like the war-horse, snorts vengeance at the minions who would dare to desecrate the soil of freemen; and his (the young buffalo's) sons, being descendants of those puritan patriots who some seventy years since made a batch of cold tea in Boston Harbour, rather than pay tax without a representation in the body which levied it; and being themselves taxed in the revenue they consume, and in the lands upon which they live, without a direct representation, they feel the humiliation of their condition.

" It being the law, however, they submit; but only

in the anticipation of soon passing from a minor to a major state, when they will be otherwise and more comfortably situated.   But in the meantime, they need a delegate in Congress, who can plead their cause and urge their claims, with words that burn and in language that will enlighten, convince, and persuade."— *Milwakee Journal.*

CHAPTER XIII.

CHICAGO, commonly called the city of cities, the capital of the Western world, and sundry high-sounding titles, too numerous to insert, I found to be a thriving town, situate on a flat marsh, washed by the lake, a muddy river, heavy and abundant showers of rain—dried again by lake winds, prairie winds, and gleams of sunshine.

Clambering into one of the train of vehicles sent down from the hotels, I bid the Illinois good morning, and whirled over the bridge at full gallop, to the Tremont House. Got established in a single-bedded room, and, having breakfasted, sallied forth to reconnoitre. Detesting flats and marshes most cordially, I was far from being enamoured with Chicago; and the pale visages of the store-keepers and clerks, as they opened their store windows, and peered up and down the streets for customers, told tales of marsh miasma, and all the ills that spread beneath its baleful influence. Nathless, it is contended that Chicago is healthy, and woe betide the luckless wight who maintains to the contrary! For my own part, as I purpose making tracks in a few days, I'll speak my mind, and, as the French commis voyageurs say—*diable me' importe.*

The first place I visited was the old block house and square of buildings, at the mouth of the river, surrounded with rotten palisades. It was here the whites were massacred to a man by the Indians; and, *vice versa,* the Indians, if not slain, were floored, bamboozled, rum-squaddled, and finally swept away from their fatherland by the white man's whisky, being another triumph of whisky-bottle *versus* tomahawk.

" When the last payment was made, some five or six years ago," said a gentleman, (unto whom you shall be introduced by-and-by,) " the streets and lanes, the prairie and the river banks, groaned beneath the weight of drunken Indians. There you might see the hoary chief wallowing in the mire beside his naked children, while groceries and grog-shops, erected for the occasion, poured forth the fire-water upon the degraded race, who sold their birthright for a few gulps of bad whisky. The moment they received the dollars from the agents, away they posted to the grocer's, drank till all was gone, and then stripped off their blankets, moccasons, and furs. Many reserving not sufficient clothing to cover their nakedness, went forth into the wilderness to brave the inclemency of the weather, and drag their weary limbs to the promised lands beyond the Missisippi. Truly the white man has been sufficiently revenged for all the injuries received from the red man at Chicago.

Sundry maps, plans, and prospectuses, having caught my eye, in a flashy store window, I halted, and a smart man, in a tight brown frock, black satin stock, and sandy whiskers, invited me to enter his office and inspect his maps, &c., at leisure. He introduced himself as Captain ———, land agent, &c., wished he could induce me to settle in the country, expatiated upon the beauty, the fertility, and rising prospects of Illinois—" the garden of America, which rivals, as one of our poets says, the garden of Eden," said the captain, jocosely, turning over the leaves of an old account-book.

I thanked the captain for his attention, assured him that I had enough of the old Adam in me to create a hankering after the garden of Eden ; assured him it was my intention to devote the residue of my days upon a farm, be it in Illinois or Tonagtaboo.

The captain proceeded, with much gravity, to examine his books, papers, and old newspapers.

" The fact is," said he, " there is such a run—such a rush of emigrants, New Englanders, and foreigners, seeking for good locations, that all the land is bought up round this district, with the exception of this quarter section, on the north branch, and this one on the lake shore, north of the city by twenty-five miles. But, ha ! ay, here I fix it at last—the colonel has a property, an estate, a park, a residence fit for a nobleman or gentleman to reside on, but, most unhappily, I believe he has already disposed of his estate," said the captain. " Excuse me, sir," said he, seizing his hat, " I'll run, and ask the colonel to step this way."

The captain disappeared, and presently returned, followed by a tall, severe, and yellow-visaged gentleman, loosely attired in dingy white, or whitey-brown linen shooting-jacket and pants. The captain introduced this gentleman to me, hoping we would become sworn brothers.

The colonel extended his brawny sinewy fist, and clutched mine. Compliments being passed, the colonel declared he would as soon part with the apple of his eye, his right hand, or any other indispensable member of his outward man as his prairie farm and wood-lots belonging thereto ; but dire necessity compelling, he was regularly tree'd, and would surrender to fate, and fate alone.   He had chosen this farm while in command of some troops, assisting the Indians to evacuate the premises.   Smitten with the beauty of the spot, he built a house thereon, bought the land at government price, improved it, enclosed it, and all that he asked for it was, three dollars and one half per acre. . He calculated the timber-lots would pay the purchase-money, seeing that timber was only four dollars a cord in Chicago, and his lot was not more than twenty miles from town.

I resolved to see the colonel's farm at once.   He would have put off the visit for a day or two, but I was anxious to see it.

"My son," said the colonel, introducing me to a tall chip of the old block, thinly attired in linen garments.

This youth declared " their horses could not gallop fast enough—one being short of wind, and the other lame of a leg ; and the short and the long of the matter is, you must hire a buggy and borrow a horse.

" And go shares in the buggy," said the colonel.

I returned to Tremont House, and presently the buggy made its appearance before the door ; the colonel gave me a letter of introduction to an excellent neighbour of his—one 'Squire ———, who would give me every information I required, tossed his son some silver to pay for his dinner, bade him be steady, and away we rattled through Chicago, as fast as our old chesnut cob could tug the jingle at his heels.

The colonel's son, a fine, intelligent young fellow, entered into long details of his hunting expeditions; how he had rode down prairie wolves, bagged prairie hens, slaughtered deer, hunted buffalo, though he frankly admitted he had never slain a buffalo.

The marsh or prairie lands over which we rode was partially enclosed, and a few fields of Indian corn, and scattered trees on the ridges or high parts of the prairie, broke the monotony of the scene ; but I looked in vain for the flowers, rich and rare, said to be found wild on the prairie. Yellow and pale red flowers of the common classes, and the Indian com- pass or rosin weed, was the only genus new to me. To this weed, or herb, the colonel's son directed my attention, frequently. It looks like a fern, the leaves much stronger, point north and south ; it bears a yellow flower, which, once broken off, the resin or gum exudes, and is eagerly gathered by young ladies, who wish to preserve their teeth. This gentleman like- wise informed me, that the Indian name, Chicago, signified skunk, or polecat ; and hereafter the citizens will be called skunks or skunkers, I calculate.

Twelve miles from Chicago we deemed it prudent to halt at a tavern kept by a Yorkshireman ; he had been six years in the country, but the world did not smile upon his tavern. He told me he had been happy, once upon a time, and only so-so ever since. He had refused twenty thousand dollars for his lot in Chicago, did not jump at the offer, and has been going down- hill fast, ever since. He refused that little fortune for a dirty bit of swamp.

" Here is another instance of character," thought I, as I contrasted the plodding Yorkshireman, brooding over his misfortunes, with the versatile Yankee, springing up from the slough of despond—to-day a pedler, to-morrow a gentleman—always going a-head.

Having dispatched our dinner of hard pork steaks, and wet potatoes, and swallowed a refresher, we started again, my friend waving his hand to the host, saying—" I'll pay when I return." This I thought uncalled for, as I had already paid our bill, in his presence.

The youth whipped right across the prairie, towards a belt of woodlands, and despising the road, we got into a slough or wet marsh, through which our horse dragged us with difficulty, through long grass, weeds, and mire for a considerable distance, till at last we were obliged to return on our trail, and steer for a house on the right roadside, having lost two hours in our experimental attempt to cross the prairie.

At last we entered the timber land, and drew up in front of 'Squire Smaus' log-house, a very small, but neat and comfortable building, with a garden and a pool of stagnant water in front. Squire Smaus had just returned from a blackberrying expedition, his phaeton or buggy stood at the door—a double-barrelled gun and pointer, and basket of berries, lay on the floor. A young lady rocked a cradle in the corner; an old lady kneaded bread in a closet, aside; two young men, in shirt sleeves, read newspapers and smoked in solemn silence. The squire sweated in an old rocking chair. I handed him the colonel's letter. The squire took the letter, looked at it askant, turned it over, shook it, fanned himself with it, laid it down unopened, put his hand upon his heart and looked as if he had received his death-warrant; at last, opening the letter, words relieved his soul.

" It would appear to me," said the squire, rocking himself, " it would seem, that you are reviewing the country, sir."

I bowed.

" The colonel," continued the squire ; " Colonel —— is a gentleman—a perfect gentleman ; yes, his farm borders on mine."

Being already aware of the fact, I assured Mr. S. I was anxious to look at it ; and, as my young friend did not know the boundaries, wished him to shew me, or send some guide along with me to the colonel's farm.

" I'll lead the way in my buggy, myself," said Mr. S., with much dignity; and having mounted his buggy, he drove along, while we brought up the rear.

The squire pointed out some stakes and landmarks, saying, " This is the boundary between our farms. The colonel's timber lot is connected with his prairie lots by this belt of timber, through which the Great Western Road is surveyed—in fact, that road runs close to his house, shaving off the garden in front."

" Pray where is the house, squire ?" said I, jumping into his buggy, and leaving the young gentleman to follow at leisure.

" The house," said the squire, " ought to be down here. We'll soon find it, I calculate." Then, whipping his horse, we drove right through some thick brush and underwood for some rods, and pulled up at a low railing in front of a deserted log hut. The door was unlatched, and creaked to and fro as the wind sighed through the broken windows; wild-flowers and briers grew over the threshold. At the rear of

M

this little edifice a patch of potatoes and some Indian corn had been trampled down by cattle, decayed and withered; a deep hole, where water might have been discovered once, was called the well, by the colonel's son, who vapoured a great deal because the hall-door was open; but, as the squire coolly remarked, "It was of no consequence whether the door was open or shut, for, save and excepting three or four shelves, the house could lose nothing by the entry of thieves, or, peradventure, a prairie wolf, seeking a night's lodging."

This latter animal, the squire declared to be the scourge of the prairie, killing his lambs and sheep, his hens and pigs, in spite of all his dogs and vigilance. We drove on through the brush, and entered the prairie; the colonel's farm seemed strangely cramped and cornered in by square fields and the worm fences of his neighbours; in fact, this garden of Illinois seemed to me the least picturesque bit of dreary flat I had ever seen. "What the deuce can a man gain by confining himself in a corner of Illinois, upon a prairie surrounded with fences?" thought I. The prairie I had pictured to myself—a vast and almost boundless plain, broken only by wild ravines and 'clumps of trees; but fences, and rail fences, and squares, and blocks, and sections, and quarter-sections — such gridiron improvements may be found everywhere at home; and I have felt as much in the country on Chalk Farm or Hampstead heath as on this prairie, in the wilds of Illinois.

Mr. S. soon turned into his own farm, and held forth about his crops—then spoke of his ailments. He had latterly been subject to palpitation of the heart, or, as he said, sudden thumpings in the stomach after meals; Job had never suffered more sickness than this worthy squire since he came West—he was a Vermonter — and I was compelled to bid him good evening, as I wished to get back to Chicago that night. My desire to accomplish this was opposed to the inclinations of my companion; he declared it was impossible—no, he would sleep at Dutchman's Point.

" Dutchman's fiddle-sticks !" said old Mrs. Smaus, making her appearance with a goodly can of berries in her hands. " Look'ee, general ; I want this here pail of blackberries to be left at Ira Isham's store this evening. Pshaw ! hear a buster rooster like you, talk of impossibilities !—why, I would walk to the city myself, before dark," said the brisk old dame, depositing the berries in our buggy.

Nevertheless, at Dutchman's Point my companion demurred he would not like to drive his friend's horse any further that evening ; but even the tavern-keeper lifted up his voice against halting there—he had only one stable, and a sick stud-horse therein; consequently, if we stayed, our horse might roam at large prairie.

" What signifies forty miles to that horse ?" continued the host. " I'll warrant I have driven him near to seventy in a day with a bigger load than that ere gimcrack buggy."

It now came out that the horse and buggy belonged to a livery-stable keeper, as I found to my cost, paying three dollars for the equipage next day. I was not sorry to get back to Chicago, where I found my chamber occupied by two ladies and three children, and my baggage kicking about the house. Next morning, I had an early visit from my young friend ; he told me his father was anxiously waiting to see me.

The colonel's office was situate in a three-story house, as dingy a brick building as might be found even in Auld Reekie. The colonel soon grasped my hand—he was delighted to see me; led me into his front room, or private office, facing the street.

"I thought you would have slept at the squire's last night," said he; "he is a most amiable gentleman, exceedingly hospitable, but rather pinched for room. I hope you found yourself at home in his house."

Some light conversation of this nature having passed, "Boys," said the colonel, slapping his thigh as if he had found a mine of gold, "have ye paid for your horse and buggy?"

"I paid for it, of course, sir," said I.

"Oh, sir! you're too ceremonious," cried the colonel; "when we free and easy folk live together we are all as brethren—'thick as pickpockets,' as the Londoners say, eh?—ha, ha! Apropos to London, bring me a bottle of porter, Tom."

Tom, being the clerk, in the back office, hastened to wipe two dusty tumblers, then ran down stairs, was seen crossing the street, and presently returning with a bottle of that delectable beverage. I assured the colonel I never drank porter in the morning.

Not so the colonel—he drank the best part of the bottle, and resumed the theme; talked about his private affairs, his profession, his lands, the government, and other matters that did not concern me in the least. Anon, he spoke of his merino sheep, his bucks, his wool—pulled forth a parcel of fine wool,—begged me to take a bit of it.

"I pride myself upon my sheep on Fox river," said the colonel; "my bucks fine, full blood, merinos, cost me five dollars a head."

" Five dollars !" said I.

" Yes, I may say five dollars, though I have paid as high as six. The prairie," continued he, " is peculiarly adapted for sheep. Come, sir, are you inclined to make me an offer for that farm ?"

I begged leave to decline the purchase ; and the colonel was evidently displeased.

" I have another farm, sir," said he ; " a beautiful spot on Fox river; there is a mill site thereon. I'll sell half of it ; or you may build a mill there, while I hold the lands—or let us build a mill there together, it would be as good as coining, at the present prices. Only think, wheat, six York shillings a bushel—flour, one dollar; why, sir, we could make our fortunes. And the farmers round about Fox river want a mill— they would assist us to dig a mill-pond and form a dam."

Finding I was rather cool about the speculation, the colonel leaned back his head, lighted his pipe, elevated his heels upon the top of a high desk, and began asking questions about England and the Eastern States; he had never visited New York, Philadelphia, or Baltimore.

" Hello ! what are you doing there ?" exclaimed a gentleman, peeping in at the door.

" Come in—come along in !" cried the colonel, turning back his head, as he introduced me to an Irish doctor with a most abominable gash over his eye.

" I have been dressing up my article in a new robe," said the doctor.

" Send it in to-night, and I'll revise it," said the colonel ; " but your last critique was too severe."

" I meant it to be so," said the doctor, freely helping

himself to a glass of porter.   "Your health, Mr. ——,
rejoiced to see you here.   Yes, colonel, I like to
bring the sledge hammer down bang upon their noses
—I'll powder their noses, and wigs too."

Four gentlemen entered the office, and were seve-
rally introduced, and shaken by the hand by me.
Another came, of shabby external : he was introduced
as a London gentleman, lately settled in those parts.
He denied being a cockney with great vehemence—

"No, no; I lived in the west-end, amongst the fashion-
ables," said he. ("The devil you did," thought I.)

"Whereabouts, pray, did you hang out, sir?"

"Islington, sir ; high ground—classic ground, near
the toll-gate."

"Then perhaps, sir, you are descended from one
of those generous men who—

> 'Open their gates did throw,'

for the celebrated John Gilpin."

"I never heard of him," said the Londoner, dog-
gedly, not relishing the laughter of his friends.

"Never heard of the immortal Gilpin !" said the
colonel, laying down his pipe.

> "'A train band captain eke was he,
>   Of famous London town,'"

said the doctor, drily.

The Londoner got up, pulled up his shirt collar,
and left the room.

"You have many poets and fine writers in England, sir," said the colonel; "but not one of them all
can approach the sublime Watts."

"Give me Bryant," said one.

"I'll back Goldsmith," said another.

"Watts, Watts!—he is truly sublime," said the colonel. "In reading and singing his hymns, gentlemen, probably you remember that splendid verse, wherein he speaks of bathing his weary limbs in seas of heavenly rest. Oh, sirs, there was an idea—a sublime idea, never yet rivalled," said the colonel, as he repeated the verse, and looked as if he really felt the want of a bath of heavenly rest; though, certes, in my humble opinion, his long weary legs resting on the table, and lank body balanced in the chair, would have been just as much delighted as his imagination, in the midst of a hot bath of clean water.

I found it was no easy matter to get away from the colonel, but succeeded at last, urging that the dinner must be over at the Tremont House, and much as I was delighted with his conversation, I was fain to resort to that unpoetical practice of chewing food.

"You are right, sir," said the colonel. "It is a great pity we cannot live without eating and drinking. I never walk out on the prairie or lake shore, in the wind, without thinking of Job's query—' Can a man fill his belly with the east wind?' The very idea makes me cholicky."

Walking by the lake side this evening, I found a regular encampment of Hoosiers. The Hoosiers are a genus of the pedler tribe, having a dash of the tinker and freebooter in their veins. Having heard the word Hoosier pronounced with respect mingled with fear, in the eastern states, I was happy to fall in with those respectable ogres. Their large covered waggons were drawn up in hollow squares on the lake shore, and their horses, tethered and harnessed, browsed upon the stunted grass. Here and there, fires were blazing, pots boiling, pork toasting. The gaunt uncouth figures of the hoosiers, as they strode about their waggons, puffing clouds of smoke from pipes, and even cigars, reminded me of the tall cavaliers and muleteers lounging about a Spanish bivouac. They (the hoosiers, not cavaliers) had sold the wheat they had collected through the country, to the corn-factors and speculators of Chicago, for six York shillings per bushel, realizing some two or three shillings per bushel more than they had paid for the same; and the empty sacks being piled upon the waggons, formed convenient beds, upon which some half-dozen hoosiers were already wrapped in the arms of Morpheus. Some of the horses were tall and well-shaped, combining blood, bone, and sinew enough for English carriage horses. I noticed particularly a span, or team, of well-matched roans, snorting about one of the waggons, till the Hoosier thrust his head from under the cover, and regarding the horses with a sour countenance, gravely asked them what they wanted—what they meant by keeping up " such a 'tarnal blowin' about the waggon?" The horses, thus rebuked, backed, till the Hoosier pulled in his head, and then they advanced, and began snorting and pawing as before. This roused the Hoosier's indignation, and this time his head, shoulders, and half his lank body, was thrust forth from under the waggon cloth: " Haven't ye had your oats?" he exclaimed, shaking his fist at the steeds—" a bushel between ye! and what do'ee want, zay?" The horses had recoiled as before; but now the off-wheeler advanced, stretched out his neck and stared at his master, while he shook himself so violently, that the heavy saddle (in which the Hoosiers ride like the French postilions) and harness rattled again. " Ho, is that all you want?" said the Hoosier, and speaking to a boy at one of the fires, he bade him unsaddle the horse, and let him roll to h——l if he pleased.

Here, as at Detroit, I am compelled to buy newspapers; though three or four of the eastern papers were in the bar-keeper's possession, he refused to lend them. Those bar-keepers are singular fish, full of airs; without the responsibility of landlord, they affect a superiority of tone, and dole out mint juleps and brandy-and-water, &c. as if they were conferring signal favours most reluctantly upon their very humble servants the boarders.

Here I record once more the obligation I am under to the Young Men's Association, for, *sans ceremonie*, I entered their reading-rooms several times during my *sejour* at Chicago, and read newspapers and periodicals to my heart's content. Chicago also furnishes a circulating library, where strangers will find the recent publications and standard works, novels, &c. of the day. Looking over books one day, I was rather amused to hear a tall, gaunt farmer from a distant prairie, ask for the last part of " Charles O'Malley, the Irish Dragoon." The man of books demurred; it was out—he could not find it. " Well, I'll wait, and put up my team till you find him," quoth the farmer. " I'll not face the girls at home without ' The Irish Dragoon.' "

The demand for " Ten Thousand a Year" was likewise made in my hearing, if not ten thousand times, often enough to shew how anxiously those works are looked for in the West.

CHAPTER XIV.

" THIS is the first time I have set foot on American ground without being hailed by runners, as the hotel porters are called, and still there seems to be a very goodly hotel beside the pillared façade of yon court-house," said I to myself, as the boat shoved off back again to the steam-boat, leaving myself and baggage on the deserted plank wharf of Racine.

Leaving my portmanteau and carpet-bag to the tender mercies of the winds and grasshoppers, I shouldered my umbrella, and marched up to the hotel; entered the bar, found the bar-keeper, and the boarders, the family, and all inmates seated at a long table, enjoying a most luxurious tea.

" Walk in, sir," said the landlady.

" Madam," said I, " my baggage must walk first." What is a man without baggage, without change of raiment, without wherewithal to make his exterior agreeable to himself, and amiable to the ladies?

" Jonathan! Ira! Thomas!" cried the landlady, turning from right to left, and from left to right, with unexpected vivacity, " fly down, and fetch up this gentleman's baggage."

I like Racine; it is one of the prettiest little spots, without pretensions, I have seen for a long, long time. Standing on high banks, or bluffs, above the lake (Michigan), its little white villas and frame houses, backed with the dark green forest trees, the wild ravine, and the river, said to be the only inducement held out by the landowners to settlers who have got up the little town. Land is a drug everywhere; but water, and water power, has a mystic charm that draws men together in this country. The river I soon discovered to be a stagnant pool, or succession of stagnant pools, separated from the lake by a goodly barrier of sand, mayhap earth and rock. When this bar is cut away, and a convenient harbour established—what then? Then, sirs, Racine will become a place of note—the root, as its name betokens, of a flourishing city, rivalling Chicago, and its rival Milwakee.

Having secured a good bed-room I retired, and was roused from my slumbers at cock-crow in the morning, by a loud crash. " Pshaw!" said I, " 'tis a dream." Anon, I slept, and dreamed of earthquakes. Bang—crash! Holloa! here is a pretty kettle of fish —the house is falling. I started from my bed, and in truth I had need—for, lo, and behold! there lay a vast piece of the ceiling upon my pillow, another, and yet another upon the floor, another wedge of the wall leaned upon the table, and, half smothered with dust, I pulled on my clothes and rushed to the door. The door was fast—that is, the upper and under sill held it firmly shut. I had some thoughts of leaping from the window. Heaven help your head—all the arms of Briareus could not open it one inch. The noise I created soon brought the maids to my assistance. Bless the women!—they are ever and aye at hand to extricate me. I found the house filled with dust, and lime, and dirt. The reason was obvious; the house had been built upon wooden blocks, or piles; the new landlord conceived his hotel would stand all the better for being built on rocks and stone. He hires two or three desperate Irishmen, arms them with crowbars, sends them under his cellar, with instructions how to proceed; they begin by knocking away the blocks, and it is only by a miracle that the house remains in an upright position. The landlord blames the Irishmen, the Irishmen blame the whisky; and in the midst of creaking sounds, mortar, and brick-dust, saw-dust, &c., we sit down to breakfast.

Rambling through the woods, I gathered some flowers new to me, and conceived the idea of forming a herbal of Wisconsin flowers. The tract through which I proceeded was little frequented by sportsmen, birds and squirrels exhibiting a tameness not at all " shocking to me." In fact, if I had carried a gun with me, I question if I should have shot or banged at the red, grey, and black squirrels, racing up and down the beech-trees, or quietly nipping off the beech-nuts and acorns, the falling of which produced a sound like the pattering of rain, which, save and except the shrill chirp of the grasshopper, and scream of the red-headed woodpecker, disturbed the solemn silence of the woods.

Sometimes I paused beside a wild ravine, filled with tangle and brushwood, and thought of the tales I had heard of *painters*, or catamounts, or lynxes, springing forth from their dens, and rending the unwary, limb from limb. A more likely spot for such small deer is not to be found in this part of the territory, as a half-breed afterwards told me; but, for my own part, I returned to the falling house, with nearly an armful of flowers and shrubs, and a tremendous appetite, the fruits of my excursion. A smell of rotten leaves and manure pervaded the house, and more especially the dining-room. This might in some measure be accounted for, by the presence of the aforesaid Irish labourers, in their working costume, at the dinner-table. They declared the lower regions, from which they had just emerged, was a sink of mire and abomination "enough to pison the divil himself." How they escaped being crushed and poisoned, I did not learn; but their persons and contiguity at the dinner-table, might have upset a stronger stomach than mine, and I have travelled too far to be very squeamish. Indeed, the house seems in a bad way; and the doors are fortunately open, but no man can shut them again—*ergo,* we must keep open house to-night for all the cats, wolves, and badgers in the country.

I had stipulated that my room was to be kept private, for my own use and enjoyment; judge, therefore, of my wrath and righteous indignation, when the bar-keeper, *sans ceremonie,* marched into my room with candle in hand, introducing an ill-favoured varlet as my room-fellow, if not bed-fellow—a stray passenger from the far west, going down south, or God knows where! I vapoured a good deal—was not the house large enough? Ay, but the rooms were full of mortar, &c. What then?—why there was mortar in my room. It mattered not; my comrade began by un-booting his sore feet. Ye gods, what I must endure ! I'll think of fragrance, and forget the hydrogen, if I can. I never felt more uncomfortable in my life.

The house quaking, and a strange man " grinning ghastly smiles" from his bed in the corner, his shock head unconscious of a night-cap, his grizzly beard, his silence, his dismal boots. And does he think I mean to extinguish the lamp this blessed night? If he does he will have counted without his host. I'll enlighten his dark mind, moreover, with a display of strength that he little calculates on. Anon, I drew forth my trusty double-barrelled pistol, adjusted the caps, and clicked the locks, then examined the point of a dagger, as if it were part of my evening service before bed. " Did you speak, sir?" suddenly turning sharply round, towards the stranger's bed. A deep guttural sound was the reply; another, and another—a snore! Sleep in the room with a snorer ye that can, it is beyond my reach—" the force of nature can no further go!"

Rose this morning in very bad humour—slept badly; resolve to quit this sweet spot immediately. Fortunately the mail-waggon starts from this to Janesville, on Rock River. Secure a seat, paying four dollars for the same; an exorbitant price for a seat in such a lumbering old concern. But two passengers—myself and a carpenter, who carries a tool-chest big enough for a meal-chest or bacon-bin. This abominable chest, or box, caused us much disquietude during the roughest part of the route, tumbling from side to side, till at last it was somewhat steadied by two girls, who seated themselves in the rear. The whip was all politeness and gallantry to the young ladies—they protested they had been tired out visiting their friends. One of them, a pretty dark-eyed girl, was glib and pert of speech; she bandied jests with the carpenter and driver, silenced them by her volubility, and drove the carpenter to commit himself so far as to sing, or make some abortive effort to squall and groan forth, " I see them on their winding way."

Mount Pleasant Post-office : here we stop to deliver the mail, and the postmaster being out, his wife asks us to enter her house, and eat some wild plums while the letter-bag is emptied on the floor, and the good woman, assisted by the carrier and the carpenter, proceeds to select and sort the letters, two children playing with the same.

" Clara, miss! what are you doing? Take your blackberry-stained fingers off the letters. Do, that's a dear! Give me that letter with the red seal."

" No, I wont, ma."

" Give it to me for this plum, dear."

" No, I wont, miss—I'll keep it."

" There! lift up the infant; don't you see the state the floor, and the letters, and the newspapers are in ?" exclaimed the carrier, as the post-mistress caught up her child, and the young ladies eating plums held up their hands and exclaimed, " My !"

We have got rid of the carpenter and his box, and proceed gaily over the prairie ; but the young ladies have grown very reserved, and the driver's jests fall " flat, stale, and unprofitable." The best part of the prairie lands in this district are settled on or taken up by speculators.

Halt at the house or cabin of a New Englander : he owns about one thousand. acres of the prairie, and seems well to do. His wife soon spread out her store of good things before us—fried pork, savoury stew of chicken, prairie-hen, potatoes, &c., tea, coffee, rich cream, pickles, cheese, cheesecakes, cherry-pie, and excellent bread and butter. Our host regulated our

seats at his table with great ceremony:—" Miss Eola
Jemima Flatwash—be seated, miss, at my right hand;
Aristibia Marianna Dido—take your stool, miss, to my
left; stranger—sit down, sir, beside my wife, &c.; and
thus the post-boy and others being adjusted at the
table, we fell upon the savoury viands like prairie
wolves. Here I met one of my Yankee acquaintances, Abimelech Boels, so altered in his outward
man, that I only recognised his guessing voice. Last
time I had seen him, he was dressed up full fig, in
Buffalo, a regular swell, puffing cigars, and talking
like a magnate of the land; now he was clothed in
fustian, sported a vagabond old chip hat, two inches
of dismal beard, and drove a team of blind horses in a
creaking waggon, laden with a winnowing machine,
for cleaning corn.

"I have made a pretty decent speculation," said he,
pointing to " that ar waggon." " I hired that consarn,
horses and yoke, for six York shillings a-day, at Milwakee, took along the machines, set them a-working
for the farmers as was hurried to get their wheat into
the market, worked some, and sold some, and now
I'm going right back with the waggon.".

" I thought you were in the fur trade," said I.

" Well, captain, I'm in the fur trade every winter;
but in the spring and fall I fly round a bit, and in
summer go loafing north-east, like the best of ye."

Mr. Boels then informed me he had fixed his eye
upon a good location near a small lake—a rolling
prairie, and some wood lots. He had fixed it, he said,
and meant to call in at the Land Office at Milwakee,
when he had disposed of his winnowing machine; and
the postman calling out that he was all right, I left
my quondam companion in earnest discussion with

the host, the beauties and perfections of the winnowing machine being "the one loved theme" and topic of conversation.

Halt for the night beside the Fox river, at the tavern kept by the father of one of our lady passengers. This man has not prospered in the West—the cause of his misfortunes stands close by his humble log house in the gigantic skeleton of a frame house, through which the wind groans lugubriously. Instead of buying stock, farming utensils, &c, this unhappy individual has expended his all upon the carpenters and blacksmiths who have erected yon unsightly fabric. He intended to have set up a hotel in the midst of this rising city of five houses, called Burlington; a dam was built across the river, a mill set up by speculators, and anon, half the population swept off with congestive fever—the sure and invariable attendant upon new mill-dams in the West. From this death-blow, the new village has never recovered, though my host believes that "the badness is all out of the mill-dam now;" and that being settled, we sat down to tea; Miss Eola declaring that she cannot stoop to help with a good grace after her visiting tour, same time she assures her fair companion that she may have "her tea free"—to sit down and make herself at home. Our hostess seems to be an amiable person with a sore foot; she rejoices at the safe return of her daughter, to whom the letter-carrier pays fierce and marked attention, which the young lady rejects quite as pointedly. Anon, the host informs me of his losses and misfortunes—his sheep have been devoured by the wolves, and last night his big dog did battle with a vagrant grey wolf, who had smelt out a fatted calf in the stable. "If it had been a prairie wolf I would have settled him with an axe when the dog bruckled him," said he; " but the grey wolf is able for half a dozen dogs, so I only pelted him with stones, till he sheered off."

Tea over, our hostess began to read the newspaper aloud, and her son, a fine boy, was all ear. She read about the burning of the Erie steam-boat—it was a glowing article, a red-hot description of the horrors of the scene and the tortures the passengers endured. Every one listened with breathless anxiety to the account—for several neighbours had dropped in—but the youth crept close to his mother, and looked up, with feverish excitement in his eyes as she read on, till at last she began to read the names of the Swiss and others supposed to be lost, and then the youth burst into tears.

" My !" exclaimed the mother, " what's the matter with the boy ?"

" I've a thorn in my foot," sobbed he, " and I rubbed it now. I'll go to bed."

" Go to bed, you goose !" said the father, not at all approving of his son's sensibility, while the postman and his dearie, who had sat aside in the shade, laughed heartily ; but the laughing was soon silenced by a box on the ear and a scratched face when that gentleman attempted to ravish a kiss from the coy damsel. He was very wroth, and she was called to order by her mother, who told her daughter she should " think shame of herself to be so rude, but that was always the way she went on"—advised her not to carry her head so high, and not to treat her guest so scornfully.

Now, for my own part, I think the said guest, or wooer, deserved the rebuke more than the daughter,

but I never interfere in a family affair. We were
soon ushered up to bed in the garret, in which we
found six beds fastened to the walls, curtained on one
side, and covered closely in at an angle of forty-five
degrees by the roof, and, through the ancient shingles,
the moon afforded the unpleasing prospect of sundry
huge spiders and creeping things hanging over our
devoted heads. The postman slept and snored like
a walrus; the big dog sat down under the window,
and bayed the moon till I wished him at Jericho—

"'Tis sweet to hear the watch-dog's honest bark,"

saith Byron—any time but at midnight under one's
pillow—

" The watch-dog's voice that bay'd the whispering wind."

In truth, this dog seems to bark at the echo
of his own harmonious voice, for, save and except the splash of the Fox river, there is naught else
worth baying at—nathless, till " chanticleer sung
cock-a-doodle doo" I could not close an eye. Breakfast over, we pursue our journey; but, ere we started,
my host took me aside and offered to sell his farm-
house, skeleton of a house and all, for ——, less by one-
half than the log house he occupied had cost; in fact,
he wanted to go further west, he said. But I was not
enamoured with the location either. Paid him my
fifty cents, and went on my way in very dubious
humour, having lost a bunch of keys somewhere between Racine and Fox river. This day our route ran
through splendid prairies; the white and yellow flowers
of the rosin weed and milk weed spread their bloom
to the sun, but not a living thing save a stray butterfly
or, mayhap, a wild bee cheered the eye. I looked in
vain for deer, prairie hens, or prairie wolves—all was
silent as the grave. Sometimes we passed clumps of

trees, and startled a few wild pigeons; the postman, or knight of the post, endeavoured to cheer on his horses with songs and hymns—he had lost two horses, he affirmed, last week, by permitting them to eat prairie grass; but this I could not credit. One of the horses he now drove was borrowed on trial, he said; and a very severe trial he put him to. At mid-day, we stopped at the house of the person he borrowed the horse from, and a long argument took place, the whip and the owner retiring to the rear of the premises for one hour, while I sauntered about the grove and prairie, in quest of flowers, &c. Returning to the premises, I found my whip and the man of the house seated almost back to back upon a bench at the stable door—each whittling away for the bare life, and a goodly heap of shavings before them. Having watched this process for some time, I begged to hint to my mail-carrier that "time and tide wait for no man," and at last succeeded in getting him away from his whittling bench, two hours having been lost thereon; and even then the bargain for the horse was not completed, because, as he said, I had disturbed them.

" The 'tarnal old chip," said he, " he sticks out for seventy dollars for this pony. I offered fifty in dicker, or sixty on time; but it was no go. But I'll be at him again when I'm a-going back—I'll whittle the nonsense out of him."

Dined at the house of a thriving New Englander, who, from small beginnings is now the proprietor of five thousand acres of prairie land; he has enclosed several fields of Indian corn with ditches instead of rails—more permanent work—answering the double purpose of staying the prairie fire and keeping off cattle; he has sunk a well, and built stables, barn, and hog-pen, on a large scale, and, like a wise man, lived, up to this, in a simple log and mud cabin. I am really at a loss to know where the good people in this country—this out of the way place—find all the good things they set before travellers, especially the New Englanders; they seem to live better here than they do at home, and riot in pumpkin pies and all sorts of cakes and meats, savoury stews, &c.; and, to be sure, wine and strong drink is not to be found on the table, but rich cream, and excellent tea and coffee, fill up the vacuum, and invariably conclude a meal fit for an alderman.

The trifling sum of twenty-five cents, or two York shillings a-head, is the moderate demand for all this—and more, for some travellers smoke the landlord's pipe, and others take gum-ticklers and gin-slings by way of a " *chasse café.*"

Near Black Hawk Grove we discovered a flight of sand-hill cranes; about thirty of them alighted on the prairie, and went stalking about like grenadiers—they are said to be very good eating. Black Hawk Grove, or the oak opening, situate on a little hill, was the rendezvous of that celebrated Indian chief, when he carried fire and sword through the regions of his forefathers. Near this place he was taken prisoner by stratagem and the treachery, saith my postman, of the Pottawattomers, and sold to General Dodge. Certes, Dodge and his men have dodged the poor Indians out of the land, and we have passed over land enough this day to have maintained all the whites and Indians in the whole territory.

Janesville: here we arrived at last, in the midst of a storm of wind and rain. The hotel was crowded with wayfaring men; some were very noisy, talking politics at the bar; others, gravely discussing the late

example that had been made of the horse thieves and
gamblers down the river. Twenty had been Lynched
into the flood—and if twenty more had been thrown
after them it would have been no great loss, say they,
for society will purge and purify itself even in a new
country.

Not a man spoke in favour of the unfortunate men
who had met with such an untimely end; and a
stranger upon the banks of Rock River had better
think twice before he disclaims against Lynch law.
For my own part, I believe some such law is absolutely necessary in a country where the executive
moves so slowly that the guilty may easily evade the
grasp of justice, seated upon that clumsy and complicated vehicle, yclept the law of the land. Here I
am happy to secure a single bed, in the midst of
upwards of twenty beds, ranged in the attics of the
hotel—bless the mark!—and slept like a watchman,
notwithstanding the deep bass, and shrill treble
snorers on everyside.

Started across Rock River this morning, with a fresh
letter-carrier, who has a one-horse waggon and two
buffalo robes, sundry sacks of letters, a severely-dressed
gentleman and his trunk, myself, and a youth, bound
for Sugar River Diggins. The horse, I say, has
enough to do to walk with this load at his tail, over
the prairies; and to make the trip more delightful, the
rain began to fall in torrents. Janesville, though the
name betokens a town, contains but three or four
houses in its bailiwick. The site of it is pretty
enough, but the grass grows high enough in the
streets and squares as yet. This dismal day we have
not had a single gleam of sunshine; even the prairie
hens, and we saw several packs, did not think it worth

their while to fly more than a rod or two, when we disturbed them. A walking-stick gun was fired at them, with little effect, and, as I thought, proved a mere catchpenny affair, though the owner boasted he had shot down deer with it. Saw a fine fox leisurely trotting along the side of an oak opening; he was nearly black. Certes, he seemed as vain of his brush, as many of our Eastern dandies, or a Broadway lounger, of his moustache, or rouch. Met a horse trotting merrily along the prairie, with some broken harness dangling about him; he soon joined our horse, with a glad neigh. We caught him, and found it no easy matter to lead him along. Five or six miles further we found the trail of a buggy; followed it, and soon discovered the buggy, upset between two trees, and broken—no owner to be seen. We continued our route through fine rolling prairie and oak openings, quite parkish, and the oak seems to be the only tree that escapes or resists the fires; however, I bserved their stunted growth and gnarled appearance bespoke the rough raising of prairie trees, exposed to winds, fires, frosts, and snows. This day we passed the debris of two houses—one a log, and the other a frame house—which had been burned by prairie fires—fate of the inmates unknown, though their carelessness is manifest to all—a simple trench or ditch round their dwellings would have stopped the fire, or turned aside the destroying element. The absence of streams and ponds of water is one of the draw-backs to a prairie farm; though water is easily found, by digging wells, even on the highest prairie; still, in my mind, a stream of water, though feeble as a silver thread, should be a *sine quâ non* to settlers in the West. Seven miles from the broken buggy, we found an old man asleep under a tree, and, having roused him up, to know what he did there, were favoured with some very hard names, and a sharp rebuke, for having disturbed his slumbers. Rubbing his eyes with his horny brown hands, and stretching himself out longer and taller every minute, he demanded—"Where the d—l we came from!" &c. &c.; then, suddenly starting forward, pounced upon the led horse, exclaiming—"Aha, ye loafing half-breeds, d'ye mean to steal my horse? I'll have ye Lynched all round for this!—where's my buggy?"

"Upset—smashed — wheel upwards — seat downwards, seven or eight miles away, on the prairie!" responded one of my party.

This seemed to recal the wool-gathering brains of this bewildered man, especially as we refused to let him have the horse until he gave an account of himself; and, after some grumblings, he told us, he was "all straight." "You see I've been to Madison with my son the printer, as prints the 'Loco Foco' newspaper; we took a horn before I left, last night, and I came right away in the buggy, and turned in here—so give me the horse, and have done with your jabber." We permitted him to take the horse, and not forget his bottle, which had been his consolation under the greenwood tree.

It was night before we wended our way through the magnificent streets, squares, and avenues of the young capital of Wisconsin. My companions, favoured by the darkness of the night, amused themselves by telling me the names of the various streets we passed through, on our way to the hotel, while I strained my eyes into the oak openings, right and left, in quest of balconies, piazzas, stoops, and colonnades.

Mr. Morrison, the innkeeper, welcomed us to Madison, led the way into his bar, volunteered whisky and water, or a cobbler, to drive the night dew out of our throats. Moreover, the good man accommodated me with a single-bedded room, a luxury I had not enjoyed for some time. Sunday morning: rose refreshed, and marched out to look at the city, which had vanished like a dream, leaving that great unsightly fabric, the capital, with its tin dome glittering in the sun, and some forty houses, of all sorts, shapes, and sizes, rained about here and there sparingly, at the corner of the *projected* streets and thoroughfares of this embryo town. Entered the capital, which I found full of chips, shavings, and mortar: from the door and raised platform, *en revanche,* we have a splendid view of third and fourth lakes—for, as yet, the lakes have been only numbered, it would seem—and there is a chain of beautiful little lakes about Madison. There is nothing grand about the scenery, but all that quiet beauty of wood and water, frequently seen in the old settled country at home. Return to the hotel, which is the largest house in the place, save the capital, and no great shakes after all. In the parlour, I found two spry-looking men seated on a sofa, covered with coon-skin. One of them hailed me directly; he said we had met before, down east, in a steam-boat, though, for my part, I never recollected having had that honour. He began, by telling all he knew about the country; and his calling or profession being that of barrister, or advocate, I did not feel inclined to woo his acquaintance; nevertheless, he resolved to cultivate mine, and we soon jogged along, like sworn brothers. Breakfast, and indeed all our meals, are taken in the cellar, or basement story of the house, where our

hostess, who is said to be a blue, deigned to preside
over the teapot.　Our party was made up of lawyers,
their wives, and certain hangers-on, employed and
expectants at the seat of government, a doctor, and
an exquisite from Chicago, in a very severe blue coat
and plucky waistcoat.　He held his head very high,
as best became him, being employed to cover the
dome of the capital with new tin, in his capacity of
tinker.　Last, not least, at our table, sat the major.
The colonel, captain, or squire, as he was called by
the guests, Bildad Morrison, our respected host—an
original root from the American bottom, as he was
wont to boast, when people spoke of their homes
down east or south—" I'm from the richest soil in
the known world—the American Bottom, in Illinois."　Then followed a grandiloquent account of
the wondrous vegetation, the fruits, roots, and shoots
of that bottomless bottom of rich vegetable matter,
where common blackberries were as big as peaches—
peaches as big as cocoa-nuts, and pumpkins grew as
big (you may stare gentlemen!) as the insignificant elevations called hills in this country.　Wisconsin
is rather flat, but then her pumpkin hills were more
than I could swallow; and I left the table, before
the forest of Indian corn-stalks and the rest of the
monstrosities of the American Bottom were paraded.
By way of dessert, it was a fortunate circumstance
that our host possessed such a garden in his luxu-
riant brain as enabled him to dispense with the
rich productions of Illinois at his table, without a
murmur; but how he had reduced himself and family
to enjoy a tomato, was beyond my comprehension.
Tomato was the word—the theme—the song, from
morning till night—from night till morning. The first

morning I descended to the bar, there sat the colonel in his white and black chip hat, set jauntily over his round, heavy, swelled face, his crooked foot resting on one knee, his twisted hand resting upon that, (he had been blown up at the Diggins, near Mineral Point,) and his expressive mouth full of a red tomato. That swallowed, he held up another love-apple tantalizingly, to a feeble little child, and, mincing his voice, he would exclaim, " Who'll have a tomato? Who'll kiss me for a tomato?" In truth, not I; having in the early part of my days looked upon that grovelling fruit as poison, and never having tasted it even as a pickle with much gusto, I was not prepared to enjoy the tomato feast, at the capital of Wisconsin.

The garden at the rear of the house seemed to produce no other fruit or vegetable. At breakfast we had five or six plates of the scarlet fruit pompously paraded and eagerly devoured, with hearty commendations, by the guests. Some eat them with milk, others with vinegar and mustard, some with sugar and molasses. I essayed to follow suit, and was very near refunding the rest of my breakfast upon the table, the sickly flavour of flat-tongue grass, sour milk, and raw cabbage, being concealed under the beautiful skin of the love-apple I had the temerity to swallow.

At dinner, tomatoes *encore*, in pies and patties, mashed in side dishes, then dried in the sun like figs; at tea, tomato conserves, and preserved in maple sugar; and to crown the whole, the good lady of the hostel launched forth at night into the praise of tomato pills.

Having mustered a party of three idlers—the lawyer, the doctor, and myself, to wit—we go a shooting, beng resolved to kill time, if we can slay naught else, with our rifles. Here the generosity of our host was tested; he had two rifles, which he never used, I wanted to borrow one of them, and leave a fowling-piece and the rest of my baggage for its safe return. No; he had made up his mind not *to loan* his rifles; but he directed me to the house of a man who might *loan* me one, as he was a Britisher also. Away I posted to the house of my compatriot, who kept a bar and billiard-table. Three rough-hewn bumpkins were actually learning to play billiards, under the eye of the marker, a soft-faced, greasy-looking youth; and the reefs in the cloth bespoke the severe play of the backwoodsmen.

Inquiring for the boss, I was directed to a fat, bloated snorer, upon two stools, within the bar; having with difficulty made him understand my position as a stranger and Britisher wanting to borrow his rifle, he extended his fat paw, and we shook hands with great cordiality. His rifle was like himself, rather the worse of the wear, the lock uncertain, and the barrel dirty.

" But you are welcome to it," said he, " such as it is."

He then invited me to drink a *sling* with him, told me a little of his disastrous history, wished he had never left old England, instead of buying farms on the prairie. He had been prevailed on to purchase town lots, ruined, beggared, " and this is all that remains of all I brought here," said he, looking round in maudlin sorrow at the bottles within the bar, and the table without.

We shouldered our rifles, and skirted the lakes in vain—not a shot did we get at bird or beast; the wild ducks fluttered away into the reeds, the bald eagles, and hen hawks watched our motions, and at last we sat down, covered with perspiration, in the vain hope of seeing deer, this being a famous "deer run," according to the doctor. "Twilight gray had, in her sober livery, all things clad ;" and if the deer did not come forth, the musquitoes did. I quietly endured their assaults for some time, till one of them marched down my back and another went to meet him, up my inexpressibles.

"A *pis aller !*" I exclaimed; "there is no deer to be met with, so let us turn our arms upon the musquitoes and on small deer."

My companions agreed it was useless to remain on our knees and elbows any longer, and as we returned we fired random shots right and left. I bagged two woodpeckers, the others robins a-piece, ditto one pigeon claimed by all, having sustained the fire of three rifles before he fell from the branches of the hemlock tree. We endured a good deal of raillery from our host and the ladies, upon our noble exploits, especially as the woodpeckers, robins, &c., were served up in a stew next morning at breakfast.

Wishing to visit Sauk prairie, where a certain Hungarian Count was located, I asked my host to furnish me with a horse.

"Perhaps you want a horse and buggy ?" said he.

I told him a saddle horse would answer my purpose much better.

"Well, there is not a saddle horse to be hired in the place," said he.

"Well, then, the horse and buggy will answer," said I.

"But there is not a horse and buggy you can loan, in Madison ; nor yet a waggon, nor cart, nor mule, nor jackass."

In truth, the only quadrupeds and beasts of burden to be seen in the streets, are hogs and oxen. The hogs, of the true snake-eating, half-rat, half-alligator breed, infest the doors ; the oxen, worn down with toil, jingle their bells as they browse about the highways and bye-ways.

Notwithstanding all this, I soon discovered our obliging host had three good horses in his own stable, yet permitted his guests to go trampling through the woods and swamps, at the risk of their being lost " to him and his heirs for ever," sooner than win golden opinions by accommodating them.

Five days have been consumed in Madison, and I see no prospect of getting out of the place ; the mails are carried to Fort Winnebago, and elsewhere, upon Indian ponies, and Indian ponies don't carry double. I began to prepare a knapsack, look to my boots, and resolved to march out of the capital at peep o' day next morning, but my good intentions were frustrated by an awful thunder-storm, followed by hail and rain ; and immediately after, a waggon, and a pair of cream-coloured horses, driven by a large, good-natured-looking man, with a smartly-dressed dame at his side, pulled up at our door ; and the reeking buffalo robe being handed out, and a chair officially pushed under the lady's feet by the host, Governor Doty and his lady were welcomed to Madison, by every one in the house.

The news of the new governor's arrival soon spread abroad, and before night his Excellency had a regular levee, the bar-room and parlour being filled with official personages, and visitors come to pay their respects. The governor had just returned from St. Peter's, where he had concluded a treaty with a powerful tribe of the

Dacota Indians. The Indians had ceded to the United States a considerable tract of land ; on which the governor intended to carry out his benevolent plan of an Indian farm ; in short, a reserve for the Indians, upon which the whites could not encroach at a future day. School houses were to be established, and farming implements furnished.

I was glad to find, even at the eleventh hour, justice was to be done to the red men of the wilderness ; and the governor rose hourly in my estimation. The weather having cleared up a little, the three chasseurs made a tour to the prairie in the governor's waggon, which he immediately *loaned* us, wishing us success.

Away we went, over roads, ruts, and logs, with the spanking cream colours, but the rain came down in torrents, and we were glad to halt at a settler's foundation, near the prairie. The old man was not at home, and my companions tied up the horses, and then entered the barn, while I made my way into the house, *malgré* a boisterous cur dog. I found the *dame du logis*, a fair-haired little woman, seated in the midst of the kitchen, parlour, and hall, reading a newspaper (not the cleanest), while her help *flew round* and arranged knives, forks, and plates, upon the table. I hailed the omen, and, as we had not dined, beckoned to my companions to come into the house, which they did very reluctantly, as they had not been invited to shelter their heads by the mistress of the loggery, who, being in that way all "ladies like to be who love their lords," maintained her seat, her gravity, and silence, till the old man came in, dripping like a wet sack, and quite as forbidding in his appearance. He was old enough to be his wife's father, and on his rough countenance, begrimed with mire and perspiration, his beard grew out in patches—

> " The upper part thereof was whey,
>   The nether, orange mixed with grey."

He had been laudably engaged frightening the black-birds from his corn-fields, and might sing—

> " They put me in a barley-field to frighten away the crows,
>   And its oh! and its oh! such a beauty I do grow."

Shortly after him two men and a boy, carrying baskets full of wild plums, entered the house ; they were the junior branches of the family, and looked as wet and rosy as their baskets of wild plums. The rain still came down in torrents, and dinner did not make its appearance ; the black pot was full of smoking potatoes, and the stove had ceased to warm the *melange,* heaps of plates, pans, and dishes hanging about it. The members of the household glanced impatiently at the door, —we took the hint—dinner was getting cold—and for the first time I left an American house, in the wilds, with an empty stomach.

" They might have offered us a few plums," said one of my companions.

" Hogs will shew their bristles," was the response of the other, as we returned towards our inn—wet, hungry, and disappointed.

One of our party declared, that in all his travels, he had never met with a more inhospitable set than the settlers we had just quitted ; while another related an anecdote.

He had been travelling in Ohio on a day like this— the rain came down awful, and he put up his waggon and team at a large farm-house; the folks, he said, were like the folks we had just seen, only perhaps they shewed more bristles all at once, for they never asked him to sit down; nevertheless he did sit down, and watch them eating their breakfast; then saw the dinner prepared and eaten. Evening came on, and with it supper for a dozen; they spread out pans of rich milk and cream upon the table, that tempted him sorely to ask for a drop of something to drink, but he refrained; and the boors and their dames began supping up the milk before him. They talked of cows and calves; one said 'he had seen three calves that were reared by one cow.' Another said 'he had seen four that were all suckled by one cow, and became fine beasts.'

" I have seen five," chimed in the hungry chasseur.

" Well, now—that beats all," exclaimed the boor. " We know very well that four calves might suck a cow at the same time; one might suck at one side, one at the other, one before, and one behind; but what did the fifth do?"

" The fifth," said the chasseur—"the fifth—why, he, great calf as he was, looked on like myself, while the others sucked up the milk." " And having said thus, I bowed to the calves and hogs, and drove away in my waggon, at ten at night, not having eaten a morsel the whole day, and my horses having fared likewise in the empty barn."

Once more we endured the raillery of the ladies and gentlemen at home. Forsooth, they had expected to have seen us return with a waggon-load of bar, of buffalo, or deer. " Mighty hunters we were," &c. As it was, we had brought home most voracious appetites in our wet jackets, and the dinner was over. Our hostess, seeing we had returned empty-handed, I suppose concluded we were not worth our salt, which, considering we paid two dollars a-day, was rather hard; so I descended to the lower regions, and discovered, or surprised, our hostess washing her caps. She was very wroth, and directed me to the cook, a brawling Irishwoman, who presided over the culinary department—that insignificant concern being beneath the notice of our literary lady of blue-stocking and cap-washing notoriety. The sorry remains of a cold shoulder of mutton, cold potatoes, and of course raw tomatoes, rewarded my perseverance.

This morning a teamster from Mineral Point halted to bait his weary *span*. Such a favourable opportunity of getting away from the capital is not to be neglected, and three of our party bargained to be carried away, bag and baggage, wherever the said teamster was bound for. Madison is only three years old, contains about three hundred inhabitants. The situation, as I said before, is picturesque and agreeable, built upon a peninsula between two lakes of pure water, having a limestone bottom. As to trade, it has none, nor is it likely to become a place of business; therefore little inducement can be offered to capitalists or speculators to disturb the peace of the community with their varied chimeras. They speak of building a church and chapel, but at present the people put up their petitions in a log cabin, which, though not quite so convenient as a cathedral, answers the same end. Our teamster has picked up a goodly load, two English women, one of them with an infant, only ten days old, in her arms—her husband a disappointed emigrant from Lincolnshire; the governor's secretary, Mr. ——, an amiable young man, travelling (I cannot say post-haste) with dispatches to Washington; the two hunters, one of whom has been staying at Madison for three weeks, in the vain expectation of finding his horse, which he lost *en route* to Fort Winnebago, but now despairs of ever seeing again; myself, the teamster, and his friend. A goodly load to be dragged along the roads by two very so-so horses; and though, for the honour of the thing, we drove out of town in a canter, jostling and rolling about like so many empty baskets, the moment we got into the sequestered road, we alighted, and shouldering our rifles and umbrellas, marched *en avant*, leaving the women and invalids with the heavy baggage. The first day's march, *en route*, we bagged eight prairie hens, some pigeons, robins, quail, and a species of snipe; winged some ducks, which we could not recover from the lakes, and nearly slew a dog in lieu of a prairie wolf. We had waded up a swamp at twilight in quest of snipe, when the heavy splashing of some long-bodied beast behind us attracted our attention. My companion had just fired at a duck, when a low growl and considerable splashing was heard: "It's a wolf—a wolf!" he shouted, " fire upon him;" and I ran through the marsh in full pursuit of the retreating wolf, gun cocked, ready to slap-bang at him the first view I got of his pate. " Dinna shoot, mon—dinna shoot my doggin," hallooed a brawny Scot, who had watched our motions, and thus saved his cur from being peppered. He invited us to enter his dwelling, hard by, and a more miserable human abode I had never seen; it was little better than a hole scooped in a bank under the root of an oak tree; here the squatter's wife offered us milk. I did not admire the appearance of the man, though he talked very big about his farm, and said he came from the birth-place of William Wallace, at hame, not being able to tell in what shire said birth-place, or his late home was to be found. This night our caravan halted at a large farm-house near Rock river. The farmers were flourishing like flaggers; they had fields of Indian corn and wheat, and oats, and pumpkins, and potatoes, and vegetables; in short, the farmers get on famously here: they have no roots and stumps to contend with, and the soil seems to be inexhaustible. We sleep up stairs—only seventeen in one chamber; beds on the floor; pillows, at least mine, was a goodly cheese; ropes of onions, in festoons, my curtains.

Breakfast upon a savoury stew of the game we shot yesterday—snipes, prairie hens, quails, pigeons and robins, all stewed up together, so that the particular flavour of each bird was lost in this splendid soup a la Meg Merriles. Cross the Rock River in a ferry-boat, below the ancient city of Aztalan, as the village, or half dozen huts and some green Indian mounds, are called. A farmer shewed me sundry bits of pottery and brick which he said, with great reverence, had been lately dug up from the ruins of Aztalan city, but I assured him his antiquities were the remnants of some Indian camp—the debris of a savage, instead of a civilized race, which he contended had established the city of his pride.

Whitewater is decidedly the prettiest little village I have yet seen in this wild country; the villas are built apart, as they ought to be, with great regularity, each having a goodly garden of rich soil; so that, in the words of Goldsmith, "Every rood of ground (may have) maintained its man," even in a town, without the aid of the noble army of capitalists and speculators and their martyrs. There are several Germans, and some very intelligent New-English folks at Whitewater. They have a mill which does not require great water-power; and if the great manufacturer can be kept at bay, they will grow up a happy community, in the midst of a fine agricultural and pastoral country.

Between Whitewater and Prairieville the country is thinly settled, most of the land being taken up by speculators. This is the ruin of the country, but it is to be hoped the tax on wild land will soon make the speculators either reside on, or sell their prairies. The teamster pointed out sundry thriving farms, which he termed Bachelor's Ruins; though, for my part, I saw nothing ruinous about the farms so called, but quite the reverse. One of the mighty hunters and myself refuse to dine at the house of an invalid; but most votes carry, and we march on, leaving our party to eat and drink beside the bed of a man laid up with fever; but whether infectious or not, they neither know nor care. We had not walked a mile before we arrived at another settler's house. The man was working in his garden, and we wistfully eyed his melon patch. The boor spoke about the goodness of his melons; I walked on, but my companion told him I was a stranger, and got a couple of water melons from him, as he said, on my account. I did not relish the jest at all, nevertheless the water-melons were very acceptable. Passing another house, I voted we should go in and demand dinner. My companion said it was my turn to go beg. I went into the house, and finding it a dirty hovel, merely asked a dowdy Irishwoman to cut me a slice of dubious-looking bread, for that poor traveller, weak with the hunger, under the tree yonder. She did so; and looking out, said something about "a hard case." I enlivened her face with a shiner, and running to my Nimrod, gave him a hunch of bread, which he munched, saying it was very sticky; and when he had finished it, told him I had begged it on his account. He was very wroth, but I told him we were quits now; for if he had begged melons for me, I had begged bread for him.

CHAPTER XV.

PRAIRIEVILLE : here we halt for the night, and find the public-house crammed full of emigrants and residents—great politicians, great wranglers. Leaving those disputants in the bar-room, I was fortunate enough to get into a single bed in a long bed-room, in which beds for seventeen were laid down. Woke up from my slumbers at a very early hour by the deep concert of the snorers in every direction, and found the fog boiling into the room through the open windows. In this place, and, indeed, all along the little Fox river, the fever and ague may be traced. Breakfast upon the game we brought in ourselves, and pursue our journey through a densely-wooded country. We have left the pure air of the prairie behind us, and now we progress very slowly over the worst road I have ever travelled—in fact, the trees have been just cut down and pulled aside, and the stumps, rocks, and ruts, render it almost impossible for the horses to tug the waggon along. This being Sunday, we have put up our guns and rifles, and walk before the waggon, perspiring at every pore and panting for breath. From time to time we pass groups of Norwegians, who have emigrated from their own forests to locate themselves in the only difficult and impracticable belt of woods in Wisconsin; they have already made some little clearing, but I think their labour and time quite thrown away. At last, *Dieu merci,* we catch a glimpse of the blue waters of Lake Michigan, at the end of the long avenue of dismal woods and infamous roads through which we have been wending our way for hours from Prairieville to Milwaukee. Even in that short route of fifteen miles I suffered more from heat and fatigue than I have yet experienced in America; for what with the closeness of the air, absence of water, and—but here we are at last, crossing a good wooden bridge into quite a gay looking town — white stoops, sign boards over stores, houses and villas perched on high banks and cheerful aspects—our waggon proudly drawn up at the door of the Milwaukee House. We are invited to enter and prepare for dinner by one host, while the other (for there are a pair of them) recognises one of our party as an old friend, and invites him into the bar.

From the stoop in front of our hotel, we look down upon the river—the lake *a la distance*—the wooded point, on which white villas already begin to rise— the marsh, through which a road has been made and lots conveyed—and the main street. In another direction we see the light-house, the episcopal church, the presbyterian and methodist chapels, and sundry gay white cottages rising out of a scrubby sort of jungle which grows on the high bluff above the lake. Altogether, it is not an unpleasing picture; and when we reflect that seven years ago there was only a single farm-house in the place and a few Pottowattomie wigwams, we must acknowledge that the Yankees possess the locomotive power of getting towns along faster than the Canadians, and to better purpose.

Many of the store-keepers, clerks, and single-men lodgers, editors of newspapers, and clericos, board at our house : certes, the charge for bed-room, board, breakfast, dinner, tea, and supper is not very exorbitant—only six York shillings a-day, and everything in very good style. Finding my host civil, though not at all communicative, I resolved to stay a few days at Milwaukee, to watch the progress of men and things in this singular place. It is no easy matter to pick information out of the denizens here; in other countries, a man may pick up some knowledge, even at a *table d'hôte;* but here every man seems wide awake—all eyes, no ears, hands and mouth generally full of his own affairs—his meals are dispatched with impatient haste, bordering on voracity—after meals, he swingeth upon his chair, squirting tobacco juice, hands thrust deeply in pockets, or whittling toothpicks—he swallows a gin-sling, and flings out of the door—he's gone, like a streak of oiled lightning. Whosoever thinks he receives information from one of these slick gentlemen, I say, has been, to use their own singular expression, " *sucked*"—left clean as an empty egg-shell, for the rule is to " gammon a stranger" who persists in asking questions, telling him something " awfully musical," and receiving as much of his plain history and adventures as he is ass enough to communicate.

The rival editors of the Whig and Loco-foco papers board in the house, and lash one another daily in the columns of their papers. One has inserted a paragraph, saying, " that his rival has not paid his board bills ;" the other demands the author of that base calumny, and openly declares his intention to shoot the author of it on the spot, whenever he finds him, and goes about armed for this purpose. Matters in this position, it is somewhat amusing to see the editors sitting balanced on their chairs in the bar, grinning defiance at each other; one picking his teeth and squirting tobacco-juice and blood on the floor; the other, fiercely whiffing a cigar with his heels in the air; while mutual friends and admirers lounge round, reading their lucubrations and red-hot articles aloud, from the columns of their favourite papers.

Several Germans have built houses and settled down here. One of them, a very intelligent, hard-working fellow, was a gunsmith; he had plenty to do, repairing old rifles and fowling-pieces. As he did a small job for me, I generally spent half-an-hour in his shop every day, inspecting the singular armoury, old French, Dutch, German, and English guns and pistols, for every man westward-bound thinks he must bring a rifle or fowling-piece with him, which presently gets out of repair, and is sent unto my friend, the gunsmith, and either forgotten, or "left till called for" in his custody.

I found the Indians generally loafing about his house; they seemed to take particular delight in looking at the guns, and watching the gunsmith as he laboured at the bench. Same time, he assured me those Indians, (Pottawattomies, from whom the town lands were bought,) were never troublesome; they preferred the ground in front of his house because it was the highest spot about the town, (except our hotel,) from which they could look down upon the stirring scenes going on below. But whenever a gun was to be tried, their joy was great—they fixed up a board for a target, and even the old men and boys tumbled head over heels, in their speed to examine the mark when the shot was fired.

This gunsmith was a native of Nassau, he had recently read Stephens's new work, and was anxious to converse about Indian antiquities, Jews, and Egyptians; but our conversations were frequently disturbed by his good frow, a tall, severe-looking woman, older than himself. The moment his file and hammer ceased to grate on the ear, a door opened, and that good dame pronounced a few mystic words, and he scrambled up his file, and worked away. Indeed, it is not clear to me but the good woman directed part of her rebuke to myself for idling her man, and loafing about the store, like an Indian.

Here I became acquainted with several Germans, and, amongst the rest, a very worthy man, a chandler, from Wirtemburg. The Germans were dissatisfied— they said they had expended their money building houses in this town; that they had originally intended to have settled on prairie lands, and farmed; many of them had been educated for that purpose at home, in the agricultural schools or colleges, but when they landed here, they could find no prairie lands—all seemed wood, and therefore they did as the Yankees did.

Now, they discovered that there were plenty of prairie only fifteen miles from them, but they could not buy a single acre of it, and were hard set to make both ends meet. They wished to know if I had purchased prairie lands, and would lease them, or farm a rural establishment of some sort on the prairie. I was grieved to see the poor fellows so much cast down, and assured them that if I did purchase lands in the prairie, I would not forget them.

All the drudgery and heavy work at our hotel is performed by the poor German girls, who are actually obliged to carry heavy logs of fire-wood, wash the house linen, and scrub away from morning till night. My righteous indignation was roused one morning when I saw a fair, delicate, blue-eyed German girl, sustaining a load of wet, slippery firewood in her white bare arms, while a clumsy, vulgar, insolent fellow, employed about the yard, was lading the poor girl with more than she could well carry.

" Come, I'll put this here crooked one on top of all," said he, thrusting a coarse wet branch into the poor girl's fair bosom.

" G-u-u-t," murmured the patient creature.

" Zay, hold on, missus!—put this'n under your arm," and another stick was thrust under her arm. " Zay, hold on; put this round one between your———"

The poor girl dropped her load in an instant; she had still spirit enough to resent the boor's indecent assault. She ran to the house with tears in her eyes, and the clown seeing me approach, retreated into a stable-loft.

Several bands of Norwegians have recently arrived in the town; these hardy woodsmen have been to the land office, and bought up lots in the woods. Meantime they lodge in a public-house, where the Germans have a rendezvous every night, and sing the songs of their distant fatherland. Sometimes they sally out at night, retiring from the public-house, and sing for an hour through the deserted streets. One night I was roused from my slumber by a band of those sons of harmony; they marched past, singing the national hymn of Norway, a wild and melancholy air, and as the singers retreated down the lake shore, the music had a peculiarly plaintive and solemn effect. I afterwards heard it was a band of Norwegians, who were thus chanting their favourite airs as they marched away into the woods in search of their new homes.

" Catch'em, say, catch'em !" said a letter carrier one fine morning, as he held up his hands, *en passant*, in the street, and tossed a bunch of keys at my head— the bunch of keys I had lost on the trail between Racine and Janesville, and despaired of ever seeing again. I note down this as a proof of the willingness to serve, help, and oblige a stranger, displayed by the rough pioneers of the western world.

This morning all the sportsmen are out shooting wild pigeons; amongst the rest, my shadow, Lebanon Slope, a young gentleman from Massachusets, who is waiting for a consignment of goods, from New York, for his new store, in which he intends to make a rapid fortune in Whitewater. He heard me speak in praises of the rising little village of Whitewater, the home of his choice, and from that moment we were inseparable. In the woods, I found Mr. Slope at my heels, bleating about Whitewater; on the lake shore his shadow was seen in the water. I clambered up the steepest and most impracticable part of the banks, and now, thought I, Mr. Slope must slope at least a mile round before he finds me out again ;—not at all; for, lo and behold ! Mr. Slope glides up the bank after me, and sitting down, pulls out his knife and whittles away, while he persists there is no place like Whitewater.

" We are all young fellows there, growing up together in the bands of harmony ; and in a few years when the territory becomes a state, we shall be men of weight and consequence; men respected—the patriarchs of the republic. Our names will be engraven upon the tablets of history; it will be recorded that we were the first who dared to establish our free institutions in the wilderness. Come, sir, you are at present little better than a disjointed member of society; join our enterprising gallant band. Go it while you are young, for when you are old you can't."

This was the favourite, and not very elegant finale of Lebanon Slope's harangue. He was a shrewd, clever fellow, and will, I am sure, succeed wherever he is.

The pigeons flew very low, whole flocks skimming over the tops of the bushes, as fast as they arrived from their long flight across Lake Michigan. The townsmen kept up a perpetual fusilade; whenever I fired, Mr. Lebanon Slope fired also, with a pocket pistol, with which he pretended to shoot birds on the wing, and as often as a pigeon fell, he would run forward and grasp it, exclaiming, " There was a shot for you! Go it, while you're young! How slick my ball went through his eye." At one period we had exhausted our wadding, so hot had been the battle, and I was fain to wad down my powder and shot with dried leaves. But Slope was ready to keep up the play, without being beholden to the trees; tearing off his shirt sleeves, he soon made wadding enough for his pistol, and pulling out his shirt bosom and collar, he threw the residue of his shirt to me, exclaiming, " Go it, while you're young!" &c. The poor pigeons are fair game everywhere, but it is when they roost at night they are killed in cart loads even with poles. I observed some vagrant hawks hovering over some of the flocks, just as they approached the shore, and struck down sundry lagging birds, as if in mere watonness; indeed I once nearly captured both hawk and pigeon, for both whirled down into the lake; the hawk got wet, and was only able to fly a short distance from the dead pigeon, when he alighted upon a rock, with drooping wings. Mr. Slope begged of me to let him fire his pistol at the bird, instead of capturing him alive, as I intended; but my friend's pistol was not so unerring this time; the ball skipped along the lake, and the wild hawk, having dried his wings in the sun, soared into the blue sky aloft, and looked out for a fresh quarry. The early flight of the pigeons predict storms and severe weather, and we soon experience the change from calm, delightful days, to rough, boisterous storms; rain falls in torrents, and we are regularly weather-bound. The lake looks like a vast sheet of foam, and the steamers and other craft have disappeared altogether.

Some wayworn and weather-beaten travellers have arrived from Green Bay; they declare the road to be in a dreadful state; between floods, and sloughs, and fallen timber, they were obliged to fag along on foot, leading their horses, and occasionally camping out, when they found it impossible to kindle a fire, owing to the rain and damps. One man had lost a very fine horse, he said, though he tied him to a tree—he broke loose, and he despairs of ever seeing him again. This was not very encouraging to me, especially as I had made up my mind to visit Green Bay; indeed, I found it would be madness to attempt the journey alone in such weather, and quietly awaited a change for the better. Seated one night at a game of chess with my friend Slope, beside the fire in the bar, the door was burst open by three dirty-looking sailors, one of whom pompously declared himself to be the captain of the Yankee schooner; he was half seas over and lame into the bargain——an Irishman to boot. Our hosts glanced timidly at each other, as the "gem" of the lake demanded a bed. They said they had no bed for him; whereupon he was supported out of the house with great solemnity. Half an hour after his exit, three of the most villanous desperadoes I ever saw, entered the bar-room, briskly. They inquired if the captain of the Yankee lodged here; then sat down by the fire, called for a bottle of brandy, swallowed the best part of it, and the leader of the gang then demanded " if that barrel of white fish had been received by the host." The host replied in the negative.

" I guess you forget the present of white fish which the captain of the Yankee sent you, gentlemen," said another of the gang.

The people of the house declared they had never received any present from the captain.

" I guess we have a score to settle right off with you," retorted the strangers, rising up.

" Will you pay for your brandy, gentlemen?" said the bar-keeper, obsequiously approaching the desperadoes.

" Go to —— with you, you d——d lubberly, chuckle-headed varmint," thundered one of the party, while the rest, throwing their arms a-kimbo, laughed outrageously, and the whole party retired, with their brandy, unmolested. I was not sorry to see the bullying bar-keeper slink aside in confusion. He was my detestation. I do not really think I ever heard him say a civil thing, or cease blustering, while I was in the house.

Among the fashionable arrivals at our hotel, we had a certain great military doctor and Indian agent, and his wife and child, from Prairie de Chien; he was *en route* to Florida *via* New York, where he intended to leave his wife; but his plans and his temper were sadly broken up by the bad weather. He chafed himself almost into a fever, at being weather-bound for a week at Milwaukee. His wife was a very agreeable, lady-like woman—an easy soul—she laughed at her husband's vain vapourings, and seemed resigned to her fate. She told me a few anecdotes of our Captain M——tt who had lodged at her house in Prairie de Chien, and was " quite a bear in his manner," she protested. She said there was another singular Englishman who had been loafing about Prairie de Chien, and the islands, for a year. " He was a man of good address," she said, " and great information." At last the governor thought he was tampering with the Indians, and had him arrested forthwith. His papers were searched, and it was then discovered that he was a man of large fortune, who had been quarrelling with his own family in London, and had deserted them all. After this, he was set at liberty, and two of the most respectable merchants at Prairie went bail for him, but he never returned to the governor again.

The Madison steamer has been lying at anchor off the mouth of our river for the last three days; she is waiting for wood, and cannot receive any assistance from shore, such is the tempestuous state of the lake; but at last, the master of the little steamer in the river resolves to make a dash out to relieve her, and we hasten on board this little cock-boat steamer, and run

o

down the river, which is deep enough to float a vessel of three hundred tons, till we come to the Bar—"ay, there is the rub"—our little steamer not only got a-ground on it, but was nearly swamped by the surges of the lake, which dashed her against the side of a large steamer which has been run hard aground on the Bar by some smart fellows of Milwaukee, who had a share in her; finding they were not paid their dividend, they made a bold stroke—actually took the steamer out of the harbour in Buffalo, in which she had been laid up, and ran away with her, pursued by two or three fast steamers, but she had half a night's start of the others, and beat them all hollow. The Milwaukee boys attempted to run over the Bar, and jammed the boat so fast, that she must be taken to pieces before the passage can be cleared; as it is, we were dashed against her clumsy sides, and were glad to get back again to the town, where we went to bed, and renewed our experimental voyage next day with better success, making desperate attempts to board the Madison, by means of a sliding plank, sometimes our boat being swept clean away from the high wall-sided steamer, and the next moment dashed up right against it, during which time we scrambled on board of her. The doctor's lady shrunk back from this disagreeable step; she vowed she could never—"no never!" take such a stride. The doctor was in despair. "Tut, tut—for shame!" he exclaimed. "You must jump, my dear;" and, with a sailor on each side and the doctor in the rear, the poor lady was bundled up the side, in spite of her cries and resistance; certes the poor doctor suffered for his want of gallantry; the lady peppered him roundly for his rudeness, and recovered her tone directly when her little girl insisted on sitting on her lap—" No," said she; " sit on your sweet papa's lap."

" Yes, she may sit on my knee," said the tender father; " she knows who she loves best. Why do you look so grave, my dear—my sweet little Kitty?" and the doctor dandled his pet on his knees, till suddenly he altered his note—" Mrs. L——,—I say, Mrs. L——, take this child, ma'am."

" Keep the child yourself, doctor."

" Madame, look at the state of my new military pants,—take the girl, I say."

" Not I, doctor; I have a new silk gown to look to."

" Stewardess—stewardess—stewardess!" roared the doctor, as he rushed out of the cabin, with his screaming little burden, while the lady coolly arranged her curls in the glass, and took up a newspaper.

Once more I land at Makinaw. The little village is quiet enough now the Indians have dispersed, and the fishermen and Frenchmen have gone off with their boats and canoes to seek for white fish and salmon. I was directed to the gate of a tavern, where they took in lodgers; entered the yard, and found two bears tightly chained near the door of this pleasant hotel. My request for a bed was treated with disdain by a fat frowsy old woman, while a stupid old boor, named Monsieur Lasley, pointed to a corner house, and signified I could get lodgings in it. This proved a stupid jest. I knocked at the door in vain; till a young woman in a neighbouring house told me, the house I knocked at was uninhabited and deserted. " What a vile, inhospitable place this is!" I exclaimed —and the good woman, anxious to save her town from such an imputation, invited me to enter her cottage. It was very small—two little rooms, a bed-room and kitchen, was the whole extent of the domicile. This young woman, and her two very fine noisy children, interested me so much, that I was not aware of the lateness of the hour, till her husband, an active pushing fellow, came home, with his cows. He said, since I had found my way into his humble shed, he would try and fix up a bed for me; and forthwith went out, and returned with a borrowed bedstead on his back, which he fixed up in a corner, and we sat down to supper, as happy as kings or presidents.

This morning I took a walk round the island with a friend of my hostess, a young half-breed, an Indian Missionary bound for Grand Passage, where the Methodists have an establishment. We explored an old fort, called Fort Holmes, on the highest part of the island. It commands the new fort completely; and, with a single gun planted here, the British retook the fort last war, and held it till the peace. The island abounds in picturesque views, and beautiful sites for villas; the air is peculiarly clear and refreshing; altogether, it is considered a healthy and delightful summer residence. We explored a singular cave, and a high picturesque natural arch, or bridge, north of the island; it looks from the lake shore like the stupendous portal of a giant's castle; the dwarf pines, and some resinous shrubs, and natural woods of stunted growth, cover the hills and valley of Makinaw, though sometimes we discovered a green spot, where our soldiers planted vegetables &c. in days gone by. The Indians look on this island with superstitious dread, and have many legends concerning it. I cannot forget—indeed, I have many reasons to remember—Makinaw and her inhabitants. The only hospitable man in the island is my host; the only woman of any feeling, my hostess. This conclusion I made, on being tricked by some rascally half-breeds and French, with whom I entered into an agreement to go to Sault St. Marie, in a canoe. My host assured me I ought not to trust them, and it was mainly owing to his exertions that my baggage was not carried off by those scamps in broad cloth, who, watching their opportunity, went off without me, this being the only time, and the only place, in all my travels and voyages, I have been served so scurvy a trick.

Embark on board the steamer, Columbus, and find a singular-looking genius reading the "Edinburgh Review," by candlelight. While the fire-wood was dragged on board, I heard some coarse jokes passing amongst the sailors, and one of them observed—"Well, I think Pat has got his last drink, now!"

"He was always thirsty," said another.

And then I learned that a man had fallen into the water, and been pulled out of it, insensible. Groping my way through piles of fire-wood, along the wooden pier, I directed my steps to where the rumbling sound of a rolling barrel and loud and noisy words, oaths, and laughter, announced that something singular was in the wind. The mob had been rolling the body of the man taken out of the water upon an empty flour barrel. They stopped at the door of a public-house; the body was carried in, and laid naked on the floor—rubbed with whisky, by the orders of one of my steam-boat friends, a gentleman from New York, who exerted himself nobly to restore animation to the body, rubbing with both hands and blowing into his nostrils. As to the town doctor, he moped about, neither doing nor saying anything.

" Will you bleed him, Doctor ?" said one.

" I will, if you like," said the doctor; and a vein was opened.

I wished them to put the body into a warm bath, but no hot water could be found, nor yet a bellows in the whole place. Makinaw could not afford even a pair of bellows. The mob began to disperse, and, by great exertions, I got the stupid old woman of the house to kindle a fire in the stove, and had the body removed to an inner room. The old French woman went round the body, wringing her hands, and crying—" Ah, mon Dieu, quel malheur! pourquoi a t'on apporte ce cadavre ici." A plate of hot salt was the last experiment I tried, but it was all useless, the vital spark having fled for ever. Every one had deserted the room, save myself and the old Frenchwoman. Presently, she said she would look after the clothes, and I was left alone, watching the dead.

There was something peculiarly stern, yet sorrowful, in the countenance of the corpse, that made a deep impression on me. Here was all that remained of a stranger, who, by a single false step, had been changed from a vain, and perhaps boastful, lord of the creation, to a helpless and inanimate mass—trodden under the foot of the lowest of the low, and spurned in the dust.

" His name is—here! you can read it, ma cher," said the old woman, as she presented me with a little Roman-catholic prayer-book, which she found in the coat-pocket of the deceased ; but Patrick was all I could make out. Patrick! Then the defunct had been Irish !—some luckless wight, who had crossed the seas, and mayhap braved a hundred dangers, to perish thus miserably at Makinaw, unpitied and unknown.

CHAPTER XVI.

THE crank little steamer, Columbus, having wea-
thered the equinoctial gale, which had blown her
out of her course, through death's door, and the
dangerous navigation, hidden flats, swamps, shoals,
stumps, and snaggs, beset Green Bay. On Tuesday
morning we rushed ashore, and sought shelter in
the Astor house, from the " pelting of the pitiless
storm." Being lightly incumbered with baggage, I
made my entré, upon the bar-room books, a-head
of my fellow voyageurs, thereby securing the luxury
of a single-bedded room to myself. Green, the
landlord, a right red-faced jovial old Boniface, flew
round the stove, thrusting huge billets of wood into
its fiery maw, and thus enabled the half-drenched
passengers, as they dropped in, to keep up the steam
till breakfast was ready. The bar-room was soon
filled with passengers and townspeople, the denizens of
Astor and Navarino. Hot politicians, they came full
fig to hear the news, give their opinions, and express
their sentiments, puffing tobacco-smoke, and squirting

the juice in every direction, and frequently excluding the travel-stained voyageurs from the benefit of the fire.

" The first act of the British, in the event of war, which, of course, is inevitable," said one of the townsmen—" the first act of the British will be, to set the Indians upon us."

" It has been always their policy to act so," responded a thin-legged old bachelor, with grey whiskers, black wig, and a long-bodied pea-jacket.

" And it is our duty," said the first speaker, " to prepare for the worst. Let us be on the alert, gentlemen ; let us look to our arms. How many stand of arms have we in the fort to-day ?"

This, and sundry inquiries of a similar description, being vaguely responded to by the gentlemen present, the first blusterer declared, that it behoved every man to look out for spies.

" Right, judge !—right, judge !" grunted three or four steady smokers.

" Ay, let all parties unite—let all parties join 'pro aris et focis,' gentlemen of Astor and Navarino. Let us look out for spies—British spies. I can remember when André was hanged for a spy. British spies are sent amongst the Indians now; I have information on that head. Let us be prepared for action, do our duty, hang them up for a spoi, as I said, and a spoi"—

Here a whiff of tobacco inhaled, choked the judge's oratory ; he coughed, belched, sneezed, while his bloated and glowing visage being wrathfully turned from one stranger's face to another, seemed to court a black eye from the clenched fist of some indignant Britisher. I felt vexed and annoyed with this man's

balderdash, and, indeed, with the severe and unfriendly
tone of the townspeople present.   With the exception
of the host, they seemed bent on kicking up a row.
I thought it unhandsome, to say the least of it, to set
upon strangers in this way, and with difficulty refrained
from speaking my mind, though the New Yorker soon
silenced them when they began to discuss the political
affairs of the Union, and in the midst of their vapouring about congress and their delegates, wondered why
they gave themselves so much trouble about matters
that in nowise concerned them.   " For ye are only
the president's children," said he ; " you have no
more influence in congress than the Indians you seem
so much afraid of."

I could have embraced the man ; even the judge,
in his grey pepper and salt raiments, slunk out of the
room, and the rest seemed extinguished in their own
insignificance ; but the moment the New Yorker
marched off, the alarmists returned in full force ; and
as no man with a roof over his head would venture out
in such dreadful weather, I was doomed to stay at
home and listen to the long tirades of the judge, the
general, the colonel, the major, the captain, and every
bellicose and pot-valiant wight, who chose to rant his
hour in our bar-room, till at last matters wore a
gloomier aspect than ever ; for M'Leod's case being
discussed for the nine hundred and ninety-ninth time,
and the prisoner duly hanged and quartered, the
boundary line wiped out from the map, and laid down
again convenient to the North pole, questions of
greater import came on the tapis.

Two of our deck-passengers, just arrived from down-
east, had been arrested in a store in Navarino, where
they had attempted to pass bogus (base coin) and

o 3

wild-cat money; and being examined before the
judge and justice, they admitted they were going to
the Indian payment. The judge declares he is surprised at nothing that he hears, and sternly informs
us—" We have, in bridewell, two very suspicious characters already. Gentlemen, you are aware of how
those fellows came here ten days ago, inquiring about
the Indian payment also. They stole a waggon—what
was their object in stealing that waggon, gentlemen of
the jury? (beg pardon, thought I was on the bench.)
Plainly and openly, it was to carry off the dollars—
the specie intended for the Indians. They meant to
intercept the agent, swamp the money-boat, (we have
no soldiers here, thanks to the Whigs, to escort even
an agent,) and so sure were they of ultimate success,
that they stole Sy Hackman's waggon. Two of the
confederates have arrived by the Columbus; did I say
two?—many—yes, many of that desperate gang may
have arrived by the Columbus, as will be seen. It is
a plot—a conspiracy; we are surrounded by spies,
blacklegs, thieves, vagabonds, soaplocks, rowdies,
loafers—look to it Mr. Agent, look to it, gentlemen of
—of—Astor and Navarino!"

The Indian agent, a thin, nervous, gentlemanly-
looking man, looked up like a startled rat. On hearing the judge's declaration, he coughed out a response
about " doing his duty, and no more ; and this being
his first expedition to the Indian country as paymaster,
expressed his great anxiety about the money-boxes,
his regret that government, in its wisdom, had not furnished him with a guard of soldiers, as usual."

" The regular troops have been removed from our
fort—it is a fact," said a tall, spare, hook-nosed, old
smoker, called the Major, who had kept up such a

well-directed stream of tobacco-juice, and latterly blood, upon the base of the stove, that I really wondered where such a reservoir of nastiness could have flowed from ; indeed, the floor was defiled in every direction. It was enough to make a dog sick, and did make two dogs sick close to the stove ; and a third, a great black pointer, chose to relieve his stomach upon the red damask sofa, upon which a hot politician sat down unwittingly, and made a great disturbance till the dogs were kicked out. "The regular troops are gone," said the major, "but there are more ; there are soldiers enough in Astor and Navarino, to guard their own. Where is our troop of cavalry? If the agent wishes it, he can have an escort of good men and true."

This idea suited the present exigency of the times ; there was a deal of irrelevant conversation about sabres and pistols, and carbines, and horses, and saddles ; and, finally, it was proposed to the agent, (who, with his clerk, sat playing draughts at a broken old draught-board, eking out the men with cents and bits of wood,) that he should call on the volunteer cavalry corps to escort him to the payment ground.

But the agent declined the honour ; he was not instructed to bear their expenses, by the government, and for his part, a *pis aller*, he would start in the morning without a guard.

This reply threw cold water on the red-hot volunteers ; they remonstrated ; nevertheless the agent remained unshaken. He was warned by the judge, the general, the major, the captain, and others, as to "the risk he ran of being cut off, waylaid, and done for, by the desperate gang lying in wait for him at the rapids."

Finding all attempts to get up a *corps de garde* ineffectual, several of the pot-valiant men marched off in a huff. But the major waxed merry upon the occasion; he said, "He had never seen an Indian payment, and from all he had heard about those payments, he had not the slightest desire to see one. He would not walk five rods to see one—not he. He had been satisfied by hearing a neat account of the last memorable payment, at which one man was burned alive, two women killed, several wounded, the whites routed, and several of our brave corps," said the major, "put to flight, and sent home *sans chemise.*"

The major here recited some verses of a burlesque poem, written upon the retreat of the Green-Bay Greys from the Wolf River Payment Ground, by a medical bard, who had been at the *mêlée* and witnessed the "scateration." I regret I did not note down the first verses, which occasioned much laughter, as celebrating the prowess and valour of sundry gentlemen in the room; they good-humouredly joined in the laugh raised at their own expense; and the major continued—

> " ————Further into the wilds,
> Penetrated Mister Childs,
> Regardless of his proper ease,
> He dash'd on bravely *sans chemise:*
> He saw the major in a slew,
> But never said, ' old friend, adieu !'
> He left the colonel, barely tree'd,
> Yet never slack'd his headlong speed.
> The night was dark, his back was bare,
> Wild Indians howling in the rear—

Despairing traders, left behind,
Saw Childs, the brave, outstrip the wind.
Three toothless squaws, 'tis understood,
Pursued the lost babe in the wood ;
While he, despising friends and foes,
Through thick and thin pursued his nose.
His nose, by instinct, downward bent,
Pursued a soul-alluring scent ;
A richer perfume, 'tis confess'd,
Than boasteth Araby the bless'd.
Oft as that perfume fills the breeze,
The ardent hunters halt and sneeze ;
Hold all aside a wry proboscis,
And calculate their gains and losses.
And thus the squaws, who follow'd after
The flying Childs, with shouts and laughter,
The moment they in full pursuit,
Seem'd wild to eat forbidden fruit,
The perfum'd air had just inhaled;
Then suddenly their courage fail'd—
Down in a stinking swamp they sunk,
Yielding our hero to a skunk."

At last, the talkers, smokers, and jokers began to drop off, one by one, to bed. They dwindled away so fast, that by ten o'clock the bar-room was deserted by all save the agent and myself. His hollow cough and worn aspect—his expiring pipe—all betokened a want of repose, and he was meditating, mayhap, on the perils and dangers before him, when the street-door opened, and, with a rush of cold wind and rain, entered a frosty-faced, severe-looking little man, in a dreadnought coat, and grasping a cudgel almost as long as himself.

"What, all alone !" exclaimed this gentleman, advancing to the agent. "Not all alone, either," continued he, glancing uneasily at me ; "but no matter. Mr. H——, are you a strong man?" was the next abrupt question put to the agent by this singular fish.

" I thank the Lord," replied the agent, looking up at the stern and searching eye of his querist, " I have hitherto enjoyed a fair share of bodily health and strength ; I have a bad cold and——"

" No, no ; I don't mean to inquire after all your ailments now," interrupted the new-comer ; " I merely thought, from your dilapidated look——"

" Sir !" said the agent.

" I merely thought," resumed the querist, " that you are not—that you cannot be a very strong man, able to contend with and repel by muscular strength half a dozen or a dozen desperate characters, and hard cases."

" Well, sir," said the agent—" and what then ?"

" Oh, nothing at all, sir ; I merely heard that, calculating upon your personal and individual strength of body and mind, you had declined our assistance— the assistance of our corps. But, sir, I'm quite satisfied about it—I see how matters will go. Some people think they are stronger than they actually are, and, counting on their strength, get awfully *sucked*, rumsquaddled, and, in the end, are happy to make a straight coat tail, and ' absquatulate ;' however, if you should change your mind, send for me, my name is Childs."

" Oh, good night, Mr. Childs," said the agent, retiring to bed, while I could hardly refrain from greeting the perplexed and dumbfoundered man of war with the classic verse—

" ——Further into the wilds
Penetrated Mister Childs."

In spite of wind, hail, rain, and snow, good and evil reports and threats, the money-boat started up the Fox River this morning. The traders began to follow her, with their bales, boxes, and barrels of whisky, as best they might. Boats, scows, and canoes, of all sorts and sizes, were put in requisition, the moment it was known the agent and the dollars were fairly started.

Our bar-room was not so closely besieged by the not politicians. My object in visiting this out-of-the-way place was to witness the Indian payment, and great was my disappointment to hear that said payment was to be made on the Wolf River, two or three days' journey into the country, with the agreeable prospect of camping out, in perspective. Being assured that it would be more agreeable to ride to the payment ground, than loiter up rivers and lakes in a canoe in such abominable weather, I betook myself to hunt for a saddle-horse; but so much had been said against strangers and interlopers by the angry judge and his clique, that even old Green began to be alarmed, and when I spoke of hiring one of his horses, to ride to the payment—heydey! the poor man was off like a shot. No, no; not he, indeed; he had never let out his horse to go half that distance. I sallied out in quest of a horse, but my search was vain, the Frenchmen saying their horses were engaged, and the half-breeds willing enough to sell, but not to let their cattle, demanding forty, fifty, and eighty dollars for little runts of Indian ponies, not worth ten dollars a piece. The boats, canoes, and the last of the Indians had already gone up the river. I saw there was no help for it, and prepared to shift my quarters, when old Green facetiously inquired if I

meant to walk to the payment ground. I demanded
my bill, and made a final sortie in quest of a steed.
The severest rebuke I experienced was from a cross
old ferryman. To this Charon I was directed by a
single-minded saddler. He said the ferryman was a
discreet member of the church, had a horse to hire
out, &c. No sooner had I explained my errand than
the ferryman broke out—"Who sent you here to insult
me in my misfortunes? Ay, I have a horse—a horse
I loaned to a particular friend of mine, to ride down
to Madison, four months ago. The horse was sent
back, only yesterday—a miserable, broken-down hack.
I'll have the tarnation scoundrel up before the court—
that I will. If I have been used in this way by a
friend, what can I expect from you, a stranger? From
where did you say you came from?"

I was glad to recross the ferry, and, totally disgusted
with the hardness of heart of the people, betook
myself to my chamber, where, from cold, wet, over-
fatigue, &c., I remained for two days, laid up with a
feverish attack.

Sunday: The weather having cleared a little, I
walked for a mile or two, and recovered my sinking
spirits. I looked, from the uplands and rising grounds,
down upon the swamps and flats upon which the rival
cities of Astor and Navarino are built, but the tide
of prosperity and speculation has receded, and left the
streets of both cities bare enough and quite deserted;
yea, verging unto ruin. White houses and painted
stoops, built at respectful distances from each other,
generally marking the corners of the streets. Here a
round and rickety plank or footway—there a slough
and a bridge—anon a row of rickety stores, all leaning
one way, for support, against the back of a meeting-

house; here and there a melancholy variety of lath and plaster churches and chapels-of-ease. "Every day is like Sunday now," said a tradesman to me, as he lamented the high and palmy days of house-building and speculation. Truly, the Green Bay cities do not flourish by the water-side; there was dry land and waste land enough in the territory, without building towns on swamps, but *chacun à son gout*. The ebb and flow of the tide is said to be observed here as in other places on the shores of Lake Michigan, though I think its regularity exceedingly doubtful, and attribute the rise and fall of water to the wind and rains.

Returned to the bar-room, and found a certain tall fellow, a half-breed, inveighing against the Indians: "They vanish before the breath of the white man," said he, "and it is to be hoped they will soon disappear from the face of the globe." He went on vapouring in this way for some time, until I brought him up short. I asked him why the red man should perish and be destroyed by the white man; why should he not be cherished, protected, and encouraged to settle down, and cultivate his own—his native land, &c. And knowing that this eloquent bar-room exquisite was half Indian, half Jew (son of a Jew pedler), I pitched into him, and poured out a vial of wrath upon his head, that completely silenced his barking; while all present seemed convinced that I had now declared myself to be the friend of the Indians, and the enemy of half-breeds and settlers. In truth, I cared not what they thought; and, recovering my spirits as the sun shone out, contradicted the judge, set the major right, awakened the general, and took my part in the conversation.

This evening we had a strong muster of townsfolk

in our bar-room, and the *politicianers*, as they are called here, expressed their sentiments freely. The election of a new delegate was at hand. Dodge, the ex-governor of Wisconsin was in the field; he was supported by the locofocoes, or the outs, while Arnold, the whig, or Doty candidate, was supported by the ins. Newspapers were read over and over again, by the politicians present; there was a vast deal of blustering and hard words bandied backwards and forwards, but the most violent disputations ended in laughter.

Both candidates had stanch supporters in the room, and one of the locofoco faction, or a Dodge man, ridiculed the present governor's attempt to alter the orthography of Wisconsin into Wiskonsan, by a special edict or act of the legislature. " He wishes to make us ridiculous in the eyes of the world," said the gentleman, and then read an article from the *Wisconsin Inquirer* :—

" A proclamation under the great seal of the territory will soon make its appearance, commanding the people of Wiskonsan not only to mind their p's and q's, but their c's and k's. ' A proklamation by James Duane Doty, Governor of Wiskonsan :— Whereas James Morrison was duly appointed treasurer of Wiskonsan, and has given bond with sekurity which has been approved of by the exekutive, the said bond has been deposited in the office of the sekretary,' &c.

The reading and spelling of this long proclamation occasioned a good deal of merriment, and the merits of the rival candidates were then discussed, the whigs saying a great deal in favour of their candidate, Arnold, whom they described as a gentleman and scholar, an acute politician, a close reasoner, a good metaphysician, a sweet philosopher, a deep lawyer, fit to urge their *klaims* and support the dignity of the territory at Washington.

" I am not a Doty man, and never will be," said a brisk little clothier, and bankrupt tailor to boot, " I never was a Doty man. I know Arnold; I have heard him make a stump speech. I see nothing in Arnold to command respect and attention; he is a mere raven's quill of a man, smart as an old shears, thin as a thread paper. What then? Let us look at our delegate, General Dodge. Ay, he is something worth looking at—a responsible personage, a fair presence, will command attention anywhere—weighs, I should say, well nigh two hundred pounds. He is the man for my money."

" Oh, ho! you want to have a heavy man, I see," exclaimed one of the whigs; " it is not the man's head you look to. No! all the locofocoes want is plenty of beef and cabbage."

" I'm sure the whigs have got beef enough, and weight enough in the present governor," drily observed the long major. " I remember the day he was appointed; in fact we boarded together at the same house in Washington, and this great big fellow came down to breakfast with a rubber tied round his head, looking as heavy and dreamy as a regular John Bull. ' My! what can be the matter with Doty?' said our landlady; ' he barely picks a fish-bone, and toys with a round of toast—sighs over the buckwheat cakes, and frowns on the molasses.' To all this the gentleman replied that indeed he had no appetite to his breakfast, being ' troubled with the weight of the affairs of state.'"

I observed old Green maintained a discreet silence; he neither said a word for or against any man, thrust logs into the stove, snuffed the candles, smiled, laughed, rubbed his red round face " almost to bursting;" he seemed to enjoy the jests of his guests, quietly cleaning the bar-room comb with his penknife, a nasty operation, and beneath a man of his parts; anon, he combed his short bay wig, then picked his teeth with a pen, introduced that implement into his ear, held the point up to the candle, cleared his nails, and in a twinkling began to peel a rosy-cheeked apple.

" What right or pretension has Arnold to be our delegate at all?" said a very vehement old orator, called the doctor. " He is an untried man. Who knows Arnold? I don't know him, for one, never heard of the name except in our history, and there it is notorious enough; whereas, we all know General Dodge——he has identified himself with the territory——he has fought for us, he has bled for us; shall his deeds be forgotten—shall the hero of the Black-hawk-war be rejected for a man of yesterday? I hold in my hand the *Wisconsin Inquirer*, and if you please, I will refresh your memories with a little of our history, which ought not to be left in the shade any longer." And the learned leech read an extract from the columns of the paper in his hand :—

" ' My men,' said the leader, ' we shall find the red-skins under yonder bank; there can be no flinching, no backing out now; remember the vow we made at the rude grave of poor ——. They will have the first fire, depend upon it. Some of us must fall; but let us march boldly up to the work, and take our chance. We all know for what we are about to contend, and what the consequences will be if we fail. Five of you must remain to hold the horses, while the rest, with myself, will march to the encounter with our foes. We must *creep* up cautiously, with our pieces ready for an instant discharge. One thought of home, and then our whole minds and energies for the immediate emergency.'

" Of the Pentacolica, perhaps it is necessary to state, that the banks are generally very bold; the point where this adventurous band was about to approach was particularly so, and entirely bald of timber. The five were detached to take charge of the horses, and the others, after examining the priming of their pieces, again set forward for the encounter. On they move, with the cautiousness of old veterans in the service. ' Be firm,' cried the leader, as they drew near the bank; ' carry your pieces to an aim, and as your sight lights upon them, blaze it into them.' Now the exciting moment has arrived—each had a thought of home, but only transient, it vanishes before the work in hand. They near the bank! but what causes that momentary hesitation and wavering? The Indians are there, but they cannot be seen yet. It is the muzzles of the Indians' pieces resting on the bank, and directed deadly towards them, ready to belch forth death and destruction in their midst. The quick ear of the savages had already discovered that there was danger near, but they had no chance to flee. They raise the bank, and are in full view of a party of Indians, about twenty-five or thirty in number, who immediately fired upon them, stretching three of their number in all the agonies of death. Nothing daunted, the survivors return the fire with the most destructive precision. The pieces discharged are flung upon the ground, and those on their backs are instantly unslung and discharged, before the Indians can reload. ' Now, my men,' shouts the leader, 'let us rush upon them, and make dispatch in ridding the earth of the survivors.' 'Tis done—they are amongst them, using their pistols and knives. It is now a struggle of personal prowess. The Indians fight well, but at great odds, and fighting, they rally round their chief, who is severely wounded, while he chants his war-song, as if to incite his followers to fight till the last gasp. One of them attempts to escape; he is nearly in the middle of the stream, swimming to the opposite bank, but a well-sped ball has done its business; he sinks—he's gone. 'Close them,' cries the leader; 'but leave the chief to me; be mine the task to dispatch him.' Upon the instant, the few remaining Indians are hurried from time to eternity; while, at the same time, a ball from the pistol of the white leader has stretched their chief upon the ground, but his spirit is still unsubdued; in an almost inaudible whisper, he continues his death-song of defiance. But the film of death has glazed his eyes with that spasm. He, too, is gone! Not an Indian escaped to tell the tale of their defeat; and thus perished by the hand of violence, men whose hands were reeking with the blood of innocence; under other circumstances, and guided by the rays of civilization and education, they might have adorned a nation."

Reader, the above is " o'er true." Many of the actors in that affray are still living near Mineral Point. They arrayed themselves under the stars and stripes, and under the same leader rendered good service, and contributed essentially to the bringing of that bloody war to a close. In that leader behold the late governor of Wisconsin—HENRY DODGE!

The solemn silence which had been preserved by the audience, during the reading of this article was unbroken for at least a minute after the reader laid down the paper; but the trampling of horses without caught the quick ear of our host; he turned to the door, but the door flew open, and a tall, dignified, bespattered, travel-stained man, with a long red blanket-lined cloak thrown over one shoulder, a battered white beaver hat cocked over his eye, and a pair of saddle-bags in his hand, strode up to the stove.

"General Dodge!" burst from the lips of the startled host, as he presented a chair; while the admirers of that great hero seemed thrown of a heap' and dumb-foundered. There was a disagreeable pause, till the ex-governor, throwing his hat aside, made some off-hand observations upon the state of the roads, the badness of the weather, the great fatigue he had experienced in his ride from Fort Winnebago. Then, stretching out his legs before the fire, he deliberately relieved himself from the burden of a high pair of Indian leggings, yawned thrice, and declared he was ready for supper. It seemed, the stanch supporters of Dodge then present had never been introduced to him, or if they had, they hung aloof through *mauvais honte*, or some-thing akin to it, until a special friend of the general's was sent for down town, who relieved them from their fears by introducing them to the general, one and all, when a general hand-shaking took place at the bar, and the ex-governor went in to supper; leaving his friends, foes, and admirers, to resume the thread of their conversation. Having consigned my watch and baggage to the tender mercies of my host, I started from Green Bay, *pied à terre*, with fifteen pounds weight of baggage, including a Makinaw blanket between my shoulders. The road was full of mud-holes, and most execrable.

Two miles from the town I overtook a waggon and pair, driven by an old Frenchman, with whom I speedily made a bargain to give me a ride for a few miles. This old fellow had been mail carrier, and knew the country well; he had two good farms, upon one of which he had located his son. As we progressed, this good fellow informed me he had fought on the British side, at the battle of Queenston Heights —where poor Brock was shot.

" Ah, quel homme—quel homme !" he exclaimed, with fervour, speaking of Brock ; " brave comme le diable, il parlait Francais comme un ange."

When the General was shot, he said he was taken prisoner by the Americans, and at the peace removed with his wife and family, to the banks of the Fox River.

" Voila Du Pere, or St. Pere !" he exclaimed, as we passed through another young city, wherein some splendid lath and plaster villas, and shingle palaces, in the wilderness, have been erected. The place was quite deserted. Thousands of dollars have been expended, thrown right away into the river also, upon a mill-dam built right across the river ; the said dam is fast crumbling away, and the first foundation of some grand mills following the general course of the tide. It seems the millers went a-head of the farmers in this country, for even now there is very little grain raised in this district, even for home consumption—flour being frequently imported from New York and Chicago. The Fox River is certainly a fine stream, and hereafter will be one of great consequence when the rapids and falls are cut down. The portage opened from Lake Winnebago to the Little Fox River, and a navigable canal opened between the Wisconsin, Fox, and Missisippi rivers; when this is all completed, and this country thickly settled, and good roads made, and Wisconsin proclaimed a state, this will be a very desirable country to reside in, I dare say.

Jolting along the road, through rain and mud, and branches of trees, and fallen trees, and bottomless sloughs, I listened to the rambling conversation of my whip. He seemed delighted to have found a good listener, and poured forth a volume of backwood history and personal adventures. In the midst of one of his rigmaroles, three deer—a stag, a doe, and a fawn—burst into the road before us. Thus, at a moment when I never expected to see a deer, cramped up in a waggon with a noisy old Frenchman, and totally unprepared, a splendid shot escaped me. The deer cantered down the road before us in single file, and dashed into the woods again.

" Restez tranquille, mon ami !" said my whip. " The woods are full of deer—*par tout! par tout!*—you'll see them everywhere further on."

Wright's ferry: Here my old whip halted to bait, and I regaled him with some *eau de vie*, while he gave me some directions as to my line of march, regretting he could not accompany me, *au payement;* he did more—he endeavoured to prevail on a Frenchwoman, one of his connexion, to let me one of her horses; and he declared he would be responsible for the safe return of her steed. This the good woman, who resided on the opposite side of the river, agreed to do, saying, that since Monsieur R—— would answer for the safe return of the horse, she had no objection in the world; and Monsieur B—— protesting on the honour of a Français, that he was sure all was right—

calling on the woman to " Regardez cet homme, un etranger c'est vrai, mais je vous gagerai tout ce que j'ai—il est brave garcon," drove off, while I entered the low-roofed tavern, and endeavoured to improve my friend's impression, by ordering dinner, and inviting the voisine, to whom I was so well recommended, to share the repast, of fried bacon, eggs, mush, maple sugar, wild plums, dried fish, and potatoes, set before us. This she declined; and while I was at dinner she crossed the ferry. I followed her—toiled two miles, up steep and slippery banks, to her house; overtook her just as she entered her garden, and reminded her of her promise.

After some hesitation, she said her husband was not at home—doubted my ability to catch the horse, and directed me to the house of another Frenchman, who could assist me. Away I went to the Frenchman's barn—found him thrashing. He put on his coat, and we struck into the woods; we now heard the tinkling of the bells; but the moment we came in sight of the horses, off they scampered, over "brake and brae," while we gave chase, and hunted them towards some enclosed fields; but it was little better than a wild-goose chase; for the horses baffled us the very moment we thought our exertions were crowned with success; and away they went, kicking, and snorting, and jingling their bells, into the woods again.

INDIANS PACKING AT THE PORTAGE.

CHAPTER XV

The Judge and the lawyer Urban were ...

... part of the day ...

... the grey-coated jade ...

... Astor, a siding ...

... had heard for ...

... to find him lower? ...

... be would never ...

... ruts. "I do care," ... he ... "I ...
will hold together as a ..."

... "You may take your ... of it" ...
simply poked ... in the ...
weak points.

"What ... they ... man still ... "
said he.

"That ... ... this and the ..."

CHAPTER XVII.

The Judge and his buggy—Indian woman's kindness—A blanket war—Little Cocaloo—Hospitable lady in the woods—Treacherous French guide—Night in a dismal swamp—Wolves—Last white man's house—Butte de Morts—A nondescript—Hard cases on the prairie—Indians—Grignons—Traders—Osh-Cosh le Brave—Voyage up the Wolf River—Our canoe—Fishing— .The camp—Indian village—The agent—A Council.

THE best part of the day being spent, I re-crossed the river, and signified my intention to sleep at the tavern. As yet only fifteen miles from the Bay. Here, to my great surprise and annoyance, I found my friend, or foe—the grey-coated judge—uneasily watching his slender buggy waggon, which had been rather roughly shaken, *en route*. He had spent the day, steering up from Astor, avoiding ruts and stumps, and, with his wife, had halted for the night at the tavern. I was glad to find him lowered a peg in his boasting. He vowed he would never have ventured so far upon this 'tarnal bad road, if he had calculated the depth of the ruts. "I declare," said he, "I do not think the buggy will hold together as far as Fort Winnebago."

"You may take your oath of it," said I, pointing to sundry cracks and crannies in the buggy, and other weak points.

"What do they say of the road still further west?" said he.

"That the road between this and the bay is a

bowling-green, compared to it," said I; "a regular waggon-splitting, racking road."

"If I had not my lady with me, I would not care," said the judge, in a choking voice.

"Sad affair, sir, to venture so far from home in so fragile a concern as yours," said I.

"It is a fact; I see my error now," said the judge; "my horse hurt his leg too."

"A man is ever more independent on foot," said I; "he has no incumbrance—no lumbering waggon—no lame horse—no awful mud-holes, to retard his progress. He carries his blanket, his fire-box, his rifle, on his shoulder, jauntily; he crosses the deep rivers in a log canoe; he basks upon the sunny side of flowery banks, and snaps his fingers at the world."

"It is a fact!—a fact!—a fact!" said the judge with deep emotion and a groan; "it is the only way to go a-head in this New Country."

"Judge, dear—Judge, my dear—bring in the robes out of the buggy," cried a shrill voice from a window, and an old woman favoured us with a sight of her sublime nose, at the casement.

"Coming, my dear!" responded the judge.

"And bring me my box, also, and my clothes-bag, for the bed is not sheeted; and you had best come help me."

While the judge was trying his hand at bed-making, three cavaliers arrived—one of whom I had seen at the bay. He was bound for the payment, and regretted I had no horse, and could not accompany them in their expedition; whereupon the judge affected great surprise.

"No horse! What!—has the gentleman no horse! Could he get no horse to hire in all Green Bay?

Well! that is very extraordinary indeed. I must say, had I known the fact, I would have loaned out my pony; in fact, there is my pony running about my fields—any man might have had him, with his saddle and bridle, for a week."

" Well, sir," said I—" supposing that I go down to Green Bay in the morning, and take your pony for a few days?" This I said, merely to sound the man a little, for I had not the remotest intention of turning back.

The judge replied not; he was taken quite aback. He pretended his wife had called him, and beat a retreat, while the three cavaliers laughed heartily.

This morning one of the horsemen volunteered to carry my blanket to a house where he intended to halt for some hours. I crossed the river, and pursued the devious track for some miles. The air was oppressively hot, and a fog hung over the river, on which wild ducks, and even swans, frequently alighted.

Leaning on some rails in front of a log-house, I addressed a good-natured looking Indian woman, in French and English. I merely inquired the distance to the little cocaloo, (or waterfalls.) She did not seem to comprehend me; but smilingly took a handful of salt, and went into a field. She pronounced some Indian words, and forthwith a little Indian pony ran up to her, and began to eat the salt, while she put a bridle on his head, and led him up to me. One of her daughters put a rude saddle on the pony's back, and, with many demonstrations of thankfulness for this unlooked for kindness, I mounted the steed and rode off, followed by a little half-breed, who, with a long stick, urged the pony into a gallop.

Arrived at the little Cocaloo *a bon heure.* I found it a

very picturesque spot—more rapids than falls. A very
fine lath and plaster chateau stands near the water-
side; it is built in the only odious flat spot in the
whole country, abounding with splendid sites for
houses, and belongs to the son of a half-breed trader,
who has considerable influence over the Indians.
Further on, I halted in front of another very neat dwelling-house, and was greeted rather uncourteously by
a rough old bear of a Frenchman, pretty much in this
style, before I opened my lips,—"*il n'y a pas de couverture ici—allez!*"

This must be the house where my blanket lined
with oilskin was left, thought I; and, consigning my
little steed to the Indian boy, I entered the yard, and
was met by a smart-looking dame. She exclaimed, in
English—"There's no blanket left here for you."

"I beg your pardon," said I, "I have not spoken
about a blanket at all;" while the old Frenchman
went on vapouring, "*Il n'y a pas de couverture ici.*" But
I still followed him, and he entered the stable, while
the lady brought up the rear, saying, that those gentlemen had said they left a blanket there an hour
ago; but, for her part, she could not find it.

"Perhaps it is *la haut*," said the old French fellow,
wanting me to go up in a hay-loft.

I did so; and while there, saw through the chinks
in the wall a man running up with my blanket, which
he thrust into the stable window, and I descended
and found it, exclaiming, "Oh, here is the blanket!"

"Very glad you found it," said the lady, as she invited me to enter her house.

I told her I had already breakfasted; but she insisted upon it, and I sat down for an hour, listening
to her political history. She said she was from Penn-

sylvania, of Irish extraction, and seemed to think she was buried alive in this barbarous country.

The Indian boy now became impatient, and Madame urged me to discharge him home, which I did with regret, sending a ring to his mother and some silver, with my best regards.

My hostess would insist on my staying to dine with her, *nolens volens*—so I agreed, and, to my utter disappointment, dinner did not make its appearance till past five—in fact, near six o'clock; then, to be sure, it was in profusion. Such a display—such a spread, I had not witnessed for some time; the whole *batterie de cuisine* seemed to be fumed out upon the table before me. Expressing great anxiety about getting on and going a-head, my hostess declared she would get me a horse and guide, and, despite of the grumblings and growlings of her servants, ordered a favourite horse to be saddled, sent for a gay Frenchman to act as guide, and for a long time strenuously resisted receiving a farthing for all her good dishes and trouble, would not accept anything for horse-hire, telling me to give the guide anything I liked when I had done with him; thus we parted the best of friends, with mutual good wishes, though we met in a very different manner. I soon discovered my guide was an arrant scamp of the first water; he jogged on pretty well for four or five miles, he then began to complain, in his vile patois, of all he had suffered when he was a hunter in the Fur Company's service. He asked me if I was a hunter. I answered in the affirmative, when he directly asked me what was the number of my lodge. Knowing that he alluded to some secret association, I declined giving him any answer, and he became very sullen and dogged. Two miles above the Grand Cocaloo, the fellow halted at a log-house, and made some inquiries in Indian, which he speedily translated into a story about a river which ran into the Fox river, and which we would have to ford, being swollen by the late rains, and quite impassable for a horse, though he admitted a man might cross it upon a tree.   Not wishing to injure the horse which my hostess had so kindly lent to me, I followed the fellow's advice, and put him into a stable.   *En avant*, was the word, and my guide, shouldering the knapsack, started into the forest at a quick pace.   This wily dog led me a pretty dance this moonlight night; we went through quagmires, and sloughs, and mud-holes, and all sorts of slippery places, till at last, in a deep and gloomy ravine, my guide threw down the knapsack, with an oath, and sat down upon it.

" How much am I to be paid for all this ?" said he, sternly.

" I have already agreed about that," said I, " in presence of Madame ———."

" But Madame ——— is not here now," said this rascal, with a sneer ; " we must make a new agreement."

" I'll make no fresh agreement with you," said I ; " I can dispense with your company—you may go back."

" You think you are in the right road—this is only a path of my own," said he ; " you'll never find your way out of this forest by yourself. Do you know there was a pedler murdered by the Indians near this spot a short time ago ?" continued he.

" And what of that ?" said I, while a dark suspicion that it might not have been an Indian murdered the pedler, shot through my mind. I grasped my pistol,

and, in a very significant way, pointed in the direction
I wished to proceed, and bid my guide lead on.   He
did so, and cursing almost every step; while I kept
my eye on him, determined that he should have only
a fair share of the battle if he was bent on fighting.
As we fagged along, in silence and distrust, a herd of
deer rushed past us, before and behind; they were
running down to the water, and the musical howling
of wolves sounded in every direction.

" They are chasing the deer," grumbled my guide;
" *la voila les sacre yeux d'un loup!*" he exclaimed, re-
coiling back, while a rustling in the bush declared
the proximity of one of those hungry gentlemen.

Here, again, I reserved my fire—if I fired at the
wolf, I should have to grapple with the rascally guide.

We soon found the slough, or creek, which he had
declared impassable, the easiest spot *en route*, over
which a rough bridge had been recently made by the
hardy pioneer who has pitched his tent at the *Butte de
Morts*, where we arrived, more dead than alive, at
three o'clock in the morning.   It was a long time before the man of the house would open his door; he
asked several shrewd questions, and at last, recog-
nising the voice of my guide, he drew the bolt, and
admitted us.

" You can sleep up stairs," said the man of the
house; but my guide declined staying in the house—
he said he knew an Indian in the neighbourhood, to
whom he would go.   I was glad to get rid of him on
any terms, paid him two dollars, for peace' sake, and
sent him about his business.   My host shook his head,
and significantly drew his hand across his throat when
I told him of my guide's singular conduct; he was a

prudent man, and did not commit himself by words; shewed me to a bed, and left me to my slumbers.

We seldom or ever see a stranger here," said my host, as we sat down to breakfast; "we. are regularly shut out from all society by that dismal forest and swamp you passed through last night, and there is not another settler's house between me and the Indian country."

He then told me he had been a land-surveyor. Making a government survey of this part of the country, he was struck with the beauty of the spot on which he now resided, took up some lots, and was

" Monarch of all he surveyed."

His wife and four very fine little boys were his only companions; he seldom or ever saw a newspaper, and made sundry vague inquiries about affairs down East. I commended my host's good taste in having fixed on such a splendid site for his house—a high bluff, commanding an extensive view up and down the river, the presence of some round Indian mounds giving an air of some antiquity to the place. When the host left the room, the boys crowded round, and the eldest, a fine lad, launched out in praise of a brown and long-bodied water dog. He could swim like a fish, hunt an otter, find a prairie hen, trace a deer, and tree a racoon, with any dog in Wisconsin. He never refused to fight but once——

" And then we were all afraid," said the youngest, blue-eyed boy.

" No, we were not, though," said another, angrily; " you never saw father *sheered.*"

Oh, no! that was a thing never heard of; and they informed me how a long, black, fierce, rough-haired animal, had regularly besieged the house one day; the dog refused to hunt him, and he kept prowling about the back of the house, and sometimes sat down in front of it, right opposite the door. My host, entering the room, confirmed what the boys had said concerning this strange animal.

"I had not a single charge of powder in the house," said he, "at that time, and I never felt so wolfish in my life; I have travelled a long way, I tell you, and never saw anything like it before or since."

"Was it a bear?" said I.

"Bear, no!—I think I should know bears pretty well by this. I tell you it was neither a bear, a wolf, a catamount, or a lynx; but, somehow, I felt a disgust to attack it single hand."

I advised my host to make sure of this nondescript, the next time it paid him a visit, and having received some useful hints from him respecting my route and conduct if I should fall in with Indians, shouldered my knapsack, and marched away.

Hardly had I marched a hundred yards from the house, when my host came after me to tell me a canoe full of "hard cases" (vagabonds) had passed up the river after the money-boat, and two of them had been to his house for whisky;" and with this piece of intelligence to cheer me on, I pursued my tramp, followed the Indian trail as directed, through open woodlands and bush, for four or five miles, till at last the open prairie lay before me, and choosing the blackest of three Indian trails, I trotted on for about a mile; when, to my surprise, I saw a line of men advancing towards me in single file. I soon perceived they were not Indians, stepped aside out of the trail, and hailed the foremost of this band of ragamuffins in

French, in which language he responded, demanding how far it was to the *Butte de Morts* ; he then demanded why I travelled alone, I said, " *Mes amis* were *en arriere*," and wishing those " hard cases" *bon voyage* (to Old Nick), pursued the trail, frequently throwing long and lingering looks behind, till the ragged fur cap of the last of those gentlemen went down in the East.

Eight or nine miles further on, I found the remains of a fire, surrounded with the feathers and bones of wild fowl. It was here the party I had met had bivouacked, *sans doute*. Climbing one of the few trees near the spot, I looked round for miles in every direction—not a living thing seemed within sight or hearing. " Oh, solitude ! where are thy charms," I muttered, as I resumed my march. Five miles further on, I halted again, beside a clear running stream, prostrate by the side of which I enjoyed a delicious draught of the pure and unadulterated, in a very primitive manner. But in the very act of swigging up the clear water, I was not a little startled to contemplate the grim visage of an Indian reflected in the flood ; and, starting up, lo ! and behold, two gaunt, fierce-looking, old Indians stood beside me. How the deuce they could have glided up so noiselessly I could not divine—for even the snapping of a dry stick could be heard half a mile off.

But the salutation, " Bo jou, bo jou !" shewed they were friendly. Nathless, there was something terrible in the countenance of one of these men, and I pointed to the streamlet, and motioned them to take the precedence, as they knew best where it could be easily forded or not. They seemed to take the hint, strode into the water, and waited for me on the other side. I could have excused their politeness, but followed their example, getting wet up to the waist. The Indians strode on before me, holding deep and earnest conversation ; their long, gaunt figures, six feet and upwards, enveloped in dirty blankets, gave them a most spectral look.

" A hay cock"—-never did *phare* greet the eyes of a more joyous voyageur than I was when I saw this simple token of civilization—-a hay-cock in a little meadow ; half a mile further on a bit of timber fencing, rails, some Indian corn, a house—ye gods and fishes, what a change came o'er the spirit of my dreams ! The smooth breast of the Wolf river lay before me, sundry canoes were paddling up it, groups of Indians refitting their skeletons of old lodges. I entered the house, and found several people sitting about in every direction, not one of whom bade me welcome. Sundry pigeon-toed squaws, and mild-looking, half-breed girls, were busy preparing victuals about an immense fire-place, the capacious chimney of which projected a considerable distance into the large rambling apartment, the walls of which were decorated with belts of wampum, powder-flasks, fowling-pieces, rifles, and sleigh and buffalo robes.

Close to a window sat two old Frenchmen, poring over account-books ; they looked like Rembrandt's " Misers " to the life ; one was the master of the house, Monsieur Grignon, the most successful and well-known Indian trader in those parts. Several Indians and half-breeds lounged about in various attitudes, some smoking their tomahawk pipes, others intently watching the motions of the fair damsels about the fire. I entered into conversation with a bluff, good-looking Frenchman, who was another of the Grignons. He informed me that he had a considerable tract of land on the Wisconsin river. Presently a soup of Indian corn and wild duck was served round, with some good bread.

"Allez vous au payment?" demanded old Grignon, speaking for the first time.

I answered in the affirmative. He then said I should be there time enough, as the payment would not be made for nearly a week, as the Indians had not received due notice, and had not come into the camp yet. I was glad to hear it, and resolved to halt in such good quarters that night. At four, we sat down to a very savoury mess of stewed wild ducks, prairie hens, and vegetables; delicious bread, butter, potatoes, coffee, and plum pies. During dinner, our host was frequently disturbed by the brusque and impertinent language of one of the Indians, who had approached the house in my company. This man, with the ferocious eye, strode round the table, his wild blanket thrown behind him, revealing various parts of his gaunt and naked body—an unpleasing sight—while his long black and grey locks streamed down his shoulders. My suspicions were not at all quieted by my host saying—"*Il est fou—c'est un fou*," and "*son père etait fou aussi*; in fact, all his family are madmen," continued he. "He wants me to give him flour and pork, on credit, of course, and the moment he is paid and gets at the whisky, he'll forget all about it, and threaten to scalp me if I say a word." Nevertheless, this mad Indian had method in his madness, for he did not leave the house until his wants were supplied. I afterwards saw him embark in his canoe, with his wife and sundry old squaws and children, and no less than five hungry-looking dogs. At sunset, we were surprised by a loud shout, and running to the door, beheld a gaily-painted canoe, sculled along by four handsomely-dressed young men; they beached their boat handsomely, and sundry Indians and a white and half-breed marched up to the house. All the Indians, half-breeds and traders, made a sort of humble salutation to a dirty, mean-looking little Indian, with a large mouth, bandy legs, a quick eye, and mean-looking brow; and while I was considering why this worshipful chimney-sweeper, in his dirty old blanket, was paid so much attention, my host's brother whispered in my ear—" C'est Osh Cosh le Brave, chief of the Menomenee Indians. His pipe-bearer soon fixed the red stone calumet to a long flat stem, richly ornamented with red and green feathers, and the chief began whiffing away like a Turkish bashaw. Observing that his coarse black hair hung down over his face, and his cheeks were covered with black dirt, I inquired if any accident had befallen his excellency, or royal highness. The answer was brief: " The chief is in decent mourning for one of his sons, lately deceased." I thought of the ancient custom of the Jews—how David humbled himself in sackcloth and ashes, &c. The contents of the canoe were soon transferred to the floor of our apartment; parlour and hall was encumbered with curiously-wrought mats, buffalo robes, blankets, neatly painted and carved paddles, &c.; while the young men sat on their haunches, in the midst of their tawdry finery, polishing their tomahawk-pipes, and sending round skunk and fishers'-skins full of nic-a-nic and Indian tobacco. The chief was in a very bad humour. He had been to the payment-ground, and was displeased because the whole tribe were not ready to receive him. He did not approve of the new mode

of taking the census of his tribe, wishing the chiefs to
receive the money, and divide it as they thought
proper.   He therefore left his band to prepare his
wigwams and lodges, and came down the river, thus
slenderly attended, to consult with his old friend and
stanch ally, Grignon, the trader.   Indeed, Grignon's
son was in the canoe with him, and I suppose it was
he that induced the chief to take such a decided step.
Just as we sat down to supper, our ears were saluted
by a loud, wild, discordant song, raised on the river
by a large band of half-breeds and Indians, who were
pushing two heavy barges, full of flour, grain, and
pork, to the payment-ground; for part of the payment
was to be made in flour, grain, and beef, pork also.
They had been a week pulling those unwieldy barges
up the Rapids.   The wild chorus of those savage boatmen resembled the Canadian songs—half singing,
half talking, half howling, and though bearable at a
little distance, was exceedingly unpleasant to hear
nigh at hand.   Old Grignon went out and invited the
head men in charge to come in to tea.   Osh Cosh
declined sitting at the table.   He was served with
wild-duck stew, tea, and cakes, on a stool in the
chimney-corner.   Tea over, Osh Cosh signified his
intention to make a speech, and profound silence
being observed, he stood up before the red embers of
the fire, dropped his blanket from his shoulders
round his loins, and raising his right hand, spoke in a
deep, yet clear and somewhat sonorous voice, without
stopping, for at least half an hour, my friend the
bluff Frenchman interpreting what he said, to me,
from time to time.   The speech, from first to last,
was in the declamatory style, and against whisky.
He said he had seen many barrels lying in the reeds,

waiting to be broached when the payment was made ; but he would set his face against any such underhand proceedings. Fire-water (iscodaywabo) was the secret poison—the knife with which the Shemookmen (the American, or long knife) destroyed his young men. He would set his face against this fire-water; he would tell the agent (or money-carrier) that he would rather see all his money thrown into the river than lose a single warrior by drunkenness and brawling. He then reverted to what occurred at the last payment: "a man, goaded to madness with fire-water, killed two women, and fired at a man; the band to which the women belonged rose to a man, rushed upon the drunken madman, what they did you all witnessed, and, I shame to say, I witnessed also," said the chief. "They threw him on the great council fire, and he was burnt. The white men fled—the pale faces were filled with fear; it is not right they should bring away such evil reports. I am resolved to preserve order in the camp, and set my face against the whisky-traders. Caun whisky—caun whisky!" and Osh Cosh sat down, in the midst of a loud, approving grunt. Anon, old mother Grignon, a squaw of high and ancient family, with a crucifix round her neck, replied, in a nasal, whining voice: her speech was listened to with great attention. She drawled out her voice till it sounded like a funeral oration, and rocked herself backwards and forwards on her low stool. My friend did not interpret any part of her speech to me ; and, fatigued with my journey, and lulled by the drawling tones of the poor old woman's voice, I dropped asleep, dreamt I was in a sinking canoe, threw out my hands at random, and saved myself from falling backwards by grasping the feathers and scalp-lock of one of the young men seated beside me. This was a pretty broad hint about turning in for the night, and one of the Grignons led me into a small, but very neatly fitted-up chamber, where, on a bed of down, I slumbered till cock-crow. Waking up, I found the Indians sleeping on the floor, in every direction. My little nook alone was not invaded; indeed, from the neat little toilet-table, and gay gowns &c. hanging round the room, I found I had been put into the young lady's chamber, and regretted that I could not apologize for the intrusion in a suitable tongue. *Certes*, Miss Grignon seemed a very amiable young lady upon a large scale—a mild and melancholy countenance, eloquent black eye. "*A tu bien dormir cette nuit?*" demanded one of the young gentlemen, presenting his good-natured phiz. I took the hint, and my reverie of the fair *dame du logis* being broken, performed a hasty toilet, and evacuated the premises. The fresh morning air was delicious, after having inhaled so much tobacco-smoke, fumes, and steam, during the night.

My host's farming establishment was very much neglected, as is generally the case with traders; he did not pay much, indeed any, attention to farming. The fine open prairie lands along the river belonged to him; the few acres of Indian corn planted at the back of his house were ravaged by the red-winged blackbirds, probably the most destructive pest the farmer has to contend with in the western country. The traders, like the Indians, seem to think it beneath them to cultivate the soil. They are an improvident race, and once married to squaws, they quickly degenerate, and become very little better than the savages. To be sure, the Grignons have maintained their ground pretty well; but, considering the vast tracts of land, and the money, support, and assistance given to them by the Indians, they ought to be the richest men in the territory.

After breakfast—a breakfast (suffer me to say) that would not be sneezed at even in Auld Reekie, the capital of capital breakfasts,—I took my host aside, and begged to know how much I was indebted to him. He seemed to be surprised, and flatly refused to take anything by way of remuneration; but I was just as obstinate; I told him I had entered his house, and been hospitably entertained, without invitation. "*Eh bien!*" said the Frenchman, cutting short the dialogue, and shrugging up his shoulders, "*un piastre.*" I would have paid three times that sum elsewhere for such good entertainment, and bidding my fair and red hostess adieu, shouldered my knapsack, when Osh Cosh spoke a few words to one of the Grignons, which was interpreted by him to me as an invitation to take a seat, to the payment ground, in his canoe. The young men were busily engaged painting or re-touching the canoe. It was made of birch bark, very long, capable of holding ten or twelve persons with ease. The young men had performed their toilet in a block house in the rear with very great care and elegance ; their dark side locks were neatly platted, red, green, and brown feathers interwoven with their scalp locks, their cheeks, chins, and foreheads plenti-fully bedaubed with vermillion and ochre; two of them wore nose-rings as well as ear-rings, necklaces of wampum, dark printed calico tunics, scarlet cloth leggings, and mocassins worked with moose hair and porcupine quills. They were dashing looking lads, and handled the paddles famously, two kneeling in the bows, and two aft, while a fifth perked himself up in the stern sheets, dipping his paddle right and left as steersman. Osh Cosh sported a white chip hat, and squatted himself down in the midst of the canoe, puffing his long calumet with great dignity and self-satisfaction, while two of the Grignons, a half-breed, and myself, stowed ourselves upon the mats, back to back, and off we went like a streak of oiled lightning.

Before we started from the trader's house, the old patriarch Grignon, espying through his spectacles a pair of ducks on the river, took down his double-barrelled gun, stole down to the river, got into a canoe, which an Indian boy, who followed his movements like a dog, shoved into the water, and guided among the reeds and long grass, while the old fellow raised the gun, banged at, and shot a duck, with which he returned in triumph to the house. *"Papa est fier,"* said an old man, as he hastened to greet the patriarch upon his success.

The banks of the Wolf River are low and marshy; flocks of wild ducks and water-fowl afford good sport to the Indians. The river itself abounds with fish, and in some places is deep enough to float a seventy-four gun ship. A sudden turn in the river brought us into the midst of a fleet of more than a hundred canoes; two or three gaily painted and plumed Indians sat in each canoe, fishing for bass. Some of the canoes looked much handsomer than our own, and as they were not laden, rode lightly on the water; reflected in every direction, the effect was exceedingly picturesque. The take of fish was enormous, the Indians with their rude tackle pulling up the bass every second. One of the chief's canoes joined ours, and the Messrs. Grignon helped themselves to two or three dozen very fine fish, *sans ceremonie.* Having witnessed the sport for some time, we continued our voyage a few miles higher up the stream, and soon saw the American flag floating from a long pole in the midst of tents, wigwams, lodges, loggeries, and cabins, straggling in every direction between the dark forest and bright Wolf River, the *coup d'œil* bringing to my mind's eye the burlesque *hors d'ouvres* of Donnybrook fair.

Once fairly set ashore, we marched through motley groups of savages, towards the council lodge, in front of which, warming his hands at a fire, I found the poor agent, looking like death; for though Mr. Child's forebodings came to nothing, still he had suffered a great deal from cold and wet, being obliged to stick by his money boxes, which were frequently transferred from the boat to the bank, and the bank to the boat, and *vice versâ,* as he toiled up the Fox River. He complained bitterly of the tardiness of the Indians, and seemed to apprehend some danger and difficulty from the hostile vapourings of the chief, Osh Cosh, who was a deep, designing fellow, he said, and the ready tool of traders and mischief makers. " If you can find no better shelter for the night, you are welcome to spread your blanket in the council lodge," said this gentleman. I accepted the offer at once, knowing I might go further and speed worse, besides being under the protection of the stripes and stars, in case of a row amongst the Indians.

The council lodge was a large circular wigwam covered with bark, framed with long rods and poles; the floor was covered with a thick layer of branches and straw, the door-case filled with a mat; windows were superfluous, for the light streamed through a hundred slits and chinks in the roof and sides of our fragile tenement. An interpreter from Osh Cosh (one of the Grignons of course,) delivered a message to the agent, the purport of it—that he and his chiefs would hold a council, and hear what the agent had to say for himself immediately. The agent's mattress and blankets were speedily rolled aside, his books opened with great ceremony, a rude table of loose boards laid on the money boxes in the midst of the lodge; his clerk, a dapper quill-driver from the inhospitable shores of Mackinaw, nibbed his pen very adroitly. Never was such excitement displayed by the traders as they peered in at the door, and a favoured few who were personal friends of the chiefs were admitted. The anxiety within was only to be equalled by the pressure from without, the sides and roof of the lodge being literally thatched with Indians anxious to see and hear the debates in this primitive house of assembly.

Presently the old chiefs began to drop in one after another, plainly, indeed meanly, dressed in blankets; every chief on making his *entrée* shook hands with the agent, and quietly squatted himself down in a corner, conversing in low whispers with his neighbour, or quietly loading his calumet. About forty of the chiefs and braves or heads of bands, had taken their seats before Osh Cosh came in; he had rubbed more charcoal on his face, and save and excepting a splendid pair of leggings and mocassins, looked dirtier and meaner than ever. Two interpreters posted themselves behind the agent, and the agent after sundry hems and haws, declared that he was commissioned by the U. N. S. government to make this payment for the lands ceded to said government by the Menomenee Indians.

This being interpreted, the Indians gave an approving grunt, and some of the old fellows began to smoke.   I afterwards understood that the agent had been guilty of a breach of decorum, having neglected the ceremony of handing round a pipe of peace.

" Say to them," continued the agent, " that their money will be paid separately to every man and woman of the tribe, to avoid confusion.   We must also register their names, and take the number of the tribe."

This did not please Osh Cosh ; he signified his intention to speak, stood up, and, as usual, girded his blanket round his loins.   He said, " When their great father sent his servants to pay them for their lands, he knew very well how shamefully they were treated.   A chief is the head of a band, he has his children to support—the band look up to him.   The chiefs alone should receive the money, they are the treasurers of the tribe, and are better acquainted with the wants of their people."

" Wheugh, wheugh," grunted the whole assembly, and Osh Cosh sat down.

" Say to them," continued the agent, " that I cannot depart from my orders and instructions, and that I hope they will see the necessity of following the plan I have already laid before them."

Here a long and desultory conversation took place between the chiefs, and it was finally signified by Osh Cosh, that the agent might proceed with the registry, and pay the Indians as he was instructed by his great father.

" Say to them," continued the agent, " that no Winnebago, Pottawattomy, or Chippewa Indian will be paid any part of this money."

" Wheugh, wheugh !" and grunts, by way of cheers,

and the council broke up, every chief shaking hands with the agent before he departed.

Declining an invitation to dinner from a gentleman connected with the council-house, I went out to re-connoitre the town.   The Indians have not much fun in them, the men stalk about wrapped up in their blankets, the boys shoot at marks with their bows and arrows, the women work, always work, even this gala time brought no holiday to the squaws; and they might be seen cutting and carrying wood, carrying water, weaving mats, cleaning skins, and patching up their temporary dwellings in every direction; others pounding and cleaning the wild rice, in large mortars or stone bowls.

By the way, it is from the wild rice that their tribe takes the name—Menomenee ; though the French have corrupted it into *Fol Avoine* or wild oats, a name which better suits the half-breeds and Canadians along those borders, than the cool and reserved Indians.

A vast number of lean and wolfish-looking dogs were prowling about the lodges, and a dire yelping was perpetually kept up, as the hungry curs were seen pilfering the provisions or anything else they could fasten their teeth in.   A trader declared that a dog had carried off his lighted lantern in his teeth the preceding night, merely to get at the oil ; and woe betide the shoe or mocassin left in the way of one of those active gentlemen.

Approaching a larger circle of Indians, I found them gambling away at the mocassin game, a sort of thimble-rig concern.   Three or four old Indian black-legs running a bullet here and there under four mo-cassins, laid on the ground ; the Indians touching with a long stick the mocassin they suspect the ball to be under, parting with their ornaments with a very bad grace, amidst the laughter of the rest, when they lose. The old blacklegs had a bank of wampum, and hawkbells, and silver gorgets, and beads, and all sorts of belts before them, the fruits of their winnings. They kept up a perpetual sort of grunting, bending their bodies over the mocassins, and striking their hands on their knees, keeping time to their monotonous " Shump, shump, shump."

Osh Cosh has hoisted the American flag over his long wigwam ; therefore matters will go off more quietly, it is augured. I was on the point of entering the chief's wigwam, when the loud and rapid enunciation of the grand medicine arrested my progress. Another of the chief's sons was ill, and the grand medicine man, as in duty bound, kept up a perpetual harangue ; it would have been considered an evil omen if a stranger entered the lodge without being formally invited on such an occasion. Well, the further we go the more we know—always learning something new. Returned to the Council Lodge and found the registry going forward in full force —the head of every family told his name, handed in a bundle of sticks, being the number of his wives and children. Apropos to wives, bigamy and polygamy are permitted : Osh Cosh has lately taken unto himself a thin young squaw, having already sons and daughters by two sisters ; they all live together in the greatest harmony.

While I sat watching the Indians handing in their sticks, an old crone, covered with wrinkles, toothless, bald, and most hideous to look upon, hobbled up to the agent and touched his shoulder. The man of business looked round, and on seeing this dim apparition

Q

almost fell off his perch.　　He afterwards acknowledged he was " badly *sheered ;*" this poor old hag presented her bundle of sticks and hobbled out.　I suppose, if her exact age could have been ascertained, she would be found the shady side of five hundred at least.

CHAPTER XVIII.

Temperance Society—Night in the Council Lodge—Breakfast at
the "Striped Apron" — Council Extraordinary — The half-
breed question—Coron, the Orator—An Indian heiress—Her
Portrait—A Council—Debate upon claims—A fortunate Trader
and happy Attorney—Prayer-meeting on Sunday—Indian Su-
perstitions—Potwalloping affair—Shift my quarters to a Pottawattomie wigwam—Cattle shooting—Butchers put to flight—A
negro Barber—Wolf River Rangers—Payment day—A Pottawattomie warrior—American flag hauled down—Agent retreats
—Drunken Indians—Last night with the Savages—My host
invites me to visit Calumet, or Pipe Town.

A MEETING of all the traders has been held in front of
the Council Lodge, and they have one and all signed
a paper, or mutual agreement, not to sell whisky to
the Indians till the payment has been made, and then
they may all start fair.   Osh Cosh and the Grignons
are the prime movers of this good measure ; and the
better to carry it into effect,'all the whisky barrels are
to be stored in the bush at the other side of the river,
and every drop seized on this, or the Indian side, is to
be thrown into the river.   We will see how long this
good resolution will be kept.

The first night I slept in the Council Lodge was
bitter cold; the keen frosty air whistled freely through
the chinks in the frail sides of our lodge ; the dogs fre-

Q 2

quently broke through the mats at the door, and prowled about us. The Indians also kept up a perpetual howling, singing, and flute blowing, round the embers of the fire, in front of the wigwam. The agent, poor man, was grievously disturbed by this noise ; and frequently, during the night, he started up from his bed, blankets, and sheets, (which he had taken the wise precaution to bring along with the money boxes,) and thrusting his head out of the lodge, he would roar at the Indians, tell them to " Stop that noise! make less noise there !" then, groping his way back to bed again, he sometimes stumbled over the snoring clerk, who would awake in a great fright, and halloo, " Thieves! mind the boxes! murder!" &c. It was next to impossible to sleep for an hour without being routed up, by some vile noise either within or without, and in the morning I rose up far from being refreshed with my first night's bivouac on Indian ground.

Got some savoury stew for breakfast this morning, down town, at the sign of the " Striped Apron," which floated gracefully above six wigwams thrown into one, by a spirited New England pedler, from the Bay. He has got together sundry cooking utensils, and a barrel of flour, some pork, and, *mirabile dictu !* coffee. He thinks he will clear his expenses, and perhaps a little more, as he charges half-a-dollar a meal. The long wigwam is the rendezvous of all the traders and loafers in the place, though the Indians seldom pass the threshold.

A great commotion broke out to day, when it was understood that the half-breeds would be excluded from the pay list, for such of the Pottawattomies, Winnebagos, and other Indians, as had taken wives from amongst the Menomenees, had hitherto been paid a share; and several of the Pottawattomies attended the payment. Their wives, and some of the Chippewa half-breeds, excited the sympathy of their red kinswomen; the squaws stirred up their husbands, the men stirred up the chiefs, the chiefs appealed to Osh Cosh, and the affair is to be settled to-day in full council.

The Pottawattomies say, if any of the half-breeds are to be excluded, all must be excluded, from the payment. They insist that the white faces have no right to interfere between the tribes—and that the children of white fathers and red mothers ought to be supported by the white fathers alone. Passing near the wigwam of Osh Cosh, I was not a little surprised to find a great, big, swaggering Frenchman, from Milwaukee, on his knees before that chief, soliciting that his wife and twelve half-breed children be put upon the pay-list, with great earnestness. Anxious to secure a good place, I hastened back to the Council Lodge, and found it beset in every direction; and way being cleared for Osh Cosh, I slipped in, and found the lodge crammed, as full as it could hold, of chiefs, and braves, and half-breeds. The agent made an abortive attempt to "clar de kitchen," and get the half-breeds out, but found it impossible. It was a very sore subject for the Indians to broach, as every white man on the ground, except myself, was connected, more or less, with Indians and half-breeds.

Osh Cosh declined making a speech: he had evidently been brought over by the half-breeds, and, during the stormy debate, lay back, resting on his elbows, eyeing the several speakers with the greatest disdain. His son, and heir-apparent, a fine young painted savage, sat behind him, and seemed sadly perplexed at having his plumed head and scalp lock crushed against the sides of our vast bee-hive.

A loud and angry debate was carried on between several chiefs, which was not translated by the interpreters. All of a sudden, up jumped a chief—strode over to the agent, and shook hands with him. He was received by the agent with cool surprise, and by the half-breeds with murmurs. A trader who sat next me interpreted part of his speech, which the half-breed's interpreter sadly changed, and hashed up for the agent's ear.

A better model of a bold and fearless orator I had never seen, on or off the stage, in ancient or modern painting or sculpture, than Coron, the red speaker before us—in the meridian of life, in the full vigour of manhood, his athletic form lightly draped with a simple blanket—now grasped on his broad chest with one hand, while the other was held forth with bold and graceful action. The classic contour of his head, piercing black eyes, aquiline nose, small, though changeable mouth—

"As sunbeams chasing shadows o'er the hill"—

the strong relief and beautiful play into which the muscles of the neck and bare throat were thrown— the whole man, reminded me of the justice of West's exclamation, when he first beheld the Apollo Belvedere in the Vatican—"a young Mohawk warrior."

He said he was the friend and well-wisher of the pale-faces, but denounced their encroachments; they were never satisfied, still crying "More land, more land!"—still forcing the red men further west, further from their great father beyond the great waters. He remembered the Green Bay treaty, and knew how it had been brought about. Osh Cosh was nothing before that time, he was only a brave, he was not even admitted into the council of the head chiefs, (loud interruption and a brawl without;) now, he was acknowledged head chief of the Menomenees—the mere tool of the Grignons and other traders, (here the speaker was interrupted by the Grignons and a crowd of half-breeds, but he still maintained his position.) He said it was new to him to be interrupted while speaking—it shewed the bad manners of the half breeds—and besides, said he, why are the half-breeds, or, indeed, any people but the chiefs and money-box keepers, allowed to push into the Council-Lodge, ("eugh, wheugh, wheugh," cheered the chiefs.) "The pale-faces," continued he, in a bitter strain of irony, "have such a regard for us poor red men that they wish to instruct us how to hoe our lands—they wish us to worship the little white man they have fixed up in their praying houses (catholic chapels) at Green Bay and the Grand Cocaloo. We have granted their grand medicine (priest) a large and fertile tract of land, not because of the little white man in his chapel, but because he is our friend, and sells us good gunpowder, and gives us advice. If the pale-faces despise us, why do they sleep so much with our squaws? (loud laughter, murmurs, and tumult.) Our young squaws bear them children, and we are beset with a mongrel yelping race; disowned by their white fathers, they follow their red mothers, they hang upon our robes, they fawn upon us, they bite their red brethren; every year we are obliged to provide for them; last payment, we agreed to pay them off, and have done with them—now, behold them, as noisy as ever, barking in our very Council Lodge."

Such was the vehemence and shrewdness of Coron's harangue, that even the chiefs who had agreed to vote for the half-breeds began to waver. Shunion (or Silver) spoke in favour of the half-breeds; he told his brother chiefs they ought to be generous, and have large hearts and open hands for friendly white-faces. A great deal of palaver and "*log-rolling*" took place, and, at last, a venerable old chief, Ko-ma-ni-kin, (Big-wave,) proposed that the half-breeds should be paid this time, and never after. Coron (or the Crown) was prevailed on to accede to the proposition; he made another speech, which I did not get interpreted as well as his first, and at the end of it he said, " Well, pay the half-breeds this once — let this be their last interference in our affairs—let them go home to their white fathers—let us not see the colour of their eyes any more."

The council broke up.

This evening, accompanied by an intelligent young fellow, who had married the daughter of a Chippewa chief, I visited the lodge and wigwams of several chiefs and Indians. I was surprised to find the interior of some of those temporary abodes warm and comfortable, abundance of mats on the floor, and the chinks and holes in the back, roof, and sides carefully stopped with moss and long grass; bear and racoon, and even black fox skins, robes, and blankets, formed beds and divans not to be sneezed at; the squaws received us with mild civility, pointing to the best mats and skins in the lodge, upon which they invited us to be seated. One of these lodges we visited belonged to a rich Menomenee belle; her father had been a chief, who died without male issue, and the tribe allotted her some land on the Winnebago lake, where she lived in single blessedness, in a neat and permanently-built lodge, cultivated a large garden, fished in the lake, and was quite an independent character; she had many admirers and many suitors; even white traders had been rejected by her. I found this paragon of perfection seated beside the red embers of a fire in the middle of a lodge, with three or four old squaws, her relations, and a young girl, who resided with her.

I was very much disappointed when I found this dusky beauty a dumpy squaw, with a little *goitre* under her chin—to be sure, she was richly dressed, in blue cloth, bedizened with beads and ribands; but her face was mild, and her fine dark eye spoke volumes: this was the reason she maintained her fame as the Menomence belle—everything depended upon her eye, glancing with shrewd and deep intelligence. In the twinkling of a bedpost, one could perceive she was laughing in her sleeve at her red brethren. Soon after we entered, my friend's vocabulary of Menomenee and Chippewa words being expended, the belle (her age was somewhere the shady side of thirty, became alarmed, and sent for one of her male friends, a half-breed, to inquire the object of our visit. Understanding our intentions were honourable, her mind was set at rest. Here my companion urged me to take a likeness of the Indian beauty; she was all compliance, lighted a yellow bees-wax candle, squatted herself down at the far end of the lodge, and, almost choked with laughter, I was obliged to kneel and sprawl before her sable majesty, with all the squaws and children in the lodge crowding upon my shoulders, while, by the pale and flickering light of the little candle, I sketched the outline of the sable beauty's head, neck, and shoulders, on a leaf of my note-book. My companion found fault with the sketch, and said it should be shaded. Doctors differ; but I was forced to shade the hair and some of her dress, whereupon the lady insisted upon seeing her picture, and was very much horrified to find it was not painted red, white, and black, on which colours she placed her fingers on her dress; and the interpreter conveyed her wishes that I should colour her portrait. It was easy enough to perceive divers colours on her dress, but her countenance was a uniform dusky hue, unconscious of a blush; and, indeed, if I had had my colour-box beside me, I should have spared the carmine and light red. Wishing to get out of the scrape as easily as possible, I told her it was too dark, and, besides, I never could paint such transcendent beauties as hers save in the sun-light. Whether the compliment was literally translated to her or not I cannot say, but the Menomenee belle favoured me with a most 'witching smile, and extended her hand to me, whereupon I took the liberty to slide a ring upon one of her fingers, received a most cordial shake in return, and retreated. Before I left the cabin, my companion had observed a tall, grim-looking half-breed peeping in at the door: at last he entered, and demanded what we did there. Seeing my occupation, he said he was a painter himself, and that the lady might have been painted by him if she liked—in short, he was a rival, an aspirant to the hand of this model of beauty.

" You had better take care of that fellow," said my companion, as we left the lodge, " a jealous half-breed is the devil to deal with."

Fortunately I was not so deeply smitten with my

dusky belle as to accept her invitation to return to her lodge next day and as often as I liked, and had no idea of gratifying my vanity at the risk of my life.

On Saturday, another council was held, which was conducted with greater regularity than the last. The bills of the traders were considered, and claims for compensation for services done to the Indians and damages done by the Indians brought before the house (or wigwam). Fifty dollars claimed by a settler near the Little Cocaloo for a cow slain by them. Not allowed; "because," said the Indians, "the white man sold the flesh of the cow, which was shot by accident, therefore he lost nothing by it."—One hundred dollars claimed by a doctor at the Bay for attending a sick Indian family during the small-pox. His claim rejected, but afterwards he was allowed fifty dollars.—One hundred dollars claimed by one Boyd, an ex-agent, for having taken care of an old Indian he found frostbitten on the ice; loud laughter, and claim rejected. A claim by a merchant of Astor, who had buried an Indian, and incurred considerable expense at the funeral, was at once allowed.*

Sundry minor claims being allowed and rejected, Osh Cosh made a speech to the chiefs, which was not interpreted; but the purport of it was, that one of the Grignons should receive half a dollar a-head from the whole tribe; and after a little delay, the agent was directed to transfer some fifteen hundred dollars to this lucky wight for services rendered; in fact, it was

* A claim made by a tavern-keeper at Madison, who had entertained Osh Cosh and his Sachems for several days, when that chief consulted Governor Dodge upon the propriety of going to war with the Sanks and Foxes, was not allowed, because that war had not been countenanced by the U. N. S.

a liberal present, and nothing more nor less.   I could not believe it till I saw the boxes opened and the dollars transferred to the safe-keeping of a gaunt, yellow, ill-conditioned man.

"What has he done for the Indians?" said I.

"Oh, he has been always their friend; his father is the old trader, but he is the gentleman of the family," said my informant.   "He has lost a great deal by the Indians; he always gives them good advice, and is glad to see them."

As to his losses I cannot speak, but as to his gains, I can bear witness; the Indians had given him a large tract of land near the Winnebago lake; they had worked for him, supplied him with game, fish, flesh, and fowl, planted his corn, built his lodges—but still he had lost a great deal by the Indians, said his friends; but it was easier to say so than to prove the fact.   At a later hour, I saw this gentleman throwing away dollars with great *sang froid* at a faro-table—a hazard and thimble-rig concern, which a nest of blacklegs got up at the "Striped Apron" in the hopes of fleecing such gentlemen as had their claims allowed by the Indians.   Finally, Osh Cosh rose up and made a long harangue: he said, "There is a man here present to whom we are all indebted; he draws up our papers, and sees justice done to us—he is our attorney, and in consideration of his services we will allow him fifty dollars."

This half-breed of an attorney sat watching the money-boxes, and the moment he heard fifty dollars, his countenance fell—never was man more disappointed; and the Indians seemed surprised when he was doled out fifty dollars for his two years' services. It was a mistake, a *lapsus linguæ* of Osh Cosh, who had used the word fifty instead of five hundred, and the delighted man of quips and quirks was soon handed a box of five hundred dollars.

Sunday : we marched from the grand lodge to the Pottawattomie wigwam, where a trader, a member of the church, had informed us he intended to hold a prayer meeting. We found a large body of painted young men playing the Moccasin game, and a sort of thimble-rig, right in front of our preacher's domicile ; they were prevailed on to move further off, and the preacher, a grave and decent looking man, invited us to enter his lodge, which smelt powerfully of salt fish and leather ; two only Indians attended the preaching, and the congregation was very thin indeed. Our preacher prayed and spoke for three quarters of an hour; he prayed for the conversion of the Indians, and frequently called them "poor and peel'd wretches," in the dark and dismal valley of sin and death. He concluded his sermon rather abruptly, saying, there is " leave to speak if any man feels inclined."

No man present feeling inclined to preach, we broke up meeting and returned to our lodges just as the Indians broke up their games. They had held a solemn feast early in the morning, which I did not witness; but during the day, I saw an Indian baptizing a dog by the river side, preparatory to its being stewed for a solemn feast. The Indians always offer part of everything they eat to the Great Spirit, and sprinkle their venison, and dog, and bear meat with water before it is dressed for a feast.

Apropos to feasting: I had taken my meals regularly at the " Striped Apron," down town, and declined intruding on my kind friends at the Council Lodge, though invited by the provider to " eat with them ;" but on

Sunday, from a sort of false squeamishness about dining in a place where gambling &c. was going on, I spoke to the merchant who furnished the *provend* at the Council Lodge table, and arranged with him that I would pay for that day's board anything he liked. He entered into my feelings on that subject, and I dined with the agent and half-a-dozen others connected with the expedition, and have never ceased to regret having swallowed a few mouthfuls of hard pork, beans, and corn-bread at that table, for reasons which I shall briefly explain. Formerly, and at the last Indian payment, a public table had been kept up at the agent's lodge, at which traders and visitors dined at the expense of the Indians, and thus a considerable sum was squandered. The same merchants who furnished the last outfit and entertainment, furnished forth this one also, and sent up provisions and knives and forks for several guests; but the new agent resolved to put a stop to this, and threw cold water on the public table. Nevertheless, the merchant provider went on, and invited several traders to " eat at the table as usual," and then handed in his account to be paid, some five or six hundred dollars; the agent refused to pay it, and a regular skirmish and many hard words ensued. All this did not reach my ear till Monday—indeed, the misunderstanding did not occur till then; the moment I heard it I flew to the provider to pay him for my dinner, but he flatly refused to receive a cent. I urged the money on him, told him I would be more obliged than words could express, if he would relieve me from the awkward predicament into which he had brought me, by making me, as it were, an accomplice and sharer in this potwallopping affair. I claimed the interference of the agent—the agent would do nothing. " He refuses to take the money from you," said he, "because he thinks it would invalidate his claim." Not knowing how to act, I went out, and calling upon an old Indian, in presence of the agent and provider, handed him a dollar, to his great surprise and delight, this being the way in which I proved to my own satisfaction that I had not robbed the Indians of a single meal.

This affair caused me so much annoyance, that I resolved to shift my quarters; indeed the Council Lodge had grown so cold and airy, that the hoar frost was on my blanket every morning, and the bear skin I had procured for a pillow was frequently pulled from under my head by the rascally dogs. Altogether it was most desirable to get into other quarters, and I marched with my traps to the Pottawattomie wigwam, and was cordially received by the preacher, a very worthy poor man, who kept aloof from the scenes of riot and drunkenness which began to break out in divers parts of the village. He was a member of the temperance society; he had brought over a few good blankets and other useful things, to sell to the Indians at this payment, and inveighed against the conduct of the whisky sellers in no measured terms. I was glad to see he was not without admirers, even among the Indians, and several of them from his own neighbourhood spent the evening in front of his wigwam, listening to his sage observations and pious ejaculations in their language, while whoops, and yells, and flute-playing, and ribaldry, sounded on all sides. This good Samaritan indulged me with a pair of blankets, and a truss of dry racoon skins for a pillow. He was from New England, and delighted to tell long stories of the wars, for he had been a soldier to boot. He invited me to spend some days with him at his village called Calumet, (or Pipe Town,) on the Winnebago Lake.

According to the articles of the treaty with these Indians, the U. N. S. government gave them several head of horned cattle. Owing to the badness of the weather and the impracticable nature of the country, the cattle did not arrive as soon as it was expected, and at last only six oxen could be procured. Formerly the young men claimed the right of hunting the cattle through the woods, and shooting them, but on this occasion Osh Cosh forbade the hunt, to the great vexation of the painted young gentlemen; the reason assigned for not permitting them to hunt was simply that the beef was spoiled with the number of balls driven through it, and accidents sometimes happened. I had crossed the river in a canoe, and was taking a sketch of the gay scene on the opposite side, when the oxen arrived; the poor animals looked wild enough, they had been over-driven, and stood near the margin of the river, while some half-breeds and the renowned Mr. C——ds, came over with long knives and hatchets, to dispatch them off hand. Not willing to preside over this piece of butchery, I walked aside into the bush, and in my perambulations came suddenly upon a painted warrior crouching among the fern. I had been surprised at the total absence of Indians on this side of the river, when suddenly from fern and bush in every direction, up sprang a host of painted warriors in gala costume, each trailing his long rifle, dropping his blanket from his shoulders, and bending his eagle eye upon the spot where the cattle slaughtering was going forward. Four of the oxen had been coolly slain with an axe; the fifth looked fierce, and had long horns, and therefore Mr. C——ds, the brave, was deputed to shoot him with his double-barrelled gun, but that gentleman having taken an uncertain aim, merely wounded the beast, and away it ran through the woods, pursued by upwards of one thousand red warriors, young and old. The first rush they made, I was hustled along with them, and " the devil take the hindmost" seemed to be the cry. But who can paint Mr. C——ds' confusion and horror, to find the whole band of savages rushing towards him ! He ran, and though his good legs had saved his bacon before, they did not save his beef now, the red men pouncing on the residue of the cows and oxen, hacking, hewing, and mangling. Mr. C——ds made his escape across the river in his canoe, and the whole brush and woods seemed alive with Indians shooting and yelling over the fallen oxen. I never saw the savage flash out so fast; the moment they dabbled their hands in blood, the Indians seemed to lose all self-control, and the most reserved and stately yelled like fiends.

A negro barber from the Bay has been detected selling whisky to the Indians; in his lodge he had several barrels of whisky concealed, and the appointed mixed force of traders and sage Indians, who have endeavoured most laudably to keep the peace, and prevent the sale of whisky, have seized upon this nigger's illicit store of the baneful fire-water, and the barrels having been rolled up in front of the Council Lodge, the agent and Osh Cosh are called on to decide as to its fate. Meantime the nigger goes about exciting the pestilent half-breeds and profligate Indians to rescue his whisky, using the most abusive and indecent language, saying he will get up a big fight for his

whisky, wishing he had his bowie knife, and, in short,
provoking some hardy pioneer to thrash him.

During this afternoon, several seizures of whisky
were made in the bush, and rolled up to the Council
Lodge by the gallant band of Wolf River rangers; but
alas for poor human nature! the band of whisky seekers
were not proof against temptation, and in the midst
of their seizures they could not help tasting, and from
tasting went on to swigging, from swigging to tippling,
and at last they cut a most ludicrous figure, marching
about from lodge to lodge, and from tent to shanty, in
quest of whisky, inveighing against the fire-water,
while they were hardly able to stand; indeed, the
major who commanded seemed to think he commanded a regiment, instead of a dozen boosy traders
in red and grey night-caps, and some half-dozen old
Indians in blankets; he carried his cudgel like a pike;
" It looks well, at least, said my uncle Toby." Frequently halting his men in front of the Council Lodge,
he would inspect them with great severity, give them
speeches upon military discipline, read what he called
the order of the day, which was the old declaration of
independence; then putting himself at their head,
march round the whisky barrels as if they were the
trophies or spoils of war, followed by a mob of drunken
half-breeds and whooping Indians. But at last the
whisky was given up, and I saw the poor major, flat
as a flounder, his occupation gone, his band dispersed,
and in a hoarse voice he exclaimed against the ingratitude of the traders, who had not rewarded him for
his zeal, even with a letter of thanks; " And after all
I have gone through," said he, " I feel as if I had
been beaten through hell with a soot-bag;" a singular,
though not very elegant phrase for a man of his

rank and standing to sport, even in the "Striped Apron."

Early this morning, the whole village was up and stirring ; flags and streamers were hoisted in front of the traders' lodges. One man, to attract notice, had taken advantage of a dead tree in front of his lodge, and covered its branches with strips of red calico, blue ribands, and gew-gaws; another hoisted a dozen striped shirts, another a red blanket, another a green blanket, and the traders strode backwards and forwards in front of the goods, bawling as loud as their lungs could bellow, " How, how, how ! How, how, how ! Nichie nobie ;"* while the Indians and their squaws surrounded the Council Lodge in groups, the squaws for once dressed in all their finery, and the young men vying with each other who could shew most vermillion, yellow ochre, and indigo on their cheeks, and feathers—red, horse, and moose hair—on their heads, wampum and beads, bracelets and gorgets, round their arms and necks. The sun shone out gloriously, and the *coup d'œil* was most enlivening ; several Indians had brought up their horses, and rode about at a breakneck rate over the stumps and logs. The Council Lodge had been metamorphosed into a pay office ; a door opened on each side, through which the Indians were to pass, and receive their pay from the agents at a long counter, upon which the contents of the money boxes, some twenty-seven thousand dollars, was piled up in goodly rows. Some of the traders, especially the Grignons, beset the door of egress, and as every Indian passed out, received the amount he owed for goods received on time. Thus it frequently happened

* " Buy, buy, buy, Indian gentlemen."

that an Indian came away from the lodge as empty-handed as he entered it, the squaws alone hesitating, and frequently refusing to part with the dollars at once.

I soon got weary of witnessing the payment, and retreated from the Council Lodge into the fresh air. I was much surprised at the sudden apparition of a tall old Indian; he stood aloof from the rest, and looked scornfully at the Council Lodge. The upper part of his face was painted white, nose, forehead, up to the roots of his hair, which was painted fiery red, and from his scalp-lock hung down an eagle's feather; over his mouth and chin a red hand was painted, indeed he seemed to have dipped his hand in vermillion and laid it over his mouth; this, on the white ground, was seen at some distance. Part of his nose had been hewn off in some old fight. He wore a muff, or collar of crow feathers, under which peeped his gorget and sundry wampum-beads, &c. His long sinewy arms were also painted; he wore deer-skin leggings, very much soiled, and trailed skunk-skins at his feet. A remnant of a green Mackinaw blanket covered his shoulders, and in his hand he carried a formidable war club, ornamented with eagle's feathers and brass; he was a most athletic old fellow, and glided about like a spectre.

A trader explained to me that this man was a Pottawattomie chief; he had married a Menomenee woman, and, with the residue of his band, had been attempting to get his name on the pay list. Failing in that, he had put on his war dress, and had a strong band of warriors lying in ambush, to cut off the Menomenees as they returned laden with goods and provisions. He was a well-known warrior, and had killed many people,

as all his trappings betokened. He had fought against
the Americans last war, fought against them in the
Black Hawk war, and was a regular firebrand in the
frontiers. At present, Osh Cosh treated him with
great disdain, and affected to despise him, though he
had been secretly tampering with him, and sent him
presents to conciliate his good wishes, which the proud
old Pottawattomie rejected, and now came openly to
bid the whole tribe defiance.

Approaching this old warrior, I began to inspect
him as I would an Egyptian mummy, and a grim
smile stole over his seamed visage, as, thinking aloud,
I said, " I wonder if he would sell this war club."

" Bai-and-bai, bai-and-bai," croaked the grim warrior.

" What!" said I, " do you speak English, my fine
fellow?"

" Two, tree words," responded he.

" What will you take for your war club?"

" Oh, two—tree—dollar, bai-and-bai."

Finding the chief's vocabulary rather limited, I
hailed one of my friendly interpreters, and the chief
then said, "he would not part with his club till night;
he would hold it for his own protection till he saw
further,—that if the Menomenees acceded to his proposal, and were for peace, he would then sell his club,"
and so saying he whisked off.

The moment the last dollar was paid, down went
the American flag, and the agent and his men rushed
to their boat, plied their oars, and sheered off from
the scene of action. Then the whisky sellers took
the field. The young Indians clubbed together, and
bought barrels of fire water, knocked in their heads
with their clubs and tomahawks, and helped their

friends all round to bowls and cups of the spirit, above proof—real fire-water.

The result may be anticipated : the whole village became a scene of riot and debauchery. I retreated to my friendly trader's lodge, and found him expostulating with a few young Indians, upon the folly and wickedness of getting drunk. Indeed, this good man's words and example seemed to have considerable effect on his hearers ; he begged of them to quit the village, bag and baggage, now they were paid. Several followed his advice at once, and others began to remove the mats &c. from their lodges ; while the Indians who lived in his vicinity lodged their money for safe keeping in his hands. One old trapper actually deposited forty dollars with him, but would not go home —no, he preferred plunging into the midst of the riot and revelry. Next morning I hardly knew him, as he sneaked up, all covered with dirt and blood, to ask for his bundle.

That evening the rain came down in torrents ; my host stood at the door of his lodge, and endeavoured to prevail on the Indians to pass on, and go home, but their drunken friends soon found them out. They came with kettles and cans full of whisky, which they insisted we should taste. My host obstinately refused, and loudly bawled, " Caun whisky, caun Ishcodaywa, bo ;" and the result was, that a good deal of whisky was spilled, the Indians forcing cans of it against our lips, while we evaded the torrent ; this was the most disagreeable part of the entertainment.

" I knew this good man would follow my advice," said my host, as a very tall old Indian approached us, followed by his family, sons, daughters, and wives, carrying mats, baskets, and papooses. The party

halted at our lodge; and the old fellow, who had evidently taken a drop too much, seized my friend by
the hand, and made a long speech, while his wives
seemed ready to sink under their burdens, and stood
patiently in the midst of the rain.

One of the company was not so patient, and stag-
gered about under a load of bedding and matting;
and the head and face being partially hid under a new
iron pot, and the lower part of the figure disguised in
a torn old petticoat of divers colours, I looked upon
the wearer as a tipsy old squaw, and was greatly surprised to hear a voice from under the iron pot, exclaiming, "Arrah! bad manners to your palaver—don't
be after keeping us standing in the rain all night."

"Holloa," said I, peeping under the pot at a pair of
red whiskers; "here is an Irishman turned squaw."
But, either through shame or indignation, the pot-
carrier answered not, but jogged off with the Indians,
and in the tumult and hubbub round us, I forgot to
inquire about him.

At night we barricadoed the door with empty barrels and logs, but the Indians still came begging for
money to buy more whisky, and the rain entered the
roof and sides of our lodge. My blanket was satu-
rated; and at midnight I sat up, finding it impossible
to close an eye amidst the wild howling, terrific shouts,
screams, love and war songs of the drunken savages
without. I never heard, or hope to hear, anything
half so horrible again. Indeed, as my host observed,
it was worse than bedlam broke loose, it was like hell
upon earth. Crowds of unhappy children crawled
round our own lodge, crying bitterly; some of them
contrived to creep into the empty barrels at our door,

and that barrier was broken down, before morning, with a loud crash.

I had been trying to dose in a dry corner, when, looking up, I saw the tall spectral figure of a naked Indian leap through the door-way; he waved a glowing faggot in his hand, and shewed his wild distorted features covered with blood and dirt. "Now is the hour," thought I, "that my ramblings will have a finale, for *certes* this mad savage is on the eve of hurling the glowing log upon my devoted head;" but hardly had the thought flashed through my brain, when the savage fell prostrate on the floor, where, with a dozen more, we found him stark and gory, snoring away the effects of his last night's debauch.

The grey morning dawned heavily upon the Wolf River; as I went forth and looked around, not a third of the tents, lodges, and wigwams were standing; all was misery and wretchedness. The ground was covered with drunken savages, stripped of their finery, torn and tangled with filth and briers. The half-breed whisky-sellers plied their vile vocations, determined to sell every drop of liquor they brought to the ground. All the respectable traders had huddled up their goods and retreated, or prepared to start away in canoes. I was not a little surprised to see the old squaws gliding about with rifles, war-clubs, and tomahawks, under their arms; in fact, they are the only efficient police, carrying off their husbands' weapons before a carouse, to prevent bloodshed if possible.

Close to a whisky-barrel, I found a young squaw belabouring a drunken Indian man, who lay very quietly upon his back, quite naked and powerless, while this athletic dame belaboured him with a long club. We took the club from her, and threw it away; then she got a stone to despatch him, this we took from her also; and at last she began whipping him with a pine branch, exclaiming all the time against his drunken habits, while she was pretty far gone herself.

Another dire battle was raging in the remnants of the lodge of a brave, who had been a gallant *homme*. The squaws were all fighting about him; they seemed all in a heap, in the midst of the skeleton of the lodge, and looked like so many devils caught in a crib. Seven or eight women, of all ages, tore, bit, scratched, and kicked, in this delectable circle; while the gay Lothario, a besotted old Indian, very quietly looked on, stoically smoking his tomahawk pipe, till it was snatched out of his mouth by one of those furies, who began to use it most unmercifully on the rest; till the beautiful *chaine des dames* was unfolded by the main strength of the neighbours.

Passing another lodge, I caught a glimpse of the plastered red head of the old Pottawattomie chief. He sat down in the ashes with a circle of old chiefs of his tribe; they were all half tipsy, chanting a low wailing song. The moment I entered the lodge they raised their voices, and their song became more lively. I reminded the old chief about the war-club, when suddenly he jumped up, and exclaimed, " No money, no dollar, for poor Pottawattomie; no blanket for him; no beef for him ;" and I was hustled, and thrust out of the lodge.

Indignant at this proceeding, I returned to the charge with an interpreter, who soon cleared up the mystery. The Pottawattomies, seeing me in the Council Lodge, thought I belonged to the agency. But when the interpreter told them I was only a

R

stranger and a Saganagh, the Pottawattomies altered their note, jumping up with a shout, they almost shook my wrists out of joint; such a hand-shaking round I never experienced before, or since.

"You shall have the club—here is the club!" exclaimed the old chief; "Saganagh, my friend; my good friend and brother; Saganagh, here is my club."

Reflecting that money would soon be thrown away upon whisky, I took the war-club, and transferred my blanket to the shoulders of the poor chief. Never was man so delighted; he almost danced with delight; a few strings of beads and tinder-boxes conciliated the squaws, and we had a regular jubilee. A squaw ransacked a roll of goods, and insisted I should have a pair of leggings made by her own fair hands. For this present I was in duty bound to make a suitable return.

"We will all go to Canada!" they exclaimed—"we will all go to Canada!" and I found it no easy matter to get away from the grateful poor creatures.

Returning to my quarters, I found my friend busily employed packing up his traps; when I explained to him the nature of my interview with the Pottawattomies, he laughed.

"Yes," said he, "the poor fellows were badly treated from first to last, but now they prefer going to Canada rather than crossing the Missisippi, where lands have been allotted to them by the Sauks and Foxes; but I doubt me much if the Pottawattomies will be any acquisition to the Canadas. They are, just as you see them—an idle, rambling race; fond of hunting. and averse to settling down anywhere; very quarrelsome, and addicted to drink, whenever they can get it by hook or by crook; *certes*, they will be no great loss to Uncle Sammy."

I had seen quite enough of the Indians; and the weather being very cold and unsettled, broke up my plan of crossing the country to the head of the Lake Superior; I embarked in a canoe with a trader, and bade adieu to the Menomenees, the last of the Pottawattomies, and the Wolf River rangers.

THE END.

T. C. Savill, Printer, 107, St. Martin's Lane.

NEW WORKS

PUBLISHED BY

MESSRS. SAUNDERS AND OTLEY,

CONDUIT STREET.

I.
SIR E. L. BULWER'S NEW WORK.
In 3 Vols. Post 8vo,

ZANONI.

By the Author of "Rienzi," "Night and Morning," &c.

"An elegant and thoughtful book. It has qualities which cannot fail of instant appreciation."—*Examiner*.

"It is at once full of poetical beauty, of lofty thoughts, and of exquisite human interest."—*Literary Gazette*.

"We need add nothing more to the evidences we have cited, of the masterly power displayed in this very exciting and imaginative romance."—*Atlas*.

II.
MR. JAMES'S NEW NOVEL.
Now Ready, in 3 Vols. post 8vo,

THE TENANTS OF THE HEART.

By G. P. R. JAMES, ESQ.

Author of "The Robber," "The Gentleman of the Old School," &c.

"This work will soon be in every library and reading-room throughout the empire, and be a theme of gratification to thousands of intellectual readers."—*Literary Gazette*.

"It is the best work that Mr. James has ever written—a deep drama of life—every line an essay, every page a lucid physiological exposition."—*Literary Journal*.

"The philosophy is sublime, the passion intense, and these two rare and masterly excellences, each singly, powerful enough to command the deepest interest, conjointly are irresistible in their dominion over us. Its perusal seems to leave behind it the flavour of experience, and we involuntarily feel that such is really the thing called life."—*Metropolitan*.

III.

THE COMPLETE PROSE WORKS OF SIR E. L. BULWER, BART.

IN TWELVE SIX-SHILLING VOLUMES,
Bound and Lettered, beautifully Illustrated.

"Of all our popular authors, there is certainly not one who has run through such a gauntlet of Translations and Piracies as Sir E. L. Bulwer. We believe that some of his Novels have been rendered into the Romaic, while almost all of them have been translated into German, French, Spanish, and the rest of the European languages. It would be a curious piece of literary statistics to trace the number of copies in which he has been thus reduplicated; and we believe we are within the truth if we estimate it at a million. The popularity of his writings on the Continent is, if possible, even greater than in England; while in Germany his genius is regarded with an enthusiasm that can hardly be credited in our sober climate. This very circumstance creates an absolute necessity for the authorized edition before us, which, produced under his own superintendence, will vindicate his reputation from all those mischances to which an author is exposed whose labours have run through so many risks of translation and reproduction."—*Atlas*.

IV.

In one Volume, bound uniformly with the Prose Works,
SIR E. L. BULWER'S

DRAMATIC WORKS.

V.

Second Edition.   In 3 Vols. Post 8vo,

NIGHT AND MORNING.

A NOVEL.

By the Author of " Rienzi," " Eugene Aram," &c.

" The best novel that Sir Lytton Bulwer has yet given to the world."—*Lit. Gaz.*
" The vivacity and variety of ' NIGHT AND MORNING' will carry it throughout the
whole world of novel readers."—*Athenæum.*

VI.

In Two Volumes, 8vo,

ATHENS: ITS RISE AND FALL:

WITH VIEWS OF THE ARTS, LITERATURE, AND SOCIAL LIFE OF THE ATHENIAN PEOPLE.

By SIR E. LYTTON BULWER, Bart., M.A.

Author of " England and the English," " Rienzi," &c.

" The rise and fall of Athens from the pen of Mr. Bulwer.   What a theatre for description !   What themes for the graphic narrator !   We cannot too much applaud his general
tone of moderation and candour. * * * These specimens, and other passages,
combine a warm feeling of the great or the beautiful with a wakeful sagacity, ever
throwing out abundance of new and fine observations."—*Edinburgh Review.*

VII.

LADY CHATTERTON'S NEW WORK.

In 3 Vols. Post 8vo, with Illustrations,

HOME SCENES & FOREIGN RECOLLECTIONS.

BY LADY CHATTERTON.

" These volumes are marked at once by talent and refinement."—*Quarterly Review.*
" Lady Chatterton's work displays an acute perception of human nature, and great
talent in selecting and applying maxims to the different circumstances of life."—*Times.*
" This work may be in truth called a miscellany of polite literature, seasoned through-
out with an amiable and sweetly religious spirit."—*Literary Gazette.*
" One of the most agreeable, picturesque, and readable books of the season."—
Monthly Chronicle.
" Three more delightful volumes have rarely come under our notice."—*Observer.*

VIII.

NEW WORK BY THE AUTHOR OF " ELPHINSTONE."

In 3 Vols. Post 8vo,

THE HERBERTS; OR, THE WAY OF THE WORLD.

By the Author of " Elphinstone."

IX.

MAJOR MICHEL'S NEW WORK.

In 3 Vols. Post 8vo,

TREVOR HASTINGS; OR, THE FIELD OF TEWKESBURY.

By the Author of "Henry of Monmouth."

X.

MR. GARSTON'S NEW WORK.

In 2 Vols. 8vo, with Illustrations,

GREECE REVISITED, AND SKETCHES IN LOWER EGYPT IN 1840.

With Thirty-six Hours of a Campaign in Greece in 1825.

By EDGAR GARSTON, Esq., Knight of the R.M. Greek Order of the Saviour,&c.

XI.

SCOTT'S VISIT TO WATERLOO.

In 1 Vol. Post 8vo,

JOURNAL OF A TOUR TO WATERLOO AND PARIS,

IN COMPANY WITH SIR WALTER SCOTT, IN 1815.

By the late JOHN SCOTT, Esq.

XII.

CAPTAIN KNOX'S NEW WORK.

In Three Vols. Post 8vo,

THE RITTMEISTER'S BUDGET:

A STRANGE MEDLEY.

By CAPTAIN KNOX,
Author of "Hardness," "Softness," &c.

XIII.

In One Volume, Post 8vo,

PEACE, PERMANENT AND UNIVERSAL,

ITS PRACTICABILITY, VALUE, AND CONSISTENCY WITH DIVINE REVELATION.—A PRIZE ESSAY.

By H. T. J. MACNAMARA, Esq.

XIV.

LADY CHATTERTON'S IRELAND.

Second Edition, in 2 Vols. Post 8vo,

RAMBLES IN THE SOUTH OF IRELAND.

By LADY CHATTERTON. With Illustrations.

" A charming book, full of picturesque descriptions, interesting observations on life and manners, amusing anecdotes, legendary lore, just feeling, and sound common sense."—*Literary Gazette.*

XV.

In Two Volumes, 8vo,

THE SOCIAL INFLUENCE OF DEMOCRACY:

THE COMPLETION OF DEMOCRACY IN AMERICA.

By M. A. DE TOCQUEVILLE. Translated by H. REEVE, ESQ.

" As a study of political science, this book stands unrivalled in our time, equally remarkable for lucidity of style, acuteness, and delicacy of reasoning, and for the moral and intellectual vigour with which it has been conceived and completed."—*Times.*

XVI.

NEW WORK BY THE AUTHOR OF "THE ANGLER IN IRELAND."

In Two Vols. Post 8vo, with Plates,

TWO SUMMERS IN NORWAY.

By the Author of "The Angler in Ireland."

" Full, satisfying, and informing in matter, as well as animated in style."—*Spectator.*
" We have in this work, for the first time, the capabilities of Norway regarding the noble art of salmon-fishing ; and although the author does not give a complete account of all the rivers in Norway, he has done more than enough to merit the gratitude of every lover of the ' gentle art.' Nor is it to the angler alone that the work will prove acceptable, for it abounds in interesting descriptions of scenery, stirring details of personal adventures, and many just and important remarks on the social character of the Norwegians."—*Metropolitan.*

XVII.

In Two Vols. Post 8vo,

ITALY— GENERAL VIEWS OF ITS HISTORY AND LITERATURE,

IN REFERENCE TO ITS PRESENT STATE.

By L. MARIOTTI.

XVIII.

New Edition, in Two Volumes, Post 8vo,

VISITS AND SKETCHES AT HOME AND ABROAD.

By Mrs. JAMESON.

" These graceful and delightful volumes afford a vivid instance of the strength and reach of the female talent of the present day. They are full of woman's keenness of observation, of her enthusiastic warmth of feeling, and of the rich eloquence of her imagination."—*Athenæum.*

XIX.

In Two Volumes, Post 8vo,

SOCIAL LIFE IN GERMANY ILLUSTRATED,

In the Dramas of Her Royal Highness the Princess Amelia of Saxony.

Translated from the German, with Notes and an Introduction.

By Mrs. JAMESON.

XX.

Third Edition, in Three Volumes, Post 8vo,

WINTER STUDIES AND SUMMER RAMBLES.

By Mrs. JAMESON, Author of " VISITS AT HOME AND ABROAD," " CHARACTERISTICS OF WOMEN," &c.

XXI.

Third Edition, in Two Volumes, Post 8vo,

CELEBRATED FEMALE SOVEREIGNS.

By Mrs. JAMESON.

" We are indebted to Mrs. Jameson for these very delightful volumes." — *New Monthly.*
" A series of admirable biographies of celebrated queens. Such a work must be popular with every subject of these queen-governed realms."—*Metropolitan.*

XXII.

Third Edition, in Two Volumes, Post 8vo,

FEMALE CHARACTERS OF SHAKSPEARE'S PLAYS,

OR, CHARACTERISTICS OF WOMEN.

By Mrs. JAMESON.

" Two truly delightful volumes : the most charming of all the works of a charming writer."—*Blackwood.*
" A beautiful and touching commentary on the heart and mind of woman."

XXIII.

Fifth Edition, Revised and Corrected,

ADVENTURES OF A GENTLEMAN IN SEARCH OF A HORSE.

By Sir GEORGE STEPHEN.

With numerous Illustrations by Cruikshank.

" One of the best practical guides to the choice and management of horses we have seen. It should be in the hands of all who are interested in horses."—*Dispatch*.

" It combines a most amusing *exposé* of the dangers of horse-dealing, with an able digest of the laws of warranty. Those who possess this work will be well armed against fraud."—*Chronicle*.

XXIV.

In One Volume, 8vo,

PETER PAUL RUBENS, HIS LIFE AND GENIUS.

Translated from the German of Dr. WAAGEN, by R. R. NOEL, Esq. Edited by Mrs. JAMESON.

" We cannot too earnestly recommend this work to the study of the artist and connoisseur. It is beyond all comparison the most complete and perfect analysis of the mind and works of Rubens which has ever been given to the public."—*Britannia*.

XXV.

In Two Vols. Post 8vo,

THE POETRY OF LIFE.

By Mrs. ELLIS, Author of " THE WOMEN OF ENGLAND."

" We can recommend ' The Poetry of Life' to all who delight in elegant and tasteful composition. It contains a series of admirable essays on various delightful subjects in nature, art, and the human mind."—*Spectator*.

XXVI.

Second Edition, with Forty Illustrative Engravings,

THE MANAGEMENT OF BEES;

WITH A DESCRIPTION OF THE LADIES' SAFETY HIVE.

By SAMUEL BAGSTER, Jun.

" A complete practical guide to one of the most interesting pursuits in the circle of Natural History."—*Metropolitan*.

XXVII.

In Octavo,

THE DELUGE.

A DRAMA IN TWELVE SCENES.

By J. E. READE, Esq., Author of " ITALY."

" Mr. Reade's ' Deluge' will find a place in the library of every true lover of poetry." —*Metropolitan*.

" A book of extraordinary interest."—*Examiner*.

" Years of labour have not been misspent in the research and consideration of the subject, and the style is worthy of the best names in this elevated part of our national literature."—*Literary Gazette*.

CPSIA information can be obtained
at www.ICGtesting.com
Printed in the USA
BVHW081808220819
556561BV00019B/4244/P